LLEWE[LLYN]
20[__]
MAGICAL ALMANAC

FEATURING

Bernyce Barlow, Elizabeth Barrette, Chandra Moira Beal, Lori Bruno, Frances Camberis, David Cumes, Estelle Daniels, Nuala Drago, Denise Dumars, Ellen Dugan, Marguerite Elsbeth, Breid Foxsong, Anna Franklin, Lily Gardner, Anne Marie Garrison, John Michael Greer, Magenta Griffith, Raven Grimassi, David Harrington, Natalie Harter, Eileen Holland, Ellen Evert Hopman, Kenneth Johnson, Ladyhawk Whispers, Kirin Lee, Mary Magpie, Edain McCoy, Ann Moura, Laurel Nightspring, Robert M. Place, Lauren Raine, Diana Rajchel, Silver RavenWolf, deTraci Regula, Michelle Santos, Sedwin, ShadowCat, Cerridwen Iris Shea, Susan Sheppard, Lynne Sturtevant, Tyger's Eye, Donald Tyson, Clare Vaughn, Jim Weaver, and S Y Zenith

Llewellyn's 2002 Magical Almanac

ISBN 0-7387-0033-9. Copyright © 2001 by Llewellyn Worldwide. All rights reserved. Printed in the United States of America.

Editor/Designer:	Michael Fallon
Black & White Cover Illustration:	Merle S. Insinga
Color Application to Cover Artwork:	Lynne Menturweck
Calendar Pages Design:	Andrea Neff
Calendar Pages Illustrations:	
Illustrations, pages: 15, 29, 38–41, 45–6, 53, 70, 75–7, 79, 104, 109, 112, 114–5, 127, 133–5, 140, 147–8, 150 161–7, 233, 241, 247, 254, 259–61, 283, 288, 296, 313, 326, 328–30, 336–8, 343–4, 350–1, 357, 368, 374	Kerigwen
Clip Art Illustrations:	Dover Publications

Special thanks to Amber Wolfe for the use of daily color and incense correspondences. For more detailed information, please see *Personal Alchemy* by Amber Wolfe.

You can order Llewellyn annuals and books from *New Worlds,* Llewellyn's magazine catalog, or online at www.llewellyn.com. To request a free copy of the catalog, call toll-free: 1-877-NEW WRLD, or click on "Catalog Request" under the New Worlds heading on our website.

Moon sign and phase data computed by Astro Communications Services (ACS).

Llewellyn Worldwide
Dept. 0-7387-0033-9
P.O. Box 64383
St. Paul, MN 55164-0838

ABOUT THE AUTHORS

BERNYCE BARLOW is author of Llewellyn's *Sacred Sites of the West* and has been a contributer to Llewellyn's almanacs since 1995. She is a researcher and speaker, and she leads sacred site seminars throughout the U.S. She is most well-known for her magical tools of enlightenment that come from the Acme Toy Company, and she swears that her cartoon totems are real!

ELIZABETH BARRETTE lives in central Illinois in an old Victorian farmhouse, where she enjoys landscaping and studying Pagan and related topics. She currently works as managing editor for *PanGaia* magazine and editorial assistant for *SageWoman,* and she writes freelance for Pagan, speculative fiction, and gender studies publications, including *Circle Network News, LunaSol, PagaNet News, Terra Incognita,* and *Spicy Green Iguana.* For more details, check out her website at: http://www.worthlink.net/~ysabet/index.html.

CHANDRA MOIRA BEAL is a freelance writer in Austin, Texas. *Chandra* is Sanskrit for "moon." She lives with a magical house rabbit named Maia and has authored hundreds of articles about everything from mermaids to law. Chandra also self-published *Splash Across Texas,* a guide to aquatic recreation in her home state.

LORI BRUNO is a hereditary Sicilia Strega and founder of Our Lord and Lady of the Trinacrian Rose Coven in Massachusetts. She also helped create the Sacred Paths Alliance Network (SPAN), a charitable organization, and the Protective Organization of Witches & Earth Religions (POWER). Ms. Bruno is a descendant of Renaissance philosopher Giordano Bruno, who was condemned as a heretic and burned on February 17, 1600.

FRANCES CAMBERIS, M.A., is a shamanic healer who has practiced her healing ways in the Chicago area since 1982. She is the founder of Wellness Management, Inc., and of the "Sensate Intiutive" approach to energetic studies. She also has an active shamanic apprenticeship program with members across the U.S. and abroad.

DAVID CUMES, M.D., has a private medical practice in California. He was born and raised in South Africa, where for a time he lived with the Kalahari bushmen. Dr. Cumes was trained as a wilderness guide and has traveled extensively in the wild, leading groups on healing journeys to Peru, South Africa, and the Sini Desert. He is the author of *Inner Passage, Outer Journey* and *The Spirit of Healing*.

ESTELLE DANIELS is a Pagan minister and member of the Wiccan Church of Minnesota. She is also a professional part-time astrologer and author of *Astrologickal Magick,* as well as a regular contributor to the Llewellyn annuals. She is coauthor with Paul Tuitéan of the *Pocket Guide to Wicca* and *Essential Wicca*. She has been active in the Pagan Community since 1989, traveling to festivals regularly and working individually with students.

NUALA DRAGO is an author, musician, folklorist, and solitary Wittan. She has been a lifelong student of ancient cultures, particularly the Celts, and speaks Irish Gaelic. She enjoys traditional Celtic music and the study of ancient recipes for food and folk medicines. She is currently working on a book-length tale of the Celtic otherworld.

ELLEN DUGAN, also known as the "Garden Witch," is a psychic-clair-voyant and practicing Witch of more than fifteen years. She and her husband raise three magical teenagers and tend to their gardens in Missouri. Ellen received master gardener status in the spring of 2000. She is currently working on a "Garden Witchery" book.

DENISE DUMARS is is a college English instructor and writer from southern California. A member of the Temple of Isis in Los Angeles, she is also the editor of *Isis 2000: The Goddess in the New Aeon,* a collection of goddess poetry. Her magazine articles can be found in such journals as *Fate, Cinefantastique,* and on the website *Fandom.com*.

MARGUERITE ELSBETH, also known as Senihele and Sparrowhawk, is a hereditary Sicilian Strega, and is also proud of her Lenni Lenape (Delaware Indian) ancestry. She is a professional astrologer, tarot reader, and spiritual healer specializing in crisis counseling,

spiritual troubleshooting, and difficult relationship issues. She has written numerous articles for Llewellyn's annuals, is the author of *Crystal Medicine,* and coauthor of *The Grail Castle: Male Myths and Mysteries in the Celtic Tradition.* She currently lives in the Southwest desert. Visit her website at http://practicalSPIRITkeeping.com.

ANNA FRANKLIN lives in a village in the English Midlands. She trained initially as a photographer and artist but was pushed in the mid-1980s to acknowledge her spiritual life. She then retrained in reflexology, aromatherapy, herbalism, and healing. Today, Anna is the high priestess and founder of the Hearth of Arianhod, which runs teaching circles and discussion groups, and she is a third degree Witch. She has written for a number of Pagan magazines and contributed to several books.

ANNE MARIE GARRISON is a full-time graphic designer, illustrator, co-owner of Witches Stitches: Counted Cross-stitch Patterns for Crafty Pagans (www.witchesstitches.com), and author of *Gods and Goddesses of the Zodiac: A Coloring Book.* She is currently working on her second coloring book, a tarot deck, new cross-stitch patterns, and other projects the gods see fit to clunk her on the head with. Otherwise, she would just as soon waste away her time singing and playing with her beautiful Virgo daughter.

JOHN MICHAEL GREER has been a practitioner of Hermetic magic for more than twenty-five years and has written numerous books and articles on occult subjects. A student of geomancy and sacred geometry, and a member of several magical and fraternal orders, he is also a scholar and practitioner in Western esoteric martial arts. He is the also director of the Ibis Center for Hermetic Studies, an educational organization, and lives in Seattle.

MAGENTA GRIFFITH has been a Witch more than twenty-five years, a high priestess for twelve years, and is a founding member of the twenty-year-old coven Prodea. She leads rituals and workshops around the Midwest and is currently librarian for the New Alexandria Library, a Pagan and magical resource center.

RAVEN GRIMASSI is a practicing Witch and author of *The Wiccan Mysteries* by Llewellyn, which was awarded Book of the Year and Best Spirituality Book by the Coalition of Visionary Retailers in 1998. His other books include the *Encyclopedia of Wicca and Witchcraft, Wiccan Mysteries, Hereditary Witchcraft,* and *Italian Witchcraft.* Raven has been a teacher and practitioner of Wicca and witchcraft more than twenty-five years, and is an active lecturer on magic, ritual, and personal power topics.

DAVID HARRINGTON has been a chronicler of the magical arts for the past fifteen years. He is also coauthor, with Scott Cunningham, of *The Magical Household* and *Spellcrafts.* He is also the coauthor with deTraci Regula of *Whispers of the Moon.*

NATALIE HARTER has degrees in anthropology and women's studies, and has been fascinated by female figures in religion, mythology, and folklore for as long as she can remember. She lived and studied at Keydong Tukche Choling Convent in Nepal, the first Tibetan Buddhist Convent to initiate nuns in the craft of creating sand mandalas, and she hopes to travel again very soon.

EILEEN HOLLAND is the author of a number of books and videos on magical, herbal, and Pagan topics. She has also contributed to Llewellyn's *Herbal Almanac.*

ELLEN EVERT HOPMAN is the author of several books, including *Tree Medicine–Tree Magic, People Of The Earth,* and *Walking the World in Wonder–A Children's Herbal.* For contact information and reviews, visit: www.geocities.com/gaias_song/willow.html.

KENNETH JOHNSON obtained his degree in the study of comparative religions. He has been a practitioner of astrology since 1974 and is the author of six books. Some of them are *Mythic Astrology: Archetypal Powers in the Horoscope; Jaguar Wisdom: An Introduction to the Mayan Calendar; Slavic Sorcery;* and *Witchcraft and the Shamanic Journey.*

LADYHAWK WHISPERS is a tarot reader, wife, fledgling author, bookstore owner, mother, and artist. She lives in northeastern Michigan

where the pine trees sing to her, and she is studying to become a master herbalist. She is a solitary Wiccan of the Natural Witch variety at forty-one years young.

KIRIN LEE is a graphic designer and a science fiction writer. She is the managing editor of a rock music magazine and coeditor of the sci-fi fanzine *Starship Earth*. She is present working on a Pagan book and a young adult novel.

MARY MAGPIE is a self-initiated Witch with a great interest in the Norse Heathen traditions. She is a member of a coven in the English Midlands and has written articles for various Pagan magazines, including *Silver Wheel* and *Quest*.

EDAIN MCCOY has been a Witch since 1981. She has studied many magical traditions, including Celtic, Appalachian, and Curanderismo. Today, she is an elder in the Wittan Irish Pagan Tradition and a priestess of Brighid. Edain is listed in *Who's Who Among American Authors* and is the author of the Llewellyn books *Witta; A Witch's Guide to Faery Folk; The Sabbats; How to Do Automatic Writing; Celtic Myth and Magick; Mountain Magick; Lady of the Night; Inside a Witch's Coven; Making Magick; Celtic Women's Spirituality; Astral Projection for Beginners;* and *Bewitchments*.

ANN MOURA was raised in a family tradition of Green Witchcraft, which she has passed on to her children. She has been a solitary Witch for over thirty-five years, and she holds bachelor's and master's degrees in history. She is the author of the Llewellyn books *Origins of Modern Witchcraft; Green Witchcraft; Green Witchcraft II: Balancing Light and Shadow;* and *Green Witchcraft III: The Manual*. She has recently completed a work on the historical roots of Witchcraft.

LAUREL NIGHTSPRING has been a solitary Pagan for more than a decade. She has spent her entire life in southeastern Ohio, and when she is not writing she spends time with her husband and their two mischievous young children.

LILY GARDNER is a lifelong student of folklore and mythology, and a writer and priestess in the Daughters of Gaia coven in Portland, Oregon. She is currently working on a collection of solstice tales.

ROBERT M. PLACE is a visionary artist, and the designer, illustrator, and coauthor of *The Alchemical Tarot* and *The Angels' Tarot*. Robert is an expert on Western mysticism, tarot history, and is a gifted teacher of divination. He has taught and lectured at the New York Open Center, Omega Institute, the New York Tarot School, and the World Tarot Congress. He has appeared on Discovery and the Learning Channel, and he is currently working on *The Saints' Tarot*, to be published by Llewellyn in 2001. He can be reached through his website: www.crosswinds.net/~alchemicalegg/.

LAUREN RAINE is a painter, performance artist, poet, and maskmaker of twenty-five years. Her work is held in private and public collections, and she holds art degrees from the University of California at Berkeley and from the University of Arizona. She is especially interested in art that facilitates self-discovery and community. Currently, she creates masks for performance and for exhibition. In her workshops she assists others to explore the mythic realms within all of us, to celebrate rites of passage, and to touch the living Earth through art.

DIANA RAJCHEL lives in southern Minnesota with her husband amidst a sanctuary for homeless plants. She is a third degree priestess in Shadowmoon Coven, a founder of the Minnesota State University–Mankato Pagan organization, and the author of the webpage *Medea's Chariot* at http://Nexus.MNIC.net/~rajchd. When not doing Witchy stuff, she works on an MFA in creative writing.

SILVER RAVENWOLF is the author of more than thirteen nonfiction how-to and fictional books relating to the magical sciences and spirituality. Silver is the clan head of the Black Forest Family. Her primary interests are divinatory tools, astrology, hypnotherapy, and getting through life in a positive and productive way. To read about Silver, the Black Forest Clan, upcoming events and books, and her

online organization, the Wiccan/Pagan Press Alliance, please visit: http://www.silverravenwolf.com.

deTraci Regula is the author of *The Mysteries of Isis* and creator of *The Egyptian Scarab Oracle*. With David Harrington, she wrote *Whispers of the Moon: A Biography of Scott Cunningham*, which explores the life of the well-known magical author. She is an archpriestess and priestess hierophant of the Fellowship of Isis. Her travels have taken her to many places around the world, and she enjoys exploring folklore and magical practices in all cultures. Visit her website at http://www.geocities.com/Athens/Academy/7133/.

Michelle Santos is an amateur astrologer, first-level crystal healer, and believer in fairies. She holds empowerment and enrichment classes in and around the state of Massachusetts. Her articles can be seen in *Bride's Magazine*, *SageWoman*, *Renaissance Magazine*, *Victorian Decorating*, and *Lifestyle Magazine*.

Sedwin is a writer and explorer of ancient Goddess spirituality. She teaches a workshop called "Understanding the Language of the Goddess," based on the work of Marija Gimbutas, and she lives near New York City where she enjoys drumming circles with friends.

ShadowCat is a priestess and Witch in the American Celtic Tradition of Lady Sheba, but she prefers solitary work. She spends her days acquiring new manuscripts for Llewellyn Publications, and her free time fussing over her five feline companions. A self-taught, self-proclaimed gourmet cook, she is also on the board of directors for the Minnesota Book Publishers' Roundtable.

Cerridwen Iris Shea is a tarot-reading, horse-playing, dragon-loving urban writer Witch who lives in Manhattan and works on Broadway. Her plays have been produced in various locations throughout the world, and her writing has been published under various names in various genres. She is currently owned by four cats.

Susan Sheppard is the author of *The Astrological Guide to Seduction & Romance*, a Book-of-the-Month Club selection, and an award-winning

poet. She lives in Parkersburg, West Virginia, where she leads the popular Haunted Parkersburg Ghost Tours. She is also an artist, painting and making Witch poppets for Laurie Cabot's shop in Salem, Massachusetts.

LYNNE STURTEVANT is a freelance writer specializing in mythology, fairy tales, legends, and folklore. She is also an accomplished craftswoman and an avid collector of folk art. She has a bachelor's degree in philosophy and lives in Virginia with her husband.

TYGER'S EYE is a solitary Wiccan and aspiring writer. She will be eighteen at the time of publication, and on her way to (gulp!) university. She thanks everyone who's ever given her encouragement, especially Christie Wright who unknowingly gave her the extra push she needed to send in her writing.

DONALD TYSON is a is a freelance writer living and working in Nova Scotia, Canada. He is the author of numerous works that cover the spectrum of Western occultism, including *New Millennium Magic*, *Rune Magic*, the annotated *Three Books of Occult Philosophy by Cornelius Agrippa*, and *Enochian Magic for Beginners*.

CLARE VAUGHN has been studying the Western mystery tradition for over twenty years. She also practices Druidry.

JIM WEAVER is a writer and collector of American folk art. Working in his herb and flower gardens helps him stay close to nature while celebrating the changing seasons.

S Y ZENITH is three-quarters Chinese with a dash of Irish in her ancestry. She is a solitary Pagan practitioner who has lived and travelled extensively throughout Asia. For the last sixteen years, S Y has made her home in Sydney, Australia. Her fascination with folk traditions both Eastern and Western has resulted in numerous articles in different genres under several names. Her work has been published both in Australia and the United States.

TABLE OF CONTENTS

Full Moon Tale

By ShadowCat

When I was a little girl, I lived on a farm in the northern part of Minnesota. The Dark River divided our property, so the township built a bridge over the river and provided a crossing to our pastures. As I was an adventurous child, my mother was terrified that I would fall into the river one day and drown. She told me, therefore, that a troll lived under the bridge, and each time she told the story she would embellish it a little more. A recent Full Moon brought the memory of Mother's story to me, which I will tell you with a bit of embellishment of my own.

This one's for you, Mom, wherever you are. By the way, did you ever know that my favorite place to be was under that old bridge and my favorite pastime was waiting for that troll to show up to claim his bridge?

Last night I was out for my evening run and as I was coming around Schwartz Pond, I heard the voices of children, laughing and chattering in the grove of trees near the pond. They emerged from the grove, brandishing "swords," no doubt found in the grove, and they proceeded to slash away at the dandelions in the grass.

As I was about to run across the bridge, one of the boys, who was now prodding the water with his sword, asked me: "Are you going to run across that bridge?" I looked into the sunset and replied, "There's still time, isn't there?" Obviously puzzled, he asked, "What do you mean?" "Well," I said, "my people believe that dawn and dusk are the times between times when the magical world blends with the mundane and the magical creatures can be seen by humans. For every bridge, there is a troll who guards it and very soon he will rise out of the pond to claim his bridge."

The young lad puffed out his chest, put his hands on his hips in a defiant stance, and said, "We're nine years old and we don't believe you! You're just trying to fool us!"

I shrugged at him and crossed the bridge with careful steps and stood on the other side. Once there, I shouted back at him: "I'm forty-one years old, and my mother told me about trolls when I was a little girl, and I still believe in them. Look! You see that mist rising over the pond? It's the troll's breath! He's coming to the top and pretty soon he's going to stand up and walk across the pond, then build his campfire right here by the bridge!"

The boys looked at me with wide eyes and mouths gaping. "And I'm getting out of here before he comes!" I exclaimed. I then looked over the pond, let out a shriek, and ran as fast as my aging legs could carry me up the hill.

As I reached the top of the hill, I turned to see what my young friends were doing. All I saw of them was the back of their heads, elbows and heels in the air, flying across the field as fast as their young legs could carry them. The most humorous part of this story was lost to these young boys. They had just had an encounter with a real Witch, and they had not a clue!

MOONSHINE

BY MARY MAGPIE

T he tides of the Moon affect us all. Waxing Moons are a time of growth; waning Moons are concerned with reduction and cleansings. It is accepted that Full Moons are potent times for magic. They usually have a powerful effect on people, and in general I try to make a point of spending some time each day outside under the moonlight so that I can absorb the Moon's power.

This night, I had gone to bed and was awoken from a strange, unremembered dream by the compelling call of a rock I'd picked up from a beach in Wales some years before.

The palm-sized stone sat on my bedroom windowsill bathing in the powerful rays of the Full Moon. In the past, I always thought of it as a greyish color, with white quartz inclusions and red iron-ore stains over much of its surface. Now I saw instead that the stone glowed ice white in the moonlight and was pulsing with a new and more powerful kind of energy.

The urge to meditate at this moment was quite strong, so I took the rock downstairs where my son was watching television. Our house is not large. The only rooms free of sleeping family members are the bathroom and kitchen, and both are very tiny. The weather was not good enough to go outdoors, so I decided to stay in the TV room and create my own quiet place. Here's what happened next:

I went through my usual relaxation routine quietly, visualizing a sphere of white light surrounding me as I sat in an armchair and rested my chin on my hands. I looked at the stone that I held. It was roughly triangular, and I held the apex uppermost.

Suddenly I felt the energy of the Moon connect with the stone, and I had the impression being lifted from my body, which remained quietly seated on a chair, half-listening to the low murmur of the television. My astral body rose up and up, out of the house, carried aloft by the energies in the stone. It traveled past the atmosphere and continued up to the Moon, where the orb's divine power greeted and embraced me. My spirit was absorbed into that of the Moon, and part of the Moon spirit became aware of my luminance shining down upon the Earth. Brightly though I tried to shine, I found it impossible to make the Earth bright enough, and I realized, feeling foolish, that it was night in my hemisphere, and that daylight was a gift of the Sun, not the Moon.

Nevertheless there were lights on the planet. Bright flashes shot up from the surface like so many fireworks. The colors were brilliant and beautiful. But they left behind wounds—deep holes and crumbling piles of rock that should have been part of the Earth's crust.

The Moon deity, who was both male and female, showed me that these bright flashes were leaks of energy where the Earth had been damaged by mining. By far the worst damage was caused where crystals were being extracted. The energy was flying from these places at a tremendous rate, depleting the energy field and the life force of the living planet.

I knew then that I was being asked to act to correct the problem. My return journey was not so easy as the outward one. I had taken the form of a tiny asteroid with a fiery tail, and, as I was flying in a fast arc, it took a while to navigate myself back into the atmosphere.

The silver thread that connected me to my earthbound body had become stretched and tangled, making my journey all the more difficult as my astral and physical bodies reeled it in to bring the disparate parts back together. I remember flying over the various continents as I circled the globe trying to find my way home.

At this point I was afraid that I would ever find my body again, but then the British mainland came into view and all I had to do then was locate my home. The shining thread was brighter and straighter now, so I let it pull me back safely.

At last I settled with a slight jolt back into my body and opened my eyes with a clear understanding of my task. First, I must bring a halt to, or at least slow down the rate of, crystal mining on the Earth. My secondary task was of rather less urgency, but one to be achieved in time. I needed to help people understand that though the Moon has qualities that appear feminine, the deity has both masculine and feminine aspects. The energies of both are of equal importance. The same goes for the Sun. So these are the purposes too of this article. I hope you will take these messages to heart.

Since my journey, I've been quietly campaigning to protect the Earth by encouraging the use of magical tools that don't need to be dug up. I have also frequently aired my strong views on environmental matters in various media and forums. May you go in peace under the light of the Moon.

FOR FURTHER STUDY

The Complete Book of Psychic Arts: Divination practices from around the world. Morwyn. Llewellyn Publications, 2000.

The Magician's Reflection: A complete guide to creating magical symbols & systems. Bill Whitcomb. Llewellyn Publications, 1999.

A History of Pagan Europe. Prudence Jones and Nigel Pennick. Routledge, 1997.

HEALING THROUGH THE ELEMENTS

By JOHN MICHAEL GREER

Many people in the Western world these days have become interested in alternative forms of healing—so many that, according to a recent study, more visits are made each year to alternative health practitioners than are made to orthodox medical doctors.

Alternative health practices are varied and diverse. For instance, both traditional Chinese medicine (TCM) and Ayurveda, the ancient healing art of India, have become very popular as part of this movement. There are good reasons for this. Both of these systems have deep links

to living spiritual traditions, and both are well suited to helping people get and stay healthy, rather than simply treating them when they are ill.

What very few people remember these days is that, up until quite recently, there was a very similar system in the Western world. Like TCM and Ayurveda, this forgotten system has strong connections to spirituality, treats the patient rather than the illness, and focuses on preserving and promoting health rather than just responding to disease. Just as TCM uses Taoist concepts such as yin and yang, and

Ayurveda uses ideas that are closely related to the teachings of yoga and other Hindu spiritual systems, their forgotten Western equivalent is based on a set of concepts very familiar to people involved in modern magical spirituality—that is, the traditional four elements: fire, water, earth, and air.

The art of healing through the elements dates back to the beginning of medical knowledge in the Western world. The ancient writings of Hippocrates include some of the fundamentals of this lore. Two other ancient physicians and writers—Galen, an ancient Greek who lived in the second century of the common era, and Avicenna, a Persian who lived about eight centuries later—established the core teachings of elemental healing. Later, figures drew from and expanded upon this tradition. Nicholas Culpeper, for instance, was a English herbalist who made it his life's work to put herbal medicine in the hands of the common people.

It was only with the rise of scientific ideas, and the rejection of magical concepts that had served humans for centuries, that the art of elemental healing was forgotten in

the industrialized countries of the West. However, this practice does still survive in India and much of the Muslim world, where it is known as *Unani Tibb,* or "Greek medicine," and in Latin America, where it remains as an important part of folk medical practice. It may yet be worth reviving as a healing art especially well suited to students of Western magical traditions.

Understanding Elemental Healing

To understand the ancient art of elemental healing, it is necessary first to remember a few things about the elements. Each element is formed by the combination of two qualities out of a set of four: warm, cold, dry, and moist. Thus, fire is warm and dry; air is warm and moist; water is cold and moist, and earth is cold and dry. In some respects, these qualities are more important than the elements themselves since anything that has the right pair of qualities corresponds to the element, and anything that is relatively warm and dry, in other words, is "fiery" or connected with elemental fire.

These qualities can be felt directly in the human body always. When the body is in its normal, healthy state, it is mildly warm and moist. This changes with illness however. A fever, for instance, makes the body warmer and may make it dry. A cold without fever, on the other hand, feels cold and moist. Every individual has a particular balance of elemental qualities, which tends to prevent certain illnesses and foster others. Every illness, in turn, has its characteristic imbalance.

When the body takes in different substances, in turn, these can change the qualities that are present in it. Swallow some cayenne pepper, for example, and you'll feel a flush of heat go through your body. Your mucous membranes will then feel more open and dry. According to the art of elemental healing, cayenne is a hot and dry herb—a herb of fire—and so it can be used to treat cold, wet, watery illnesses like the common cold. Similarly, yarrow is cold and dry, and thus can be used to break the heat of a fever.

These concepts—elements, qualities, the balance of the body, and the way that different herbs and other substances affect that balance—are the core ideas of the old elemental healing. There's much more to the whole system, of course. Every herb or healing substance, for example, has two properties. The first is its elemental effect, or the way it affects the warmth, coldness, moisture, and dryness of the body. The other is its specific effect, which includes all the other effects it has on the body. The different specific effects help the healer choose between different warming and drying herbs for a given cold and wet illness.

Once you get more involved in this method of healing, you will find that the elemental effects of healing substances are divided more precisely. There are four degrees of warmth, coldness, moisture, and dryness. The first degree is mild, the second is moderate, the third is strong, and the fourth is so strong that it can damage the body if it's not used carefully or counteracted with other herbs. Cayenne, for example, is warm and dry in the third degree, which makes it a strong treatment for wet, runny head colds. Chamomile is also warm and dry, but only in the first degree, so it's a milder and gentler treatment for less intense conditions.

In conclusion, it is interesting to note that almost everyone in America actually knows one bit of folklore that comes straight out of the ancient art of elemental healing. According to the traditional lore, the process of digesting food increases the warmth of the body. Eating thus tends to help counter cold illnesses, but worsens hot ones, which is why we still remember today "to feed a cold, and starve a fever."

FOR FURTHER STUDY

Culpeper's Medicine: A practice of western holistic medicine. Graeme Tobyn. Element, 1997.

The General Principles of Avicenna's Canon of Medicine. Mazhar H. Shah. Naveed Clinic, 1966.

Hippocrates' Latin American Legacy: Humoral medicine in the New World. George M. Foster. Gordon and Breach, 1994.

The Traditional Healer's Handbook: A classic guide to the medicine of Avicenna. Hakim G. M. Chishti. Healing Arts Press, 1991.

Ritual Breads

By Magenta Griffith

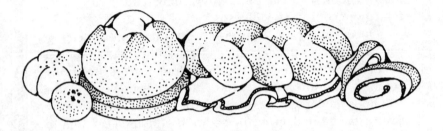

A large symbolically shaped bread is an excellent contribution to any seasonal ritual. My coven has used the bread god to symbolize John Barleycorn, the god of vegetation who rises every spring and is cut down every autumn to feed the people. We have also used kore bread to celebrate spring for many years. Here's how to make these special breads.

The Bread God

2	packages yeast or 2 tablespoons dry yeast
½	cup warm water (put a drop on your wrist to test, like a baby bottle; warm, but not too hot)
6	cups of white flour OR 3 cups white flour and 3 cups whole wheat flour
3–4	tbsp honey or sugar
1	tbsp salt
3	tbsp oil
3	eggs, beaten (reserve 1 tbsp for glazing loaf)
1	cup milk or water
	Extra flour

Hand mixing method: Dissolve yeast in warm water, allow to stand for 5 minutes to proof (test that the yeast works). Put flour in a large bowl, make a well in the center, and pour in the yeast mixture. In a separate bowl, mix the eggs and reserve one tablespoon for the glaze, if desired. Then add sweetener, oil, salt, and water, and mix, then add wet to dry and mix well. Turn out onto a lightly floured surface, flour your hands and knead for 10 minutes. Add more flour if needed. Dough should not stick to the board, but also should not dry out or become crumbly.

Electric mixer method: If you have a heavy-duty electric mixer with a dough hook, you can use this method. Dissolve yeast in warm water in mixing bowl, and allow to stand for 5 minutes to proof. Mix the eggs together and reserve 1 tablespoon for the glaze, if desired. Add the eggs and rest of the liquids and sugar or honey, and mix using the dough hook. Add salt, then flour, one cup at a time as quickly as possible to avoid overkneading. Add up to 1 cup more flour, a tablespoon at a time if needed to keep dough from sticking to the bowl. Knead about ten minutes.

Both methods: Place the dough in an oiled bowl, cover, and let rise in a warm place for 1 hour until doubled in bulk. Punch down and knead for 1 minute. Now comes the shaping of the bread god, somewhat like working with Play-Doh.

For this, turn out the dough onto flour surface. To make one very large figure, divide the dough into three parts. (To make two smaller figures, divide the dough in half, then into thirds, and go through this process twice to form two figures.) Roll each piece of dough between your hands into long ropes. Lay these parallel on the surface.

Leave some length at each end, and braid the middle into the body. Use the three strands at one end to shape the arms and head, on the other end to form the legs and either a phallus or a vulva. You can use dried fruit for eyes, nipples, or other details. Be creative.

Baking: Place the bread god on a baking sheet that has been greased and dusted with corn meal, and allow to rise uncovered in a warm place. If you are forming it into one large bread god, you may not have a big enough sheet. In this case, you can overlap two baking sheets, being careful to always move them as one.

Allow the bread god to double in size, about 1 hour. Twenty minutes before baking time, preheat oven to 350°F.

Before you bake, mix the reserved tablespoon of egg with 1 tablespoon of water, and use this mixture to glaze the loaf. You may also sprinkle poppy seeds or sesame seeds on strategic places, if you want the effect of hair on the god's head, beard, crotch, or chest. Bake 35 to 40 minutes, or until the bread god is nicely browned and sounds hollow when tapped. If you have a hot oven, check after 30 minutes.

Carefully transfer the bread god to a wire rack and cool. If you have used two sheets, be especially careful when removing it from the oven.

This is a versatile dough. Feel free to experiment with other shapes, like a Sun Wheel, a spiral, as well as the traditional braided loaf. In this last case, simply divide into three parts, roll into ropes, and braid as you would hair. Don't be afraid to be creative.

Low Fat, Low Cholesterol Variation

You can eliminate the eggs in the above recipe. Simply increase the liquid to 1½ cups. I would advise using low fat or skim milk in this case rather than water. The oil can be decreased to 2 table-spoons, but the bread needs oil in it. You can use milk to glaze the unbaked loaf, or you can leave it unglazed.

Kore Bread

This recipe is a variation of a Russian bread made in the spring, usually for Easter. The abundance of eggs is both practical and symbolic. The egg is a symbol of everlasting life, of life renewed, and of new life yet to come.

Also, hens start laying more eggs as the days get longer, so in the spring, the farmers have more eggs than they know what to do with.

1	cup water
½	stick cinnamon
4	whole cloves
4	allspice berries
1	bay leaf
10–12	coriander seeds

Mix ingredients in a pan, bring to a boil together 5 minutes. Strain, set aside and allow to cool.

In a sauce pan, scald 1 cup milk, add 1 cup butter, then cool the mixture to room temperature. In a bowl, dissolve 4 tablespoons dry yeast and 1 tablespoon honey in 1 cup warm water, and set aside to proof for five minutes.

10–12	cups flour
1	tablespoon salt
1½	cups honey
2	teaspoons oil of anise
	Peel of 1 orange, grated
10	eggs

Mix flour and salt in a large bowl, add dissolved yeast, honey, the milk mixture, anise oil, orange peel, and the spiced water. Mix in a heavy duty electric mixer with a dough hook for 15 minutes, adding eggs one at a time. Remove from the mixer, and add the rest of the flour with a spoon, turning onto a floured surface and kneading in the last of it until you have a soft dough.

Put the dough into a buttered bowl, cover, and let rise until doubled in size, about 1 hour. Punch down, let double again, punch down again, and let double in size a third time.

Turn onto a floured surface and knead briefly. Divide the dough in two, then divide each half into thirds. Let the dough rest under a towel for 10 minutes.

Roll 3 pieces of dough into 24-inch strands. Braid these together, then join the ends to form a kind of wreath. Transfer to a well-greased cooking sheet, and repeat with the rest of the dough. Cover the dough, and let rise until doubled, about 1 hour.

Gently push 4 dyed eggs deeply into the quarters of each wreath, and if you'd like, put one in the center of each. I like to use naturally dyed eggs. To do this, place eggs in a pan of water with the skins of several yellow or purple onions. Boil the water to produce a pleasant reddish brown, or purplish red color, respectively. You can also use a heaping tablespoon of tumeric to produce yellow eggs. (Use a metal pot; tumeric is a permanent dye.) The eggs must be pushed deeply into the dough so the baking won't force them out.

Beat together 2 eggs and 1 tablespoon milk, and brush the surface of the loaves with this mixture, avoiding the eggs. Sprinkle generously with sesame seeds.

Bake in a preheated 350°F oven for about 1 hour, until done. The crust should be golden, and the bread should sound hollow when tapped. Gently remove the bread from the pans and cool on a wire rack.

Makes 2 large braided loaves. You can make a half-recipe for one loaf, but it's almost as much work for one as for two.

FOR FURTHER STUDY

Beard on Bread. James Beard. Knopf, 1995.

Bread Winners. Mel London. Rodale Press, 1979.

Winter Wonderland, or the Magic of Snow

By Edain McCoy

Whether you love or hate snow, if you have access to it this winter and are not employing it in your repertoire of natural magic, you are missing a great magical opportunity.

Snow shares similar properties with water since, as you well know, it is ultimately the solidified form of this element. Yet snow falls from the sky and blows about, giving it air qualities too, and it blankets the ground in silence and stillness, giving it earth aspects. Therefore, snow automatically gives you the power of three elemental energies in one natural substance.

You'll likely find dozens of uses for snow magic once you begin experimenting. Start your magical winter journey by trying or adapting any of the snow spells I've listed below.

Snowball Slowdown Spell

If you have a situation or issue you wish to put on hold, take a representation of that problem and pack it tightly in the center of a snowball. You can use a symbolic object, such as a piece of paper on which you've written the problem down, or a stone or herb or

other symbolic object in which you've poured the energy of the issue or your feelings about the problem. Next, take the snowball indoors and store it in your freezer. Before you shut the freezer door say:

Frozen deep in icy state,
Pressing problem now must wait;
Snow that blankets and cloaks the bane,
Until I release the energy again.

Don't try to put your problem on hold forever. Problems don't just go away. In fact, they have a sneaky way of regrouping their energies and attacking from another direction. Find a way to cope as soon as is reasonable. When you're ready to deal with your problem, release it from its bondage by setting the snowball out in the sun to melt.

SNOWFLAKE SPELL FOR ATTRACTIVENESS

To enhance personal attractiveness, collect some falling snow overnight in a small bowl. Take the bowl inside and stir in some vanilla. As the vanilla and snow melt together, imagine them becoming a catalyst for giving your face a lovely wintertime glow. Wash in the mixture each morning after a new snowfall to attain winter beauty. After you pat your face dry, look into the nearest mirror and smile while you say:

Face of mine with radiant glow,
Project beauty where'er I go;
Skin is soft and eyes do shine,
Attractiveness now is mine.

SNOW BLANKET BANISHMENT

To remove an unwanted person from your life without causing them harm, go outside when snow blankets the earth and make two small snow figures, or "snowmen" as you may call them. Make them no more than a few inches tall. As you make them, invest one with the energy of yourself and the other with the energy of the person you wish to have out of your life. Make sure the first figure faces your home and the other faces the opposite direction.

Between the two figures make a wall of snow high enough that if the figures had eyes in the back of their heads they could not see each other over the embankment. Visualize the direction and path of each figure diverging from the other, taking each towards its own happy, fulfilling—but wholly separate—life, as you say:

Out of sight and out of mind,
Know my thoughts are not unkind;
Our paths must take us separate ways,
So we may live in happiness all our days.

I let you go with blessings true,
Hoping you find the best for you;
I wish you love and wish you peace,
As of now our relationship does cease.

Take the figure representing you, and remove it from the ground. Hide it outdoors where it could not be found if the other figure were able to sprout legs and come searching. Return to the other figure and complete the snow wall around it, leaving only a small opening for a pathway leading in the opposite direction from your hidden figure.

SNOW ANGEL WARDING SPELL

Protect your home and property by empowering snow angels to do the warding for you. As you did in childhood, lie flat on your

back in fresh snow, and flap your arms and legs side to side and up and down. Then add the visualization of an angel standing guard near your home to protect it both physically and psychically. Get up carefully, and, as you look down at your imprint, you'll see it resembles an angel. Do this on all four sides of your home if possible. Leave a small bit of protective herb such as cinnamon, bay, or garlic at the "heart" of the angel to empower it further.

First Freeze Protection Spell

In the days before modern sanitation and antibiotics, it was not uncommon for airborne diseases to devastate large populations throughout the warm months of the year. This phenomenon would end only with the coming of first freeze—when the germs were killed by the cold. The "freezing ills" archetype is found in snow, which can be used both magically and medicinally to help heal wintertime colds and flus.

To do this, fill a small bucket with snow from the ground outside which has not been disturbed by any tracks or footprints. Visualize it as a healing balm for fever and flu. Let it melt on its own at the bedside of the person who is ill. Stir in a small bit of peppermint, rosemary, or eucalyptus oil as it melts.

Immerse a clean washcloth into the melting snow mixture, and use it to gently wipe the body of the person with the fever. This helps bring down the fever through the natural cooling power of water, and it helps magically because of the oils and visualizations you added. Be sure to keep envisioning your patient's fever coming down and the illness going away as you do wipe the snow over over him or her.

If your patient is up to chatting, talk about favorite common subjects. If the patient needs quiet, chant a spellbinding couplet over and over in your mind as you administer the healing snow.

Fever fade and sickness flee,
Health and strength restored to ye.

Snow Removal Spell for Stalemates

Collect a large bowl of snow to help move yourself forward out of a situation that seems in stalemate. Remain outside with it while contemplating all the details of the situation. Do not attempt to visualize a solution yet.

Bring the bowl of snow indoors and divide it into seven smaller portions. Place six of them in your freezer and place the seventh in a small bowl of its own. Set the bowl in front of a white candle. Gaze at the snow as it melts in the glow of the candle's warmth. Visualize your stagnant situation melting with the snow, the future bright like the candle's flame. Again, do not visualize an outcome, allow the powers of the universe to find the way out of a tough problem. Repeat for the next six nights.

MELTING SNOWBALLS, MELTING PASSION SPELL

To halt passion between two people, take a small piece of paper and write down their names. Separate the names from each other by cutting them apart with a pair of sharp scissors. Douse each piece of paper with vinegar and lime juice, then wrap each around a small bit of ashes or salt. Wrap each name up in its own snowball, and throw the snowballs away in separate directions. As you do this, say:

> *Flames of passions, quenched in snow,*
> *Love does flee, and lust does go;*
> *Happy do the ties now break,*
> *Passion's tremors no longer quake.*

FOR FURTHER STUDY

Bewitchments: Love magick for modern romance. Edain McCoy. Llewellyn Publications, 2000.

Earth, Air, Fire and Water: More techniques of natural magic. Scott Cunningham. Llewellyn Publications, 1988.

Earth Power: Techniques of natural magic. Scott Cunningham. Llewellyn Publications, 1983.

Making Magick: What it is and how it works. Edain McCoy. Llewellyn Publications, 1997.

Natural Magic. Marian Green. Element Books, 1989.

POSITIVE PROSPERITY

BY CERRIDWEN IRIS SHEA

When it comes to sabotage, no one is as good at damaging ourselves as we are. We know how to get in our own way better than anyone, and how to block ourselves from what we most need and want.

Love magic is, of course, very popular, but so is prosperity magic. The most difficult aspect of love magic is avoiding interfering with someone else's will, and the most difficult trap in prosperity magic is to truly believe that we deserve prosperity. Of course, as magical people, we do not want to gain our own prosperity by causing others to lose theirs. So, how do we train ourselves, and, even more, allow ourselves to be prosperous?

SOME THOUGHTS ON PROSPERITY

It is hard to believe that, contrary to the media diet we are fed each day, there is enough of everything out there for each of us to be prosperous in our own way. We see poverty, war, starvation, abuse, and the excess of those who have too much. It's difficult to see how the world can get back into prosperous balance when there is so much imbalance.

The key to this is that each of us make our own little corner of the world as pleasantly balanced as possible. But how?

Consider these concepts as the keys to balanced prosperity: time, energy, nurturance, and sustenance.

TIME

We should all be certain to take time to sit down with pen and paper and list all the things that make us feel prosperous. This can take several days. Be brutally honest. Write what you want, not what other people want, or what the media has told you to want. If you want five cars, write down "five cars." Remember, having five cars doesn't mean you're a terrible person. It has created jobs for people in the factories, for mechanics to fix the cars when they break down, for people at the gas stations, and so on. This is an economic contribution that helps others with their own prosperity Having five cars without proper emission controls, on the other hand, is another kettle of fish altogether.

As with energy, the object itself is not good or bad. How you choose to use it, however, defines its function. Maybe having fresh flowers in the house makes you feel prosperous. Maybe it is having flannel sheets in winter, or being able to eat out once a week, or take a trip somewhere. Maybe it is owning your own house, or simply not having to worry about the bills every month.

Whatever it means to you, write it down. Take your time with the list, revising it over a few days, or a few weeks, and adding and deleting as you see fit. Certain things will resonate every time you look at the list. Certain things will feel unimportant and can be thrown away.

Keep honing the list until you feel it's quite complete. Remember, this is a list of what you want, not what you think you can have. Don't set up roadblocks, especially this early in the process. If you find yourself chastising yourself for an item on the list, write about it in your diary. If you still want it, put it on the list without guilt.

Once you're satisfied with the list, choose one letter to represent each item and draw it on a stone or a piece of paper—something you can carry with you. If you can, set up a prosperity altar, even if it is as simple as a scarf with a few objects that make you feel prosperous, or a bulletin board with photos stuck on it. Take the actual list and burn it in your cauldron (this can be done in a circle or simply in sacred space), so that your desires are carried up to the gods.

ENERGY

At this point, you need to expend a little energy. You can't just burn a list, carry a talisman, and expect the items to manifest. There's more work to be done. Think about these questions: What can you do to achieve or procure the items on your list? Can you put your change into a dish at the end of the day, then every few months roll it up and put it in the bank? Can you cut out spending money on some regular habit—such as a daily bag of chips or can of soda?

Every little bit helps. Once I had dishes of change all over my home. I finally rolled it all up and discovered I had nearly $100! Very easily, little bits can turn into big bits. If you like fresh flowers, but can't afford to buy them every week, can you buy seeds and a pot and grow them? Are there other ways to save money? Maybe instead of eating at the most expensive restaurant in town, there is a small independently owned cafe with good food. Is there a possibility of a promotion at work? Or maybe it's time to look for a new job.

When you experience the feeling of prosperity, whether it comes in the form of a good meal or a good paycheck or from checking something off your list, remember how it makes you feel. Remember the warmth, the joy, the security. Remember you deserve it. And remember to say "thanks."

NURTURANCE AND SUSTENANCE

Nurturance and sustenance have a lot to do with prosperity. To bring in, you have to give out. Often, it is a case of clearing out the old to make room for the new. Or it may be that generosity of spirit sent out brings back more of the same.

There are many ways to give out small doses of prosperity. Give to your community. You don't have to write a check to an organization in order to be generous. Can you devote some time to a benefit? If you're busy trying to juggle work and family life, could you bake some cookies or donate something handmade? Can you help a neighbor carry groceries or shovel a sidewalk? Can you simply listen when someone in line at the store is desperate for a sympathetic ear? All of these things are important.

Sure, you're not going to be perfect. There are days when all you can bear to do is get away from everyone and go home. But you'll find that random acts of kindness are, in themselves, magical acts, and that what you put out will come back to you in ways more interesting and wonderful than you can imagine. When you make your own corner of the world a better place, you create a ripple effect that causes other people to do the same. Pretty soon, you will see the difference you make. And, since we are all one, everything good anyone does affects everyone else for the better.

As with anything, there are fine lines to walk. You want your acts to come out of genuine kindness, not out of your own sense of self-preservation, greed, or guilt. It's not a case of "if I'm nice to twelve people, I will be closer to getting that SUV." You want to do things for people who appreciate them, and without making them feel guilty if they don't respond in the way you wish. You don't want to be a doormat nor a martyr. You simply want to be a person.

You also need to allow yourself to receive. Some people get so caught up in the giving, they feel that they aren't allowed anything in return. In fact, you are. It keeps the energy flowing. If you never give or never receive, the energy gets stuck. You must find the negative pat-  terns in your past, in your environment, and work to change them. You have the power to change anything you don't like in your life. You deserve to be prosperous and happy.

FOR FURTHER STUDY

Silver's Spells for Prosperity. Silver RavenWolf. Llewellyn Publications, 1999.

To Light a Sacred Flame: Practical witchcraft for the millennium. Silver RavenWolf. Llewellyn Publications, 1999.

Everyday Magic: Spells and rituals for modern living. Dorothy Morrison. Llewellyn Publications, 1998

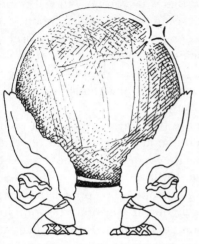

The Enochian Ritual of John Dee

By Donald Tyson

All that we know about Enochian magic is the result of a partnership between two men. For a period of seven years, from 1582 to 1589, the mathematician and scholar John Dee conducted a series of ritual séances with a paid crystal scryer, the alchemist Edward Kelley. The angels communicated with Dee through Kelley, a highly gifted spirit medium who was able to see and hear the angels with ease, not only within the depths of the crystal globe, but at times outside the stone as well. Dee's psychic ability was limited, only rarely did Dee see or hear the angels. This forced Dee to rely on Kelley for communication with the angels. This was a fortunate pairing, for it was with Dee that the angels sought to communicate—he was their chosen prophet.

The angels first contacted John Dee in his bedroom on the night of March 8, 1581, somewhere between ten and eleven o'clock, as Dee recorded in his diary:

It was the 8 day, being Wensday, hora noctis 10, 11, the strange noyse in my chamber of knocking; and the voyce, ten tymes repeted, somewhat like the shrich of an owle, but more longly drawn, and more softly, as it were in my chamber.

This interesting though inarticulate spiritual communication was repeated several times. Dee began to scry into a crystal ball in an effort to see and hear the spirits more clearly. Crystal scrying has an ancient and honorable history in England. The Druid Merlin was known to own a crystal globe in which he foresaw events. Crystal gazing was an accepted means for communicating with spirits along with other forms of scrying such as water divination and mirror divination. The idea was that spirits found it easier to appear if they had some sort of physical medium as a focus. The crystal acted as a little window into the realm of the spirits.

Dee did not record in his diary the ritual procedures he used during his own solitary attempts at crystal scrying. It was the custom to use ritual when scrying in the crystal, so we may assume that Dee employed a ritual structure, though it was probably quite simple. At a minimum it consisted of a prayer and invocation. Dee very probably prepared himself for the sessions by cleansing himself, and may have put on ritual articles of clothing or jewelry. Whatever procedure was used, it proved at least partially successful. He recorded in his diary:

May 25th, I had sight in [chrystallo] offered me, and I saw.

What he saw in the crystal was not recorded. Dee's successful attempts at scrying were infrequent. He realized he needed a scryer with a talent beyond his own if he was to achieve a fruitful communication with these spirits. He experimented with the psychic abilities of Barnabas Saul, a medium who at the time was having troubles with the law. On October 8, 1581, Saul gave Dee information concerning chests of books that had recently been discovered in Northamptonshire, but Dee recorded of Saul's vision: "I fownd no truth in it."

Dee reported in his diary that the next night, while lying in bed in front of a fireplace, Saul "was strangely trubled by a spirituall creature abowt mydnight." The Enochian angels were willing to attempt to communicate through Saul, but found him to be an unsuitable instrument.

The attempts by the Enochian angels to reach Dee through Saul ceased at around the same time that Edward Kelley arrived at Dee's house in Mortlake. On March 6, 1582, Saul came to visit. Dee recorded in his diary: "He confessed that he neyther hard or saw any spirituall creature any more." Two days later, Edward Kelley, traveling under the false name Talbot, arrived at Dee's home along with a mutual friend named Clerkson. Saul left Mortlake that same day, at around two or three o'clock in the afternoon, presumably after Kelley's arrival. It would be interesting to learn what took place between Saul and Kelley when they confronted each other.

It was on the night of March 8, the same day Kelley arrived at Mortlake, that one of the Enochian angels first visited him. It probably appeared to Kelley while he was lying in bed. Kelley was able to see and hear the angel clearly enough to learn from it all about the deceit of Saul.

The first contact of the Enochian angels with John Dee occurred exactly one year to the day prior to Edward Kelley's arrival at Mortlake. Kelley came to Mortlake to discuss with Dee an alchemical manuscript in Kelley's possession called the Book of Dunstan, which the alchemist believed to contain the secret of the red powder. Dee was renowned throughout Europe as a scholar of recondite subjects. However, given the coincidence of dates, I cannot believe that Kelley's arrival was mere chance. I believe the Enochian angels somehow contrived to initiate his journey to Mortlake in order to bring Dee and Kelley together.

No matter the circumstances, it was immediately obvious to Dee that Kelley was the perfect scryer to communicate with the spiritual beings who had for the past year been trying to reach him. Kelley first scried into the crystal two days after his arrival at Mortlake, on March 10, 1582. The crystal was an egg-shaped globe of polished but cloudy quartz, set in a frame that took the form of a vertical band of gold with four supporting legs and a cross on its top. The scrying session occurred in Dee's study, probably in the late afternoon. The time of day can be inferred since the angel Annael appeared to Saul on December 21, 1581, and told him to scry with the crystal bathed in the sunlight from the western window in Dee's study.

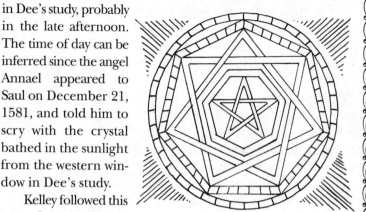

Kelley followed this procedure. He placed the crystal in its frame on the outer corner of Dee's writing desk, in a beam of sunlight. Dee sat down behind the desk to record in a diary Kelley's observation, and all that the Enochian angels might say to Kelley. Thanks to Dee's rigorous adherence to this practice, the Enochian conversations have the accuracy of legal transcripts. Kelley did not sit, but knelt on the floor in front of Dee's desk. Kelley began to pray and invoked aloud the angel Annael into the stone. When this did not bring immediate success, Dee arose and went into his oratory, a small room attached to his study, to pray. Within fifteen minutes, Kelley reported seeing an angel in the depths of the stone. This angel revealed itself as Uriel, and immediately began to transmit part of the Enochian system of magic.

In the following months, Dee and Kelley communicated regularly with the angels. Apart from the extemporaneous prayers that Dee recited to open and close the ritual, there was little outward formality. Dee did always maintain an attitude of reverential awe when communicating with the angels, as he was convinced throughout that they were the true angels of God. Kelley could never convert Dee to his own opinion that the Enochian angels were liars and deceivers.

Through Kelley, the angels transmitted instructions for the construction of ritual furniture and instruments. These were designed to make communications with the angels more certain. The chief of these was the elaborately inscribed "Table of Practice," a wooden table with four legs that was painted in various colors, with Enochian letters on its top. Its overall shape was cubic; thirty-six inches on each side. Dee finished it on April 29, 1582. Upon it were set (or perhaps painted) seven elaborate seals, called the "Ensigns of Creation," arranged in a large circle. The Ensigns corresponded to the spheres of the seven planets of traditional astrology. Within the circle of the Ensigns was the most important of the ritual instruments, the "Sigillum Aemeth" (Seal of Truth), a wax seal nine inches in diameter.

The Sigillum Aemeth is the power object of Enochian magic. It was inscribed with a detailed and beautiful design in the form of a pentagram set within a heptagon set within two interlocking heptagrams set within a larger heptagon. All of these shapes were surrounded by a great circle of forty segments. The names of several Enochian spirits appear on the seal, as well as individual letters and numbers. At its very center is the name Levanael, a spirit of the Moon. Enochian magic is lunar magic. Monday, the day of the Moon, was the day chosen by the angels for the most important scrying sessions. The entire elaborate structure of Enochian magic is based on the number seven and on the seven planetary spheres in a cycle beginning with the moon and Monday.

The scrying crystal was laid upon a small cushion on top of the Sigillum Aemeth, which acted as the key to open the crystal and allow the true Enochian angels to appear within its depths. This was not the same crystal that had been used by Barnabas Saul, but a new crystal that miraculously appeared on the floor of Dee's study on April 28, 1582. While scrying in the old crystal on that day, Kelley happened to look toward the western window, and noticed a gleaming object on the floor. He had a vision in which a small angel with a flaming sword in hand picked up the object and extended it toward Dee. The angel Michael told Dee through Kelley, "Go toward it and take it up." So Dee approached the window. At first he saw nothing, but then he noticed something on the floor. It was the crystal that would become his "principal stone."

It is quite likely that Kelley placed this crystal on the floor. But in my opinion, he was possessed by one of the Enochian angels while doing so, and retained no knowledge of his actions. Dee simply accepted the appearance of the stone as miraculous. It became a part of the ritual furniture, along with the Table, Ensigns, Sigillum Aemeth, and other ritual instruments such as a magic seal ring and a lamen, both designed to be worn by Dee during the Enochian rituals.

The principal showstone was placed on its cushion on top of the wax Sigillum Aemeth in the center of the Table of Practice, surrounded by the seven Ensigns. The Ensigns were not visible, but hidden beneath a cloth. Candles were lit to cast light on either side of the stone. A red silk carpet lay on the floor under the table. Kelley sat at the table and scried into the stone, while Dee recorded the sayings and doings of the angels. Prayers were used to open and close the ritual. Dee probably wore the seal ring and the lamen. There is no mention in the Enochian transcripts of casting a magic circle around the table, but one may have been used. Kelley was a necromancer, and would have been well familiar with magic circles.

Many details were left unrecorded by Dee. It is impossible to reconstruct the ritual precisely. On the other hand, we are fortunate that the records kept by Dee over a period of seven years have preserved so much of Enochian magic. We at least know the instruments constructed by Dee under the directions of the angels. Without Dee's transcript of the conversations with the angels, neither Enochian magic nor the Enochian language would even exist today.

A Charm
Against Violent Weather

By Elizabeth Barrette

Hurakan,
Bringer of storms,
God of the whirlwind—
We call on you.

Your name is the word hurricane,
So we turn to you for protection.
You created the world,
You created humans and animals,
And you gave us fire from your own hands.
Pray do not destroy us now!

Set your blessing upon us
As a shield;
Accept our offering of incense,
And show us mercy.
Hurakan,
Defend us from the coming storm!

Totem Animals

By Bernyce Barlow

There are as many totem animals as there are animals—some very familiar to us, others not. Generally, it is wise to use as totems the animals that are known in your own country. As a rule, totems should be animals we can study, spend time with, and draw power from with ease.

You will probably have many questions about totem animals: What exactly is a totem? How do I get one, and can I have more than one? What do I do with a totem animal once I get one? And aren't totem animals just the same as familiars? These are all good questions to explore.

Native American Traditions

Within the Native American traditions, totem animals are closely identified with animals that bring you power, healing, and protection both in the physical and spiritual world. Having a totem gives you strength and power to deal with a difficult world. One thing to keep in mind, however, is that according to these traditions your totem chooses you—you do not choose your totem.

Ordinarily, a totem animal is acquired during a vision quest. A vision quest is a supervised time of fasting, prayer, and meditation where a participant and an intercessor spend time alone in the wilderness calling on and waiting for Spirit. Usually this takes place over a period of four days.

Traditionally, the totem makes its first appearance during a person's first vision quest. This sometimes happens in dreamtime, at other times in visions, and occasionally in the physical world.

At times, the totem animal shows up only after the quest. Nevertheless, it is the goal of the first quest to bring in that totem.

Ideally, therefore, the first quest is taken during adolescence so the participant may use the totem animal during the process of personal development and growth during his or her early years.

In some shamanic teachings where a vision quest is not involved, your totem animal should come to you through a dream or a vision. In these cases, it must come to your four times during the same dream.

Some shamans lead folks to their totem animals in this manner instead of through a vision quest. Through drumming, fasting, sleep deprivation, heat, or hallucinogenic drugs, the participant is put into an altered state and encouraged to travel mentally towards the heavens or deep into the Earth through a natural crack or hole in the ground—such as an animal hole, a tree root crevice, or perhaps a deep vertical cave. During this journey it is hoped that the totem will appear, usually four times but not always depending upon the culture as the ways of shamanism differ very little from country to country.

According to the Native traditions, after you choose your totem you must carry something that represents the animal with you at all times. That is, if you have a horse as a totem, a bit of horse tail is not hard to come by. Unfortunately, there are certain animals and birds that are protected by law which you cannot legally carry or have in your house—like eagles, or gray wolves. If your totem is an eagle you will have to carry something that represents the eagle instead. It is wise to find out what is legal and what isn't from your state's Fish and Game Department.

TOTEM ANIMAL CHARACTERISTICS

Specific animals embody specific characteristics very often similar to your own personality and physical character. For example, the bear is a powerful animal that is given the traits of leadership, physical strength, endurance, hibernation, nurturing, long-range travel, and fierceness in battle. One who has had bear medicine brought to them during their quest would study these attributes and develop them. The probability is that the person chosen by the bear already has these characteristics, and the bear would therefore further strengthen those traits in the spirit world as well as in the physical world. A warrior in battle would call upon bear medicine for aggressive and fierce endurance. But the same warrior may call on the bear to help travel deep within oneself, just like the bear does in hibernation. The bear likes berries, fish, and honey. These foods may be the very foods needed for an individual who carries bear medicine to ward off illness and strengthen parts of the body that may have a tendency to succumb to illness or weakness.

Medicine people often call on their patient's personal totem along with their own totem during healings. If the medicine person has a bear as their totem, they may call upon that bear to give strength to the person receiving the healing.

Sometimes totems travel in tandem. This is true of the wolf and the raven who are hunting partners in the winter. The wolf has difficulty finding prey in the deep snow of winter, so the raven will spot the prey from overhead during flight, circle above or call out to the wolf so she can locate its food source. Furthermore, since a raven cannot crack open a carcass of an elk or moose, the wolf kills the prey, rips it open with its teeth, and shares the meal with the raven. So, those who have wolf medicine sometimes align with the raven as a totem tandem—especially if they live in a region whose snows bring on a harsh winter. A good rule of thumb is if one animal cannot survive without the other, claim both their medicines.

Very often a totem animal will stay with you for life, but there is a chance you may have a profoundly life-changing experience—such as a profound illness or accident, or a death of a loved one. In this instance, a different animal may come to take the place of your totem.

A totem animal is not a familiar, although similar traits run in both. There are times a familiar and a totem can closely mimic each other, especially if you have a cat for a familiar and a cougar for a totem. Although a familiar can reflect the personality of its owner, and protect him or her in the spirit world, a familiar is not a totem animal. One cannot draw upon a familiar's medicine in the same way as he or she can draw on the medicine of a totem.

KEEPING YOUR TOTEM ANIMALS

Shamans and medicine people suggest that to keep your totem animal happy and powerful you should spend time meditating on it, visualizing your totem doing what makes it happy and healthy. You should sing your totem songs about itself. And when you dance, imitate the animal. For instance, if your totem is a horse, prance around to a drum beat as a horse would. If you have long hair, put your hair into a ponytail, and visualize that you are the horse, prancing or running. Paint pictures of the animal on your drum, or keep a photo or picture of it in your house or wallet. Tuck a bit of horse tail into your magical bundle or medicine bag.

It is believed actions like this keep your totem strong and gives it a willingness to help you when you call upon it for wisdom, help, protection, or healing. Some healers or medicine people don't like to talk about their totems because they feel it is a way for another shaman, sorcerer, or Witch to attack or use their medicine against them. You should always therefore be careful in revealing your totem animal to others. Make sure you trust the person that you share with.

You may ask: Can I use a totem from a different part of the world? Sure you can, if it comes to you. When focusing on regional animals as potential totems, it is easier to study that animal. It is also easier to carry a physical piece of its body in your medicine bundle or bag. There are no snakes in Hawaii, so if a snake chooses to become your totem, you must rely on the mainland to get a piece of snake skin to put into your medicine kit.

Still, shamanism has been used for thousands of years to heal and protect millions of peopls, and, to put it simply, the stuff that has not worked through the centuries has been tossed out, while the stuff that has worked has been kept. Keep in mind, then— what works on one side of the world usually works on the other side. The similarities in the healing aspects of totems and the various shamanistic techniques are uncanny. And, as it is only recently thanks to TV and to picture books that those living in North America really know much about the kangaroo and those in Australia know anything about cougars, it remains to be seen how effective such animal totem are across cultures.

Totem animals are sacred. If you do not already have one and feel this is something that would benefit your practices of personal empowerment, seek out your totem wherever and whatever it may be. Just call it in.

Remember that your animal, bird, insect, or fish chooses you, and when it does come you must give it the respect it deserves. For indeed, there may come a time when you will want to claim its power to bring you into yours.

Good Workout Tarot Meditation

By Kirin Lee

S taying motivated for workouts is a major challenge for many people. You get stuck in a rut with the same old routine, and it gets boring. Changing your routine helps for a while, but eventually, boredom creeps up on you. This happens to everyone, from the daily jogger to the serious bodybuilder.

This tarot meditation is effective in winning the battle and conquering boredom, therefore keeping you on track to your goal. Do this meditation as often as needed to motivate you in weight loss, muscle building, or just staying in shape.

What you will need: a tarot deck, candle holders, orange, black and purple candles, and crystals (optional).

The Meditation

Choose one or more tarot cards from the following list, according to your workout goals. Use one candle for every day you work out. Use one black candle in the group if you are trying to overcome bad eating habits that slow progress. A black candle can also be used if you are working to build strength. One purple candle is used for personal power, or if you are a trainer or fitness professional that needs a mental boost. The rest of your candles should be orange, for mental and physical energy, and for endurance.

Place your candles in an arc on your altar or a table top. Space corresponding crystals between them if you wish. Lay your chosen cards in a row before the arc of candles. Place them in the order of importance to you, right to left.

Now cast a circle. Sit at the table or before your altar and take a moment to collect your thoughts. Light the candles from right to left. As you do, feel their energy flow toward you. Shift your focus to the first card. Think about its purpose. Visualize yourself going through the process represented by the card. See yourself reaping the rewards from successful results. Take your time, and when you feel you are ready, move on to the next card. Repeat the procedure with each card in turn. When finished, clearly visualize the way you want to look and feel after all of your hard work. Be realistic in your goals. If setting a time limit on your goal, make sure it's a reasonable one. Achievement in smaller stages gives better rewards in the end without fear of disappointment.

Whenever you feel your motivation lacking, repeat this meditation. Keeping up on the latest workout information also helps. Read fitness magazines and find a book discribing excercise variations. Use the meditation to help you get started on creating new workout routines.

CARD LIST

Ace of Wands—Represents a fresh start, a new beginning, or a new excercise program. This card should be used by those starting out on a new routine. Thinking about trying kickboxing, spinning, or bodybuilding? This is your motivational card

The Star—This card represents faith in yourself, the ability to see through the here and now to what could be.

Death—Represents the end of a harmful lifestyle. Use this card to visualize new opportunities for yourself and a new lifestyle that will transform your body and mind. Use this card to give up harmful vices such as smoking or overeating.

The Hermit—This card is for seeking and finding the perfect workout routine for you, or finding a new one to replace an old boring one. Visualize yourself overcoming health problems with excercise. Fitness professionals can use this card to help them keep clients interested.

Strength—This card helps you visualize dynamic energy and unlimited energy to perform your workout. It also represents the overcoming of physical disabilities and learning to work your routine around them.

The Lovers—This card represents physical productivity and the building of a strong body and mind. Use it to reorganize your routines after an injury, and to motivate yourself to start again. Fitness professionals can use this card to aid them in keeping clients motivated after setbacks.

The Empress—This card is used to get in touch with your body and see what it wants or needs in a program for fitness and nutrition. The focus here is on feelings and inner promptings or intuition.

The High Priestess—The focus for visualization with this card is overcoming injury or illness to continue training. It will help you start up again, or keep going, even if it means starting over.

The Magician—This card helps you visualize the results of hard work and serious training. Let your desires and fitness goals for the future come out here. This is a good card for beginners.

Two of Wands—Use this card to direct energy toward improving yourself, your image, or your training technique. This card helps you focus on making excercise a lifelong priority. It will help you focus on losing weight, building muscle, and increasing strength and endurance.

Nine of Wands—The focus of this card is on character, stamina, and self-discipline. All these are things needed if you are to reach your health and fitness goals.

Ace of Cups—A great card for beginners, especially in bodybuilding. The focus of this card is on mental and physical discipline. It will help you gain the faith in yourself necessary for you to reach your goal.

Ace of Pentacles—This card is useful for continued motivation in your workout routines and practices. This includes nutrition programs and focusing on how it will all come together later. It is an especially useful card for long-time exercisers and for those in intense training programs.

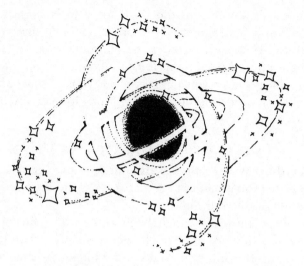

THE MAGIC OF THE VOID

BY KENNETH JOHNSON

I t's a place that is not a place, a state of consciousness much sought after, and yet entirely nonexistent. After all, "void" means nothing, right? It's part of a New Age nomenclature which may well stretch on into infinity.

So what is the void, anyway?

That depends on who you talk to.

THE 1960S VOID

I suspect that most members of the New Age community first learned about the void back in the 1960s—that is, if they're old enough for that—whence it came bursting into the collective consciousness thanks to Tim Leary, Richard Alpert, and Ralph Metzner's interesting, though sometimes fanciful, translation of *The Tibetan Book of the Dead*. This notorious "Harvard three" made the void sound like a perpetual psychedelic fantasy of colors and lights.

But according to *The Tibetan Book of the Dead* itself, the void is actually something quite different from this psychedelic fantasy. In fact, it isn't a something at all. It's a nothing.

In classic Buddhism, the word for void is *sunyata,* which means simply "emptiness." But there's a catch to this particular emptiness. It actually signifies the emptiness that occurs after you have poured something out of a container. So the void is where you go after you empty out all your garbage, all your thoughts, all your conditioning, everything human or imperfect, and so on.

THE TRUE NATURE OF THE VOID

If everything is a creation of the mind, then what is left over? What is there that had not been created by the busy, active, restless entity that is your mind?

And the answer is, you guessed it, the void. The void is the primal state of emptiness which occurs when everything else is cleared out. It is not quite the same thing as Nirvana, which is covered elsewhere in this present volume—see page 131. This emptying is, in fact, the goal of most Eastern meditation.

There's also a void in the Western tradition. And no, I don't mean just a gap in our knowledge. I mean a conceptual void, similar to the ideas of the Eastern philosophies.

It is mentioned in the first chapter of Genesis in the Bible: "The earth was without form, and void; and darkness was on the face of the deep." Is this the same void? You bet. The actual Hebrew term is *tohu bohu,* and it is a peculiar void indeed. Way back in Babylon, the primal chaos, or void from which all things sprang, was perceived as a dragon, and the dragon's name was Tiamat. The Hebrew Bible contains a great deal of common Near Eastern myth disguised as theology. Tohu bohu, therefore, is none other than the cosmic dragon Tiamat—meaning chaos and the void are seen in the Western tradition as a kind of serpent or dragon, a formless chaotic energy from which all things began.

And the dragon is a lady. Tiamat is a female dragon, and one suspects that tohu bohu was the same. In Babylon, a godly patriarch named Marduk kills the dragon, and in the Bible Yahweh does the same thing—except that the dragon has taken on a different name and is referred to as Leviathan.

So focused rational consciousness exerts its control over the mystic, mysterious, serpentine, and feminine depths of energy which is the void.

Some of you would like say at this point: This is not necessarily a good thing!

But do take note of the fact that this Western void seems decidedly feminine in character. After all, the dragon was a lady. Can we say the same thing of the Buddhist void?

W. Y. Evans-Wentz, the original translator of *The Tibetan Book of the Dead,* says that: "Bliss is the father, and the void which perceives it is the mother. Radiance is the father, and the void which perceives it is the mother. Intellect is the father. Void is the mother."

East or West, all the same.

The void is where you go when you lay down the heavy burden of the intellect and return into the eternal empty space of the cosmic mother.

Happy trails to you.

FOR FURTHER STUDY

Buddhism: Its essence and development. Edward Conze. Harper, 1959.

Near Eastern Mythology. John Gray. Bedrick Books, 1985.

The Tibetan Book of the Dead; or, The after-death experiences on the Bardo plane, according to Lama Kazi Dawa-Samdup's English rendering. W. Y. Evans-Wentz. Oxford University Press, 1927.

ALTERNATIVE MAGICAL NAMES

BY EILEEN HOLLAND

T here is no obligation to assume a magical, craft, or secret name. Many practitioners, however, do take follow the practice. After all, magic is transformational, so a new name is one way to celebrate the positive changes that magic makes in your life.

Finding your magical name isn't something that you need to stress over. Names, like familiars, have a way of finding magical people. When the right name for you comes along, you'll know it. You'll feel the rightness of it.

New names can honor gods, ancestors, animal totems, culture heroes, spirit guides, the place where you live—whatever is meaningful to you. If a certain culture has particular resonance for you—say Norse, Celtic, or Egyptian—you may want to choose a name from that culture. Be aware, however, that some say it isn't a good idea to take the name of a very powerful deity like Isis, Odin, or Kali. Others say this is up to you—that only you can judge whether or not you are able to handle such power. It is always a good idea to research any name that appeals to you, learn its history and meaning.

If you have been hoping that an unusual name will find you, here are some choices names from geology, history, meteorology, oceanography, and mythology.

NAMES BASED ON THE ELEMENTS

Any element can be looked to for a magical name.

Earth—Alluvia, Arroyo, Beck, Brae, Cairn, Chalcedon, Clay, Crag, Crystal, Dolman, Dune, Gemma, Greenwood, Grove, Jet, Ley, Mesa, Moraine, Obsidian, Onyx, Ravine, Savanna, Shale, Stone, Sylvan, Sylvana, Tarn, Telluria, Topaz, Tor, Vale.

Air—Aether, Anemone, Argon, Boreas, Cardea, Gale, Hurikan, Keen, Khamseen, Mesembria, Miasma, Myst, Notus, Scirocco, Skye, Tempest, Typhon, Vortex, Windflower, Zephyr.

Fire—Agni, Ardent, Baelfire, Blaze, Candelifera, Censer, Chandelle, Dittany, Ember, Firefly, Flame, Flint, Forge, Magma, Phoenix, Prometheus, Pyrrha, Salamander, Scorch, Smoke, Smolder, Sylph, Tallow, Taper, Torch, Vesta, Vulcan.

Water—Amberella, Amphora, Aquamarine, Avalanche, Brine, Brook, Cascade, Chalice, Delta, Deluge, Dylan, Hailstone, Hoarfrost, Llyr, Maelstrom, Monsoon, Niagra, Nile, Oasis, Oshun, Pearl, Rain, Riverine, Scald, Serac, Storm, Telchine, Tide, Torrent, Trill, Tsunami, Wave, Weir.

Names from the Deva Kingdom

Any flower, herb, or tree can be used from magical names. Herbal names are common in the magical community, but plants not usually heard include Agrimony, Aloe, Amaranth, Anise, Betony, Buckthorn, Chervil, Damiana, Elecampane, Gentian, Germander, Lovage, Mastic, Medlar, Melilot, Oleander, Pomegranate, Savin, Samphire, Tamarind, Tarragon, and Yarrow.

You might want to choose the name of a plant that is considered especially magical, such as Aconite, Belladonna, Blackthorn, Bryony, Galangal, Hellebore, Mandrake, Nightshade, Rowan, Vervain, or Wolfbane.

Folk names of plants provide unusual magical names: Absinthe (wormwood), Anciana (pear), Azadarey, Buckrams (wood garlic), Camphire (henna), Catmint (catnip), Dwale (belladonna), Gallion (ladies' bedstraw), Malina (apple), Maythen (chamomile), Personata (burdock), and Sanders (sandalwood).

Names from Myth and Legend

Legendary and historical figures are archetypes that make powerful magical names. Male power names include Anu, Cernunnos or Kernunnos, Shango, Cuchulain, Gilgamesh, Hercules, Marduk, Poseidon, Samson, Taranis, and Thor. Female power names include Ambika, Boadicea, Cartimandua, Delilah, Durga, Galiana, Kali, Macha Mong Ruadh, Morrigan, Myrine, Nessa, Onomaris, Oya, Scathach, and Vashti.

Female Amazon names include Aella, Antandre, Antianira, Antiope, Clymene, Evandre, Harpe, Hippolyta, Lyce, Melanippe, Myrina, Omphale, Otrere, Pantariste, Penthesilea, Polydora, Thalestris, Thoë, and Xanthe.

Male centaur names include Ancius, Argius, Centaurus, Chiron, Crotus, Dexamenus, Elatus, Eurytion, Hippotion, Hylaeus, Nessus, Oreus, Phrixus, and Thereus.

Satyr names include Astraeus, Gemon, Lamis, Leneus, Lycon, Napaeus, Orestes, Pan, Petraeus, Phareus, Pithos, Poemenius, Satyr, Satyrion, Satyrius, Satyros, and Silenus.

Names of nymphs include Abrya, Andrastea, Anthracia, Asteria, Asterodia, Chian, Chryse, Cranaë, Dryope, Echo, Harmonia, Leuce, Marica, Menthe, Moria, Myrtoessa, Neda, Nephele, Orphne, Perdix, Phiale, Philyra, Phyllis, Pitys, Rhene, and Thisbe. Names for dryads include Beldis, Clytia, Daphne, Egeria, and Erato. Names for naiads include Abarbarea, Amalthea, Argyra, Caliadne, Callirrhoë, Cleocharia, Creusa, Cyane, Diopatra, Drosera, Lara, Lotis, Melite, and Naiad. Names for oceanids include Acaste, Admete, Argia, Asia, Calypso, Caphira, Chryseis, Daira, Electra, Eudore, Ianira, Ianthe, Idyia, Petraea, and Rhodia. Names for nereids include Autonoë, Dynamene, Evagore, Evarne, Galene, Glauce, Panope, Pasithea, and Psamanthe.

The names of male fairies include Aillen, Amadan Dubh, Brown Man, Cluricaun, Credne, Donn, Fachan, Finvarra, Ghillie, Kelpie, Luchtar, Melwas, Oberon, Puck, Rhys Dwfen, Tamerlane, Trow, Tylwyth, Urisk, and Wichtlein. The names of female fairies include Aeval, Aine, Airmed, Aoibheal, Banshee, Bendith, Caer, Clethrad, Cliodna, Donagh, Eri, Glaistig Uaine, Grania, Mab, Summer, Titania, and Una.

NAMES FROM HISTORY AND GEOGRAPHY

History and mythology have provided these male names and titles for magical adepts and gods of magic: Aba-aner, Abbarais, Apollonius, Carinondas, Carrefour, CuRoi,

Damigeron, Dardanus, Djedi, Djeheuty, Ea, Enki, Fintan, Gwydion, Hermes, Hermes Trismegistus, Hifmoses, Irin Mage, Khonsu, Magus, Marduk, Merlin, Mithras, Musa, Necta-nebus, Numa Pompilius, Simon Magus, Thespion, Zamolxis, and Zoroastres.

Names of Witch goddesses and female adepts include: Angitia, Aradia, Arionrhod, Aset, Berchta, Carman, Cessair, Circe, Dalukah, Diana, Ertha, Etain, Greine, Hallawes, Hecalene, Hecate, Helice, Maia, Margawse, Marie Laveau, Medea, Medusa, Morgana, Nemain, Nimuë, Rhiannon, Tlazolteotl, Vivienne, and Yemaya.

Some names from geographical places incude: Abydos, Alexandria, Amenti, Babylonia, Byblos, Carthage, Delphi, Eire, Erin, Giza, Ionia, Karnak, Nubia, Olympus, Persis, Petra, Salem, Saxon, Sedona, Sumer, Tara, Troy, Tyre, and Umbria.

Some names from well-known magical priests include: Adapa, Anmutef, Astronomus, Babalawo, Balahala, Balsam, Brendan, Camma, Flamen Dialis, Galli, Heirophant, Imhotep, Kristophores, Manethon, Nebseni, Neocoris, Orpheus, Osorkon, Pastophoris, Petosiris, Plutarch, Psonchis, Ramesses, Rom, Semeref, Semnothite, Stolist, Tchatcha-em-ankh, Zaclas, and Zarathustra.

Some names from well-known priestesses include: Althea, Boadicca, Cleopatra, Devadasi, Dryope, Enheduana, Entu, Heira, Hypatia, Io, Ishtarith, Jezebel, Cassandra, Mambo, Nadith, Nefertiti, Phryne, Pythia, Qadishtu, Sagae, Shamanka, Sibyl, Tcherau-ur, Thastius, and Volva.

Male Druid names include: Amergin, Calatin, Cathbad, Dubhtach, Emrys, Lochru, Myrrdin, Niul, Olc Aiche, Ono, Rechrad, Senias, Sitchenn, Tages, Taliesin, Trosdan, Tulchinne, and Urias. Female Druid names include Aoifa, Biróg, Bodmall, Camma, Druidia, Dryade, Fidelma, Gáine, Ganna, Geal Chossach, Milucrah, Sin, Smirgat, Tlachtga, and Veleda.

Some names of those killed during the Burning Times include: Agata, Appollonia, Babel, Barclay, Barthelemy,

Brigida, Bruno, Chantraine, Duncan, Elspeth, Horne, Isobel, Jennet, Joan, Jordemaine, Kilian, Kirstin, Lachlan, Macette, Marable, Margarethe, Margrat, Melchoir, Mirot, Og, Osborne, Powle, Redfearne, Sabina, Sylvanie, Veronika, Visirer, and Wyles.

NAMES FROM ALCHEMY

Alchemical names include: Alchemilla, Alembic, Antimony, Argent, Cinnabar, Electrum, Khemeia, Luna, Magistery, Qemt, Quicksilver, Regulus, and Zaphara.

ANIMAL NAMES

Animals, both real and mythical, provide a good source of magical names. Dragon names for males include: Dracunculus, Drake, Draco, Firedrake, Mandrake, and Ladon. Female dragon names include Delphyne, Dracena, Mandragora, Medea, and Tiamat.

Wolf names for males include: Fenris, Lycaon, Lycastus, Lycomedes, Lycotherses, and Lycus. Wolf names for females include: Faula and Lupa.

Raven names for males include: Adam, Bran, Bram, Corvus, Kronos, Morvran, Vron; raven names for females include: Badb, Eriu, Etain, Macha, Medb, and Nemain.

Bear names for males include: Arcas, Artaios, Arthgen, Arthur, and Wachabe. Bear names for females include: Andarta, Artio, Brauronia, Callisto, and Ursula.

Serpent names for males include: Ananta, Mahanaga, Ophion, Ouroboros, and Python. Serpent names for females include: Kundalini, Lamia, Pythia, and Serpentine.

Horse names for males include: Abraxas, Aethiops, Arion, Bellerophon, Chrysippus, Hippomedon, Hippomenes, Melanippus, Pegasus, Phaëthon, Sterope, and Xanthus. Horse names for female names include: Epona, Hippodaemia, and Hipponoë. Amazon and centaur names also tap into horse power for magical names.

Sun, Moon, and Star Names

Astronomy and mythology are sources for magical names taken from the Sun, the Moon, and stars. Solar names include: Amaterasu, Ammon, Apollo, Arinna, Aten, Corolla, Daystar, Greine, Helios, Inti, Ra, Saule, Shams, Sol or Solara, Sunna, and Sunflower.

Lunar names include Albina, Bendis, Cereus, Hecale or Hecalene, Hillel, Hina, Ix Chel, Lunah, Moonlight, Moonstone, Moth, Nannar, Nyame, Phoebe, Selene, Sin, Thoth, Yarisk, Zarpandit, and Zirna.

Astral names include: Aldebaran, Algol, Altair, Andromeda, Antares, Aquila, Ara, Arcturus, Astra, Capella, Cassiopeia, Celeste, Circlet, Cygnus, Eridanus, Hesperus, Lyre or Lyra, Mira, Nebula, Nova, Orion, Perseus, Polaris, Saah, Sagitta, Sirius, Sothis, Star, Stella, Triangulum, Ursa, and Vega. Each zodiac sign is also the name of a constellation, and thus a potential astral name.

Composite Names

It has become fashionable in neo-Pagan culture to join several words together in order to create personalized names. Some examples of this are: Mystic Greenwood, Tempest Blue, Ebon Morvran, Myrrha Moontide, Emrys Buckthorn, Dark Weir, Veleda Thorn, Chryse Daystar, Autumn Windflower, Celtic StormCrow, Cairn Firefox, Aldebaran Mage, Midnight Baelfire, and Riverine Fae.

Overall, be creative in making your choice. And be sure that what you choose has magical resonance to you. That's the most important thing, always. Good luck.

MAGIC AND SYNCHRONICITY

BY ROBERT M. PLACE

Magic, real magic—not sleight of hand or trickery—is illusive and hard to define. The term is derived from the Greek *magus,* a word referring to a sorcerer. The Greeks borrowed this word from Persia where it was the name of a member of the priestly class. This brings out one of the essential problems in defining magic: Is it separate from or one and the same as religion?

The dictionary further defines magic as "the use of means (charms or spells) believed to have supernatural power over natural forces." This seems to fit the common conception of magic, though the definition contains a disclaimer in saying "believed to have." This is as if to say some people believe in magic but we officially do not. Therefore, the second essential problem with understanding magic is the fact that our culture sees it as a misconception or false belief. Although magic is an important part of ancient culture and of some modern cultures, and though many people in our own culture continue to believe in and practice magic, it is officially considered a superstition.

MODERN MAGIC

Most studies of modern religious thought start with a discussion of the theories of the British folklorist and author Sir James Frazer. In 1890, Frazer published *The Golden Bough,* in which he placed magic on the bottom rung of an evolutionary anthropological structure and stated that humans, finding themselves helpless in nature, first attempt to control nature with magic. According to Frazer, as culture advances, humans realize that magic is ineffective and abandon it. They then develop a belief in a higher power outside of their control, which they attempt to appease. This is called religion. When sufficient knowledge of the real workings of the world are attained, humans abandon this second superstition and enter into the wisdom that is called science. In this final stage, the culture aims at real power over nature.

Of course, this breakdown is a bit too pat to be useful. For instance, most primitive people believe in a higher power or powers and use both magic and technology in conjunction with this belief. Most historians, meanwhile, trace the origins of rational scientific thought to the philosophers of the classical world, such as Pythagoras and his follower Empedocles. As mathematician and magician, Pythagoras is responsible for initiating a religious, scientific, and magical culture simultaneously—one that became the root of modern Western culture.

In fact, the distinction between magic and religion is an artificial one created in the West. Saint Augustine helped to create the medieval Christian worldview by describing magic as a continuation of Pagan culture and therefore unchristian. His view persisted, and near the end of the Middle Ages, the papal bull of 1320 defined magic as heresy, subject to the censorship of the Inquisition. This happened in spite of the of the fact that the essence of the Christian mass is the magical transformation of the bread and wine into the body and blood of Christ, that saints were all reported to have performed miracles, and that many Christians were involved in alchemy and Hermetic tradition. In order to think of magic as evil and unchristian, it was necessary to see it as something separate from religion and to redefine sanctioned magic as a miracle of God. Although this separation does not exist in any other culture, it continues to influence modern Western scientific thinking. Today, scientists think of magic as an ignorant superstition.

MAGIC AND RELIGION

It is impossible to separate magic from the esoteric aspect of religion. This esoteric aspect has the power to create a personal inner experience, one that can lead to psychic transformation and growth in the quest for enlightenment. Today, modern Westerners have increasingly turned to other cultures for this experience. Although this outside influence has been good for the health of our culture, the separation from our own esoteric tradition is unhealthy.

Aleister Crowley, a notorious twentieth-century magician, defines magic in his *Magick in Theory and Practice* as: "The Science and Art of causing change to occur in conformity with will." Crowley believed that because magic makes use of cause and effect experiments in the practitioner's attempt to control nature, there is a closer analogy between magic and Frazer's final scientific stage than between magic and religion. In fact, Crowley's definition of magic is not that different from the dictionary's. To Crowley the charms and spells of the magician only seem to supernatural to the "vulgar," but both definitions admit that they cause change in the natural world.

I believe that magic is synonymous with what Jung calls "synchronicity." Carl Jung, in his introduction to the Wilhelm and Baynes edition of the *I Ching*, says that when we successfully consult this Chinese oracle we are experiencing synchronicity. This word is defined by Jung as: "A meaningful coincidence of an external event with a psychic event, such as a dream, fantasy, or thought." These events coincide in time in a way that gives them meaning for the observer. That is, they seem like communications between a divine force and ourselves, and they confirm that there is a connection or interaction between our psyche and physical reality. Jung feels that these occurrences are not part of a cause-and-effect relationship. Instead, he insists that they are acausal acts of pure creation. He adds that when synchronicity happens an archetype is activated, but we should not think of the archetype as causing synchronicity. Synchronicity is simply what happens when the archetype emerges into consciousness. With this definition, Jung breaks from previous definitions of magic which all try to define magic as a cause-and-effect relationship instigated by the magician. Here, we come to a deeper and more profound view of reality, one connected to the quest for higher consciousness.

Archetype is a term that Jung borrowed from Plato, who did not trust his five senses to give him accurate information about reality. Instead, Plate reasoned that the sensual world was entirely composed of temporary, time-bound objects and that the forms or patterns that these objects posses are timeless and therefore real. These are the archetypes.

In other words, if we look at our house cat what we are seeing is a temporal creature. Yet, this cat contains a form that we can distinguish from other animals and that we can see is consistent with others of its species. Its essence is the immortal or divine cat, which, as long as there are cats, will never die. This is what Plato calls the real cat or archetype. Plato said that number is the bases of form and the essence of archetypes. This view is confirmed by modern scientists who discovered that an archetypal form is communicated to each living creature through a pattern of molecules, called DNA, contained in the center of each cell.

When we include the observations of modern quantum physicists in this discussion, we too find that the number of electrons and protons in an atom determine what substance it will be. Yet when we try to determine the nature of these subatomic particles we find that they are made of an illusive nonstuff which has the disquieting, acausal habit of slipping in and out of existence. These facts pull the rug out from under our materialistic worldview and show that there is a connection between psyche and matter. All physical reality, therefore, is the expression of the numerical thoughts of the universe—what the alchemists would call the *Anima Mundi*—and our thoughts are a manifestation of the thoughts of universe.

When Jung explored the unconscious mind, he discovered that at its deepest layer there emerged psychic patterns or personalities that were the same in all individuals and that can be found in religions and myths throughout time. At the deepest level of the unconscious, he, like the quantum physicist exploring matter, found that he lost sight of the archetypes as they merged into the vast sea of the collective unconscious. For this phenomenon, he used the alchemical term *Unus Mundus*.

When we use an oracle, such as the I Ching or the tarot, we bring these unconscious archetypes into consciousness through the use of symbols. This gives us the opportunity to intervene and create the future that we desire. When we perform magic, we use symbols to manipulate the inner world of the psyche and affect change in the outer physical world. When we succeed in this, the changes seem miraculous. By using symbols to manipulate the psyche, we are activating the archetypes—in fact in many magic rituals we deliberately contact them as gods, angels, or demons. The magical event is the manifestation of an archetype, or, in other words, synchronicity.

As I said before, Jung feels that synchronicity, or magic, is an acausal act of pure creation. This concept is almost impossible for our Western minds to grasp. Saying that it is acausal is akin to saying that it just happens. Is magic just an illusion created by our ego to convince it that it is in charge? Rather, perhaps our magical actions are a manifestation of the archetypes. Jung has supplied evidence to support this view by demonstrating that most people perform daily rituals and yet remain unconscious of their symbolism. Notice next time you meditate—when you quiet your mind the archetypes will emerge out of nothingness, the empty void. This void, the Unus Mundus, is the real creative power. This is where inner and outer reality comes from. If we want to effect change, this is where we must go with desires. We must dissipate the ego and go beyond desire. So how can we manifest our desires if we no longer have them? This is the paradox of magic. Magic must take place in the middle zone, where the archetypes emerge out of the unconscious, and our desires are not yet dissolved.

In general, in spite of what Jung says, I have found from experience that the archetypes respond to my expectations of them. If I treat them as individual personalities that can cause change, change happens when I ask for it. If I treat them as manifestations of the Unus Mundus, then acausal synchronicity happens.

Again, this is reminiscent of quantum physics. When scientists conduct an experiment to prove that subatomic quanta are solid particles, they find that they are. When they conduct an experiment to prove that these same particles are immaterial waves, they find that they are. In both cases, reality responds to the expectation of the observer. The observer is intimately connected to result simply by having expectations. This is magic.

FOR FURTHER STUDY

Ancient Philosophy, Mystery, and Magic. Peter Kingsley. Clarendon Press, 1995.

The I Ching. Wilhelm Baynes (introduction by Carl Jung). Princeton University Press, 1950.

Magick in Theory and Practice. Aleister Crowley. Dover Pub., 1976.

Man and His Symbols. Carl Jung. Doubleday, 1964.

Psyche and Matter. Marie-Louise Von Franz. Shambhala, 1992.

Magical Herbs for Stuck Situations

By Clare Vaughn

Almost everyone has at some point in their lives been caught in a situation that appeared to be hopeless and stuck. In reality, however, any situation can be unstuck by judicious action, whether mundane (writing a letter or note) or magical (making a charm bag or talisman).

If you choose to become unstuck through magic, herbs can help. Many magical traditions prescribe certain herbs for these occasions. Half a dozen of these herbs are readily available to buy or grow, and can be used by any type of magical practitioner. These herbs can handle a wide range of situations and meet many needs.

Cinquefoil (five-finger grass)

When to use it—In any stuck situation. An old folk proverb says: "Anything the hand of man can do, five-finger grass can undo." It has been used in European and American folk traditions to counter both hostile magic and mundane meddling. Cinquefoil breaks all kinds of directed negative intention, from hexes to office rumors. It jump-starts stagnant energies, opens doors, and breaks stagnation.

How to use it—Magically, it is effective when used externally as a floor wash, amulet, charm bag, incense, or potpourri.

Special information—Cinquefoil has numerous species, some native to North America. Some cinquefoils are common weeds. Shrubby cinquefoil is a popular landscape plant. Look for a bush or shrub with small five-part leaves and five-petaled yellow flowers that look like wild roses.

Agrimony

When to use it—A close relative of cinquefoil, agrimony is useful in stuck situations, and it may be easier to find than cinquefoil. It is especially effective with stagnant problems in the workplace. Agrimony can have quick effects, especially if drunk as a tea. As a flower essence, it treats mental suffering.

How to use it—Either internally or externally as a tea, tincture, flower essence, floor wash, amulet, or charm bag.

Special information—Agrimony treats slow, grinding stress. Use agrimony when you feel yourself gritting or grinding your teeth. Even if the situation doesn't immediately start to resolve, you will experience noticeable relief.

Ground ivy (alehoof, gill-over-the-ground)

When to use it—For stuck situations manifesting in the body. Stagnant energies causing illness will dissolve when treated with this common garden and landscape plant. It is also used to treat headache pain, muscle aches, infected wounds, chronic sores, and ulcerations.

How to use it—As a tea, salve, or tincture. You can add to its physical properties with magical efforts designed to help it do its work.

Special information—Ground ivy needs to be used fresh for best effect. It grows readily in many garden conditions, as well as in planters or hanging baskets.

Violet

When to use it—Like ground ivy, violet flowers and leaves have been used for centuries to ease the physical ills rising from stuckness in the body. Violet's special virtue is in treating the effects of stuck emotions, particularly grief. It also soothes neck and shoulder tension, headaches, tight chest, aching ribs, and other physical expressions of grief.

How to use it—As a tea, salve, tincture, potpourri, or eaten fresh in salads. Magically charge flowers to increase their effect.

Special information—Don't use store-bought violet oil in your magic, as these are synthetic. Violets do not yield essential oils.

BORAGE (BEE-BREAD)

When to use it—If you are stuck through fear or lack of courage, borage is your herb. It is a noted tonic for heavy-heartedness and low self-confidence.

How to use it—As a tea, flower essence, potpourri, or eaten fresh in salads. All of these can be magically charged.

Special information—Borage's star-shaped, intensely blue flowers are among the loveliest in nature. Borage is easy to grow and reseeds itself freely.

CAYENNE PEPPER

When to use it—When a situation is stuck due to inertia, cayenne will blast it free. This potent herb promotes free circulation of blood and energy, and lifts tiredness.

How to use it—As flower essence, food seasoning, vinegar tincture, amulet, herbal charm bag, floor wash.

Special information—If you can't handle hot spices, try taking cayenne flower essence. It has a very mild bite.

SAMPLE RECIPE: HERBAL CHARM BAG

Stuck situations often make the people who are caught in them feel hopelessly trapped. A herbal charm bag can help.

1   fresh leaf (or ½ tsp dried) cinquefoil

1   fresh leaf (or ½ tsp dried) agrimony

½   tsp dried borage (optional for fear)

⅛   tsp cayenne powder (optional for inertia)

Mix the herbs well and wrap in a scrap of fabric. Place the fabric in a small bag. If you want to bless the bag, or charge it magically, do so. Wear the bag around your neck, carry it in your pocket, or place it somewhere in your work area. When you are feeling stressed about the situation, touch the bag or remind yourself it is there. Carry it when you are taking action to help resolve the situation. Use it daily as long as you feel a need for it.

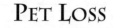

PET LOSS

BY MARGUERITE ELSBETH

Death is not something to be feared; rather, the demise of the physical body is only one aspect of the synchronistic cycle inherent in all of life. Still, the passing of a loved one always brings sadness, and the death of a cherished animal can be as devastating as the loss of a human family member.

DEALING WITH THE MOURNING AFTER

The first thing that happens when a much-loved pet dies is the onset of grief and attendant feelings of denial, anger, guilt, depression, acceptance, resolution, and even relief. Initially, you may reject the fact that the animal has died. And if your pet dies suddenly then the loss may be even more difficult to accept.

Anger and guilt often follow denial. You may inadvertently direct your anger toward people you love and respect, or you may blame yourself and others for your powerlessness in the face of death. Finally, depression is the most difficult part of grief, leaving you feeling drained of energy, or wondering if you can go on.

Fortunately, these unpleasant feelings will fade away, and you will begin to resolve and accept your animal's death. However, grieving is a personal process having no particular timeline. Therefore, it is important to take your time before you return to a state of emotional balance. Know also that Nature is our best teacher and healer.

THE CIRCLE OF LIFE

Nature constantly demonstrates that just as the four seasons ebb and flow, returning full circle back from whence they started, all life is born, expands to fullness, recedes, dies, and is born again. This natural circle of life reassures us that death is a gateway opening into the next level of spiritual evolution, and the soul continues on after death.

Many religions also teach us that when the body dies, the spirit returns to our heavenly birthplace, our spiritual home. Practitioners of earth-based traditions, such as shamanism, believe that people and animals return to the spirit world where they are cared for and watched over by the ancestors. If you believe that there is an afterlife for people, your beloved pet must be there also, waiting for you.

THE ANIMAL SOUL

Those of us who have shared a close relationship with a beloved pet know that animals are endowed with feelings and intelligence equal to or even surpassing that of human beings. Indigenous peoples believe that animals are filled with the spirit or life-breath of the Creator, and that animals have a soul—the vital, living essence that makes all creatures what they are. This animal soul has a strong emotional quality; it reveals itself through instincts and feelings. We too have an animal soul.

Contemporary science refers to this animal soul as the primal brain. Through it, we are connected to everything in the cosmos, including our departed pets. True, most of us cannot perceive the spiritual realms with the ordinary senses; we need to use supersensory perception to see the events, creatures, and things that have vanished from this Earth. Yet, the soul is interwoven with the subconscious mind, which is in charge of all our involuntary bodily functions, emotional behavior patterns, and instinctual reactions. It is also the place from which our dreams spontaneously emerge, and therefore dreams can be a potent venue for receiving messages from the spirit world concerning the welfare of our deceased pets.

DREAMING YOUR PET

Sometimes pets return to us in our dreams. If your animal lives a long and happy life, and then naturally passes as a result of old age, it may visit you from a beautiful dreamtime place, such as a sunlit meadow filled with wildflowers wherein it is content and well tended. However, if your pet dies suddenly or unnaturally, through an accident, illness, or other event, it may be confused for having left the body so quickly. Your pet's soul may then be inclined to wander in a disembodied state, in search of familiar surroundings. In these cases, you may suffer from disturbing dreams, wherein your pet appears in a dark, desolate place, or trapped in a situation from which there is no escape.

Should the latter be true, or if you have not yet received a dream message from your departed pet, then you may wish to call on your pet in the otherworld to see how it is doing, and thus reassure yourself in the process. Here is an effective method for contacting your pet in dreams:

Set a small table by your bedside.

Gather a white candle, a photograph of your pet, and all its favorite belongings—collar, leash, nametag, blanket, toys—and arrange them on the table.

Each night before you go to sleep, prepare a small portion of your pets' favorite food.

Set the food bowl on the bedside table you have prepared, and light the candle.

Relax and take a few deep breaths. Then gaze at the photograph, recalling the tender times you shared with your pet.

When you are done, call your pet's name out loud three times, using your most doting voice.

Blow out the candle, and go to sleep knowing that soon your pet may visit you in dreams.

Whatever happens, remember that your pet still loves you unconditionally, and will always be among your closest companions as you travel the road of life.

FOR FURTHER STUDY

The Association for Pet Loss and Bereavement (New York City). http://aplb.org.

The Lost of a Pet. Wallace Sife, Ph.D. Howell Book House, 1998.

Daily Meditations

By Breid Foxsong

M ost of us feel stressed from time to time. Some days are worse than others, but in this hectic world there is rarely a time when you are not pressured by deadlines and too many activities packed into too few hours. To reestablish a sense of balance and stability, try doing a daily meditation. It doesn't have to be a religious meditation; it doesn't even have to take more than a minute or two of your day. Think of it as a way to clean your mind the same way you clean your body.

You don't like meditating? Trust me, you are not alone. The most common frustration of beginners is that their mind races and their body fidgets. As with anything, the more you practice the better you become at whatever it is you've undertaken. In fact, disciplining your mind is very similar to disciplining your body. It is difficult to start, and there are "muscles" that need to be exercised. But just as regular exercise helps tone the body and keeps it fit, regular relaxation and meditation will allow you to improve with ease. You can also use the meditation time to concentrate on your daily agenda so that you can focus your energy where it is most needed.

You do not have to be an ascetic or a saint for meditation to work. To start, it is a good idea to have a place reserved just for your meditation. Although it is possible to meditate at your kitchen table, coffee cup in hand, or in the bathroom brushing your teeth, these are not ideal circumstances. A quiet secluded spot outdoors is wonderful, as is a quiet corner of the house. If you have room to set up a small altar, so much the better. Wherever you choose, it should be used only for your daily meditation.

Remember that "practice makes perfect," and that meditation is not a cure for all the worlds' ills. Do not expect too much the first time out. There are many methods of meditation to consider. You do not have to be still to meditate. Neither do you have to be sitting, standing, or folded up into a pretzel. The only requirement is that you be comfortable and do not have to concentrate on anything except what you are doing. Over time, try several different methods of meditation, and see which works best for you.

Once you've chosen your spot and method, use all of your senses. Look at a fire or a candle until you can see pictures in the flames. Feel the air around you as you walk outdoors and look "through your skin" at the sky. Lie next to a stream and picture yourself flowing with it into the ocean. Listen to a tape of drumming or Gregorian chants, and let the sound take you away. Practice emptying your mind, or filling it up with one idea or concept. Burn a favorite incense. Once you discover the best techniques for you, practice it.

Here's a simple method to try: Start by focusing awareness on your heart until you can feel your heartbeat. Then, without losing contact with the sensation, slowly add awareness of each of your other senses. Maintain the position as long as you can.

Concentrate on yourself without other people to distract you. Some people find it easier to relax with music or an environmental tape in the background, and some don't. Once again, you decide. If you do use music, be sure that the rhythm is slow and steady. Remember, don't tell anyone what you see or experience during your meditation. Decide this beforehand and stick to it. Also, don't talk to yourself about what you are seeing or feeling. By "narrating" the experience, you are separating yourself from it. If you follow the spirit of this rule, you can draw the experience deep inside of you instead of dissipating it in words. You can become it, and from there you can share it in other ways much richer than words. Simply absorb the experience.

The primary rule of any form of meditation is to be in your body. All other rules are corollaries of it. Then when you find the "still point" of mental silence, you can bring spirit and flesh together directly. Thus is the essence of meditation. Doing this daily will give you a way to center and focus your life that will allow you to tackle the hardest problems with energy, logic, and balance.

Magically Charged Herbal Tinctures

By Clare Vaughn

Anyone who has put St. John's wort and vodka into a glass jar and set the jar in sunlight to steep has magically charged a herbal tincture. A herbal tincture is a natural way to absorb the energies of a herb or other magic item to make a health-giving medicine.

The actual process of charging a tincture is not difficult. The critical ingredients for success are knowledge and intent. Know what energies you want to put into the tincture, and why. You may need to do advance research and planning, but always formulate your intent to charge the tincture with healing energy. Hold this intent as clearly and steadily as you can while you charge, and you're well on the way to success.

Once you have the actual magical intent clear in your mind, the question is what method you want to use to charge the tincture. You can choose from several different options, either singly or in combination, based on your preferences and magical tradition. In all of the discussions below, I assume you are charging an ordinary small glass bottle of tincture, but you could equally well charge any amount in any container.

TOUCH CHARGING

The touch charging method involves charging the tincture directly through your body. You can use your own energies, or bring outside energies through yourself. To charge a tincture using this method, take the tincture bottle in your hands and spend a moment aligning yourself with the energies of the tincture. Summon the energies you want to charge the tincture with, and send the charge through your hands into the tincture. Hold this until you feel that the tincture is thoroughly charged. Allow the flow of energies to taper off and stop. Set down the bottle, and release any energies you may be bringing through yourself.

PRAYER CHARGING

The prayer method brings higher energies into play by requesting the aid of a divinity or angelic being to help you charge the tincture with healing energies. Hold the tincture bottle and ask the aid of the being(s) you want help from, using any prayers or blessings you are comfortable with. This method is particularly helpful if you have trouble holding focus, or if you are afraid of doing something wrong while charging the tincture.

INVOCATION CHARGING

With invocation, you are bringing divine or angelic energies directly down into the tincture. Instead of asking a spirit to help you charge the tincture, you are asking it to charge it for you. As with the previous method, use whatever level of contact with the tincture you prefer; use whatever actual method of invocation you are comfortable with. Some traditions of prayer cross the line into invocation, and most methods of invocation also involve prayer, so this method can become a more intense version of the previous method. You may find with practice that you want to move from one into the other during a single charging operation.

Ritual Charging

Some magical practitioners prefer to use a full-blown scripted ritual to charge items such as amulets or talismans, and this method is useful for tinctures also. It requires a chunk of time, but the investment may be worth it. Select your ritual, make your preparations, and treat the bottle of tincture as though it were a blank amulet

or talisman waiting to be charged. Perform the ritual in the usual fashion. It is wise to temporarily shield the tincture in silk while doing the closing phase of the ritual, but you can unwrap it again once you're through and ready to put things away.

Sun and Moon Charging

Using the Sun and Moon to charge a tincture requires no energy output from you, and no ritual unless you want to use one. Make sure the tincture you want to charge is made from herbs that work with the proper luminary. For example, a tincture of St. John's wort would benefit from standing in sunlight but not from exposure to moonlight, while a tincture of mugwort would benefit from sitting out all night in moonlight but not from being put in the Sun. If you plan to use moonlight, consider which phase of the Moon will be best for your intention: The waxing Moon is best for increase, waning Moon for decrease, and so on. Once you have made your plans and are ready to carry them out, expose the tincture to the light in question for at least a couple of hours. Your tincture can stand for up to an entire day (sunrise to sunset) or night (moonrise to moonset) at one time. You can also repeat these exposures every day or night for a set period of time—a week, a lunar quarter, or other duration.

GEMS AND METALS CHARGING

Charging with gems and metals requires no energy from you, and no ritual unless you want one. It does require knowledge, though. The only metals you can safely use to charge a tincture are gold and silver, both of which are nontoxic. Likewise, use only hard gemstones which will not dissolve in alcohol. The sole exception to this rule is the pearl, which may dissolve, but which like gold or silver is safe in tiny doses. If you're not sure the gemstone you have chosen is safe in alcohol, soak it in a little pure water instead and add one or two drops of this water to your tincture. Soak the gemstone, gold, or silver in the tincture for two hours, and then remove it and rinse it clean of tincture residue.

FINAL SUGGESTION

Ready to make a plan and put it into action? Here is an example, start to finish, of how to magically charge a tincture. This is a suggestion for one way to charge a mugwort tincture intended to help shrink ovarian cysts.

To start, take the bottle of tincture outside on the first night after the Full Moon, just before moonrise. Place the bottle where it will get as much direct moonlight as possible. Invoke the power of the waning Moon to shrink and reduce that which is too full, and ask the Moon to fill the tincture with its power. Expose the bottle to the moonlight from moonrise to moonset, being sure to take it back indoors before sunrise. Repeat each night until the dark of the Moon.

FOR FURTHER STUDY

Herbal Healing for Women. Rosemary Gladstar. Fireside, 1993.

Natural Magic: Potions and Powers from the Magical Garden. John Michael Greer. Llewellyn Publications, 2000.

DIVINATION

BY ESTELLE DANIELS

WHAT IS DIVINATION?

D ivination is the art of telling the future and is also a tool
for self-exploration. The word derives from two Latin
words: *divinare,* which means to foresee, and *divinus,* or
pertaining to the gods.

Divination is a tool. Some people think divination is an
end in itself. If you are just fooling around, then it probably
is. But used properly, with reverence and positive intent, divination will enable you to accomplish a great deal. With
proper intent, you will be able to use the information you
gain from your divinations to make things better for yourself,
for your friends, and for the world.

Divination certainly is a manner of telling the future. But
divination can also be used to determine what may be hap-
pening at present or in the past. You can use divination to
check up on people who might be out of touch or out
of reach at the present moment.

Furthermore, some people feel that when you are working a divination you are in some way
receiving a message from the
divine—whatever
you perceive the
divine to be. If
you treat divina-
tion reverently
and with a good
dose of respect,
you will get bet-
ter results than
if you take it as

a game. Not only is your question answered, but often you may receive an answer to something you didn't ask about. Be open to these cosmic messages, and you just might find your life is more smooth and less upsetting than otherwise. When the cosmos speaks, it pays to listen.

METHODS OF DIVINATION

You can use a focus for divination, like a crystal ball, or tarot cards, or you can just use pure psychic talents. Most people use a focus point, which allows them to channel your psychic energies through a medium, and it makes it easier to get ideas and impressions. Because people are varied in their skills and interests, there are many divinatory systems which have been developed and used throughout history.

Most societies have had some mechanism for fortune-telling. The need to be able to predict the future is universal. Some societies controlled or repressed divination. Some societies celebrated divination or even went so far as to make divination an industry. The ancient oracles around the Mediterranean were an important source of revenue for the places that hosted them.

In the ancient world there were two types of divination: direct, or natural, divination—consisting of dreams, necromancy, oracles, and prophets; and indirect or artificial divination, which was divided into two categories—the observation of animate phenomena, haruscipy (reading the entrails of sacrificed animals), augury (reading the flight patterns of birds), and taking notice of human birth marks or deformities; and the observation of inanimate phenomena, such as casting of lots and dice, observation of weather phenomena, terrestrial events (like earthquakes), and celestial phenomena.

USING DIVINATION

In general, you can use divination to get information about a person or situation, or you can use divination to explore your inner self. Dream interpretation is a good method for self-exploration. All you need is a notebook, perhaps a good dream dictionary, and patience.

Jungian psychology advocates using divination as a tool for personal-self exploration. You can do readings for and about yourself. You can ask what aspects of yourself need work or modification. You can ask how important people in your life have affected you. You can ask about past lives and the people in them.

A divinatory reading about a troubling person or situation which is troubling may help provide some understanding. Sometimes a reading can give insight and perspective, and cause you to see a person or situation in a new light. Anything which helps increase self-awareness and understanding of the world is beneficial for personal growth, even if what you find out isn't as nice or pleasant as you thought.

Most people practice divination for themselves and possibly a few friends. They have their tarot cards or other tools, and they use them when they feel a need. They can ask about the future, past, or present. They can ask about themselves, friends, loved ones, or national figures. Around election time predictions of who will win are always popular.

Asking about the future is always tinged with a bit of uncertainty. Most readers feel that what you find out about the future is what is most probable given the present conditions. We don't usually have enough information at hand to make fully informed decisions; after all, a giant asteroid could hit the Earth tomorrow and end everything.

Some people practice divination for the public at large as a way of helping others and also possibly making money. If you choose to read for money, you should be aware that most municipalities have fortunetelling laws on the books, which are there for good and just reasons. Honest readers state their readings are for entertainment only, and they are not usually violating any laws.

Divination answers a strong need in humans. It has been around as long as mankind has been aware and thinking. And sometimes it seems that the more complex and hectic life is, the more urgent is the need for finding out about the future.

CHOOSING DIVINATION

Divination is useful for many things, but how does a magical practitioner go about choosing a divinatory system?

There are several criteria to look at. The first is availability and price. It does no good to determine you will be the best thrower of knucklebones the world has seen, if you cannot get a set of knucklebones. The most widely available system of divination available today is tarot.

There are hundreds of tarot decks available. Some people just decide to do tarot, and pick up a deck they like. Some people choose to get a deck and book set, which is more convenient, though more expensive. Most decks come with a small booklet which gives a few meanings for each card and details how to do a few simple spreads. That may be all you need. There are many good books on tarot, both general and specific to certain decks. Some people want more indepth information about the deck's symbolism and how the cards interrelate. The Internet has many good sites on tarot. A few even review decks and give good information.

There are other divinatory systems which are easily available, but pricey. You have to weigh your resources against your needs. It does no good to look at a sealed product. The description on the back may be good, but after trying the system, you might not like it. Some people go to a reader to see how a system works, and what kind of information they can get. Psychic fairs are good for this. You can ask for a reading from a friend who uses the system, or perhaps borrow it yourself and practice. It's better to see the system in action, so to speak, rather than buying something blind.

A second criterion to consider is the ease of use of a divinatory system. Astrology is a wonderful system, and there are hundreds of books available to read and enjoy, but it takes time and practice to be an effective astrologer. If you don't want to have to learn to cast charts by hand, though, there are lots of good programs available for your computer. On the Internet there are a number of good freeware programs which also calculate charts for you. But you still have to be able to make sense of all the squiggles the computer generates. Many people have taken the time and energy to study astrology and become fairly proficient at it. You don't have to be at professional level to use astrology effectively in your daily life. Many good almanacs have descriptions and ideas on how to use the Moon in the signs as an aid to making your life easier. But to be able to completely interpret a natal chart, or to effectively compare two charts to determine the general level of compatibility, takes time and study. It isn't something a person is going to pick up and master in a weekend.

Tarot can be used fairly effectively even by a beginner, if you are willing to use the book. This is perfectly acceptable. The pictures themselves speak to the meanings of each card, and these make it easier to memorize and understand what each card is about.

There are many other easy, do-it-yourself types of divination out there. And most actually work well.

Another criterion to consider is portability, especially if you travel often. Cards travel well, just put them in your bag and carry them wherever. Having an elaborate crystal ball may be fun, and you may be good at it, but if the ball is big and heavy, and has an elaborate stand and is breakable, you won't want to be carrying it around with you. If you just want to do readings for yourself and a few friends at home, a big, fairly permanent is fine. But you need portability if you like to do readings at psychic fairs or parties.

The fourth criterion to consider is comfort and familiarity. Runes are a good divinatory system, but they are less familiar than tarot or astrology. The use of runes actually died out except in scholarly research until they were "rediscovered" in the late eighteenth century. Modern rune work is based speculation.

There are several good divinatory systems based upon oriental methods, but these cultures are not necessarily easily understood by Westerners, though it helps to understand the mindset behind *I Ching* and *feng shui*. Some people find they are drawn to a certain system, even though they have no understanding of the culture it came from. If you feel it's right for you, then go for it.

The final criterion is long-term interest. Choose a system that will hold your interest. You can become an expert in reading a Magic Eight Ball in about five minutes. Do you want to make a lifelong study of its mysteries? Probably not.

Many people grow with divinatory systems as they use them. Some are so complex and multilayered that they can provide a lifetime of interest. Astrology, feng shui, tarot, and the runes work best after a long period of study brings growing understanding. If you just want a system which gives you a quick reading on immediate issues, and you aren't interested in long-term study, then choose something simple. If you want to become more accomplished and knowledgeable, then choose a complex system. If you are interested in lifelong study and interest, take up one of the systems with more levels of complexity.

Finding a divinatory system that is right for you can take some time and effort, but if you are careful and choose correctly, you will have something to use for a lifetime.

Introduction to Artistic Spellcraft

By Anne Marie Garrison

You can use art to enhance your spellcraft. Just follow these eight simple rules.

Rule one—Be clear about your intentions. Know what you are asking the universe to help with and why. Meditate and divinate several times to make sure you are doing the right thing. As the old saying goes: "Be careful what you ask for, you might get it." Be specific in your requests, such as: "I will soon have reliable, affordable transportation to work everyday." But do not tell the universe *how* to solve your problems ("I won't accept anything but a new red sports car"). If you already know how to solve all your problems then don't ask the gods for help.

Rule two—Form a very clear and affirmative statement of intent. For example: "I, Moon Dragon, child of earth, child of the universe, am part of the divine, and it is part of me. Therefore, in the name of Morrigan (or other god or goddess), I call into my life the perfect doowangle (or other object of desire). May it (or he or she) be beautiful, bold, and true (or other qualities of your choosing). As above, so below. So mote it be!"

Rule three—Visualize your spell coming true. See yourself enjoying the benefits of having your needs fulfilled. Don't fret. Know that it is not only possible, and with proper planning it will happen.

Rule four—Plan properly. Make a list of things you will do to help your intent. Set goals and a schedule. Pick the most advantageous time to do your spell by checking with an astrologer or other diviner. Gather art supplies and other ritual implements. Take some time to research visual symbols that can be put into a physical spell. Obvious ones include: hearts for love, dollar signs for prosperity, Suns for happiness, pentacles for protection. Don't worry about how much or little artistic talent you have. This is just for you! Nobody has to see it unless you want them to. The idea is to lose yourself in the creative flow. Visual language (not verbal) is the most direct way to access the magical subconscious mind.

Rule five—Remember the rule: "As it harm none." Be sure that your spell will not harm or interfere in the free will of others. Avoid spells using any names other than your own. It is okay to ask for love in your life, but it is not proper to demand that "John" or "Sue" fall madly in lust with you. Similarly, if you feel that someone has wronged you somehow, ask the universe for justice or resolution and leave it up to the gods to decide the best way to take care of the matter. Spells should not be undertaken for purposes of revenge or power over someone. What you send out returns to you threefold.

Rule six—Here's the fun part: Do the art-spell working. Start with a self-purification, cast a circle, and light some appropriately colored candles or incense. Put on some tranquil music. Invite the spirit helpers of your choice to join you. Choose an appropriate affirmation. Speak it clearly and loudly. Chanting will also work. Draw, color, paint, or collage your spell-page while concentrating on your symbols and colors. Write your affirmation, and feel free to embellish your art with pasted photos, beads, glitter,

fabric, small plastic toys. Have fun. Let your inner ch
When finished, thank your invited guests and close t[

Rule seven—Hang your magical art somewhere sp[
can look at it and meditate on it for a few minutes [
Repeat your affirmation out loud, visualizing your wish coming
true. Periodically add to the artwork if you desire. Do not take it
down until your goal is achieved, no matter how long it takes.

Rule eight—When finished with the art, thank the gods. If you
are doing this spell to help a friend, you can frame it and present
it as a gift. Otherwise, you can ritually burn, bury, or cast away the
remnants of your spell. If you magically disempower your art, it
can be pasted it into a scrapbook. That's all there is to it!

Note: Parents, please do these rituals with your kids. Kids love
to color and it is an easy way to "get inside" their heads and really
communicate with them. Feel free to modify the rituals to make
them appropriate for the age and ability of your children.

Here are some commonly held ideas about the meanings of
various colors to get you started. Use what works best for your needs.

White—Purity, light, heat, energy, chaos, all colors of the
spectrum working together in harmony, winter, cold,
snow, ice, frost, death, the bone mother.

Pink—Self-love, self-respect, friendship, feminine energy.

Red—Passion, will, courage, war, blood, fire, lust, sexual-
ity, masculine energy.

Orange—Creativity, heat, fire.

Yellow/Gold—Ego, confidence, happiness, air, intellect,
springtime, sunshine, solar energy, creativity, leadership, wealth, the harvest.

Green—Prosperity, money, life, fertility, growth, summer,
earth, healing.

Blue—Emotions, healing, cleanliness, water, eloquence.

Purple/Violet—Spirituality, Spirit, royalty, nighttime,
mist, fog, dreams, the collective unconscious.

Black—Death, the underworld, earth, dirt, the void, the
passing of time, the abyss, ultimate peace, comfort.

SACRED BATHS

BY BREID FOXSONG

S ince the beginning of recorded time, baths have been a method of not only cleansing and purifying the body, but of fortifying the spirit. A sacred bath should be different from a regular get-into-the-tub-and-scrub bath in that it is designed to clean the spirit and mind as much as the body. This cleansing can be accomplished in a variety of ways, but it is often combined with the principles of aromatherapy to enhance the experience.

Water being one of the four sacred elements—along with fire, earth, and air—you can create a combination of all four elements in a hot bath to make it into a sacred ritual. Of course, the involvement of water in a bath is fairly obvious—it's what one bathes in, after all—but involving the other elements in your bath is a bit tricky.

Fire, since it does not coexist well in the same space as water, needs to be approached obliquely. Your hot water tank, which is usually in the center of the house, is a representation of the ancient hearth fire; by using water heated by that flame, you are bringing in the energy of fire to your sacred space. Air and earth are combined in the bath salts by using a scent which evokes a specific emotion or frame of being (the air), and using the salt (the earth) to both ground and focus that scent. Bathing in ocean water is a traditional cure for depression and purification, so why not create your own "perfumed sea" in the privacy of your home?

Making your own bath salts is easy. For each batch you need a cup of Epsom salts, two tablespoons of baking soda, and no more than twenty drops total of essential oil. You can combine different oils to create specific moods or spells, but the total should never exceed twenty drops or the scent may become overpowering.

Mix the Epsom salts and the baking soda together thoroughly. Then add the essential oils and mix again. Pour the mixture into an airtight jar or bottle and close it tightly. Don't forget to label it—there is nothing worse than trying to remember just which mixture was created for some special ritual. To tie the tag, you can use a ribbon which indicates the purpose of the salts—blue indicates relaxation, for example; orange indicates empowerment, and so on.

You can use a single scent or a combination of oils when making your bath salts, and you can focus on the therapeutic effect or the fragrance, or both. The magical aspects of the scent and the way that it makes you feel are equally important. The power of aroma to evoke a variety of emotional senses and physical responses has been known for thousands of years. But you will have your own reaction to individual scents. The study of aromatherapy can fill up years. You do not need to be an expert in the use of essential oils to create blends, however. Here is some basic information that may be useful to you as you creatively compose your own unique bath salts.

Making Your Own Bath Salt Blends

When creating a blend you will want to consider first the purpose of the blend, then the desired therapeutic effect and the type of fragrance desired, and finally the concepts of a balanced blend.

First of all, you should familiarize yourself with the fragrance and effect of essential oils. Breathe the aroma and note how it makes you feel—calm, uplifted, focused, sensual?

Note the scent: Is it light, dark, fresh, strong, sweet, bitter? Does it evoke a specific memory or emotion? To test the aroma of an individual essential oil you can breathe directly from the bottle, remembering to swirl the oil first, or place a drop on an unscented tissue and breathe.

You may experience olfactory overload if you are testing the aroma of many different essential oils. You can restore your sense of smell by smelling coffee beans, or, believe it or not, your armpit in between sampling new scents.

When blending for therapeutic or magical effects, determine the essential oils that may be useful. *Cunningham's Encyclopedia of Magical Herbs* is a good reference, as is any basic aromatherapy book. See the "For Further Study" section at the end of this article for more suggestions.

List the oils in order of priority when several magical effects are desired. This will help determine the number of drops of each essential oil you will use. Test the fragrance as described above.

Some pointers for creating a balanced blend: You may want to use essential oils with a strong fragrance—such as peppermint or basil—sparingly. Lavender may be useful for toning down strongly scented oils. You can add just a drop or two of any essential oil to create an appealing fragrance in your blend. In the case of oils, "less is more."

Essential oils will merge over time, and the fragrance may change in your blend. As you experiment with your blend creations, keep a log of the number of drops you use of each essential oil in the fragrance blend, and make notes on both your initial experience and the therapeutic effect after time has passed. You may be surprised to find that a blend you did not like at first turned out to be a masterpiece. With good notes, you will be able to duplicate it!

SOME PRE-TESTED BLENDS

Here are some examples of combinations for bath salts that I have enjoyed. Add the essential oils to a cup of Epsom salts and two tablespoons of baking soda.

Pre-ritual Bath

6   drops rosemary oil

4   drops myrrh oil

4   drops sandalwood oil

2   drops frankincense oil

4   drops geranium oil

This makes a fragrant blend to bring pure thoughts to mind.

Relaxing Bath

9   drops marjoram oil

9   drops thyme oil

This one makes a good stress reliever.

Invigorating Bath

9   drops grapefruit oil

6   drops lemongrass oil

4   drops rosemary oil

Have a wonderful time experimenting with creating your own recipes.

For Further Study

Aromatherapy for Dummies. Kathy Keville. IDG Books Worldwide, 1999.

Aromatherapy. Clare Walters. Barnes & Noble Books, 1999.

Encyclopedia of Magical Herbs. Scott Cunningham. Llewellyn Publications, 1985.

Magical Aromatherapy: The power of scent. Scott Cunningham. Llewellyn Publications, 1989.

Dr. Leo Louis Martello

By Lori Bruno

Born September 26, 1930

Born into the Summerland June 29, 2000

Where do I begin to write about a legend? A man who gave tirelessly of himself for the fight for human rights, animal rights, gay and lesbian rights, and for Witches worldwide to worship in complete freedom?

Leo Martello was an amazingly compassionate man. He never turned away anyone who genuinely needed his time and effort in the pursuit of a just cause. He fought long and hard for the freedom of Witches and Pagans. He coined the very phrase: "Out of your broom closets and on to your brooms!" He was always humorous, but in that humor there were always wise lessons. He was fond of saying: "The coward finds a way out; the brave find a way." And he was himself brave and always in the forefront of controversial or difficult movement. It is to his credit that he stood up in the initial movement for gay and lesbian rights in New York City's "Stonewall Riots" in the 1970s. A spirit of light imbued the mortal body of Dr. Leo Louis Martello. He was equal to a million Suns and was crucial to the craft's beginning in this country. He was not one who jumped on the bandwagon because it was the "in" thing to do. Many write about the craft; however, Leo possessed an inner fire—the "heartfire" of the true Witch.

To have known Leo Louis Martello was an honor, and ever a challenge. Leo was a loving man, yet sometimes caustic. Leo taught this way. Sometimes he was a tough teacher, but it was to make you strong, and he did it with love. I soon learned I could never hide myself from him. He could see right into me and knew me for whom and what I was. If at times he was critical, it was never intended to hurt, but rather to help me to grow to my true potential. He once said these wise words to me: "Never let your failures poison your heart, nor your successes poison your disposition." With Leo you could make no excuses and take no shortcuts. To him, only cowards made excuses.

To me he was a beloved teacher, high priest, and father. After my own father died, it was Leo who taught me. He was there for me, a beloved mentor. No one can ever take his place. Leo Martello now sits with the Ancient Ones, and they surely are telling him: "Welcome, our son. You did well. Join your ancestors, all those who paid with their lives to bring the Ancient Ways back to a breeding Mother Earth."

As I write these words, it is with great respect and a very sad heart. There isn't an hour of the day or night that I do not miss him.

My comfort is knowing he walks now in the Elysian Fields and the Summerland with his beloved pets and all of his animals. Tears well up in my eyes as I remember the dream I had in August, at Lammas, when he came and asked to kiss my beloved Tasha, a snow-white Samoyed who lived eleven years by my side. I awoke to find Tasha not her old self. She refused food and would only drink water. We took her to the veterinarian, and after tests discovered she had cancer of the pancreas and liver. There was no hope. As I held her close to me, and I knew that he had come from the other side to take her to run with him in the beautiful fields before she would suffer on this earthly plane.

Tasha passed away in my arms, and that night, in my dreams, I ran with Tasha in a beautiful wheat and poppy-filled field, and we came to a wooden bridge. How I wanted to cross that bridge as Tasha ran ahead of me, but my legs could not move. And as I looked across where Tasha ran, there was my beloved high priest, second father, mentor, and wise one, waving to me, saying, "Go back and do what you have to do."

THE BIOGRAPHY OF LEO MARTELLO

There have been many times since Leo's passing that his spirit has been made known to the members Our Lord and Lady of the Trinacrian Rose Coven. If it were not for him in 1992, we would not be the coven we are today. We are a Sicilian coven, whose beginnings stem from ancient Sicily. Our name comes from the ancient name of Sicily—Trinacria, meaning "three capes." We are all priests and priestesses of the ancient secret Sikelian Goddess. The Sikels were the first inhabitants of Sicily. Primarily, we are all a sacred priest- and priestesshood. To the people of my tradition—the Mago and Maga, Strega and Stregone—Leo had true heart, and heart is the true magic, and anything else is technical. The gods see the human heart, and here alone you are truly judged in your rites. Leo Martello was one of the blessed ones with his endless and boundless heartfire.

To understand this heartfire, I must say something about Leo's history. For this we go back to 1930s America, during the time of the Great Depression. Poverty was rampant in the United States. Joblessness, homelessness, and hunger were prevalent. It was a most terrible time for anyone to come into this world.

Leo sprang from a Sicilian immigrant father who had a farm in Massachusetts. Leo was baptized a Catholic. In his book *Witchcraft: The Old Religion,* he states that many of the Strega and Stregone hid under the very eyes of the Roman Catholic Church. His parents divorced when Leo was very young; consequently, Leo's father put him in a Catholic boarding school. The six years he spent at the boarding school were the unhappiest of his life. Needless to say, he did some mischief here and got into no little trouble. However, through this experience, at a very young age, Leo became strong and determined to move forward and never look back, and never let sadness poison his spirit—as we Sicilians and Italians say, "Avante!"

Leo had many psychic experiences as a child. In his early teens, he began his study of palmistry and tarot with a Gypsy woman. Aside from being a Sicilian Stregone and Mago, Leo in time became also a learned hypnotist, graphologist, publisher, and author. His publications included works on the craft, as well as books on hypnotism and handwriting analysis. When he was sixteen, he began making radio appearances, and giving handwriting analyses and selling stories to magazines. Later, he made television appearances. At the age of nineteen, he won a gold medal for the best fiction written by a teenage author in New York City.

Leo was educated at Assumption College in Worcester, Massachusetts, and at Hunter College and the Institute for Psychotherapy in New York City. He managed all of this on his own, supporting himself with a variety of odd jobs.

Leo's grandmother on his father's side, Maria Concetta, was a well-known Strega Maga and high priestess of the secret Goddess of the Sikels, in her hometown of Enna, Sicily. Enna is the place where the sacred Lago Pergusa and the cave from which Hades took Persephone to the underworld are located. Maria Concetta was reputed to have helped many people in Enna. It was also said that Maria Concetta, who loved her husband very much, was the cause of a local evil mafiosi's death when he threatened to kill Maria Concetta's husband if the husband did not pay protection money to him. The mafiosi dropped dead of a heart attack. We can only speculate whether this was Maria Concetta's doing—after all, what goes around comes around. This may seem terrible to some, but in those days, sometimes it was necessary for the Strega to take justice into their own hands, and Maria Concetta was a Maga. She protected her own.

Leo's father said that Leo physically resembled grandmother Maria Concetta. He surely had her temperament and psychic abilities. Leo's father also told Leo there were cousins in New York City who were of the Ancient Ways, and who wished to meet him. Thus began the journey that was to change his life forever.

Leo met his cousins and they told him they had been watching him for years for his potential in the Old Religion, or as it is known, "La Vecchia." On September 26, 1951, Leo was given initiation into his cousins' secret Sicilian coven; he then became a Mago, a Stregone, or male Witch. The initiation involved a blood oath never to reveal the secrets of the coven or its members or any of the secret teachings. In any and all of Leo's books, he has never revealed the secret Sicilian teachings to which he was privy. He was never an "Ynfamia," or "Oath-breaker."

In 1955, Leo Martello was awarded a Doctorate of Divinity degree by the National Congress of Spiritual Consultants. He became a minister of Spiritual-Nonsectarian, and served as Pastor of the Temple of Spiritual Guidance from 1955 to 1960. He left his position there to pursue his interests in witchcraft, parapsychology, psychology, and philosophy, thereby no longer accepting the theology of the National Congress of Spiritual Consultants.

He also used his talents as a graphologist, or handwriting analyst, to examine handwriting for various corporate clients. He was founder and director of the American Hypnotism Academy in New York from 1950 to 1954, and was treasurer of the American Graphological Society from 1955 to 1957.

In 1964, Leo Martello decided to travel to Morocco in North Africa. From 1964 to 1965, he resided in Tangier, Morocco, to study oriental religion, magic, and witchcraft.

In 1969, before he published his first book, *Weird Ways of Witchcraft,* Leo sought permission of his Sicilian coven to go public as a Witch. Subsequently, he contacted and was initiated into the Gardnerian-Alexandrian, Alexandrian, and Traditionalist witchcraft traditions.

He was the first public Witch to champion the establishment of legally incorporated tax-exempt Wiccan churches, civil rights for Witches, and like all mainstream religions, paid days off for Witches on their holidays. To strengthen and further this cause, Leo founded the Witches' Liberation Movement and the Witches International Craft Association (WICA). In 1970, he launched publication of the WICA *Newsletter and Witchcraft Digest.*

Leo Martello was a very outspoken man with a colorful way of saying thing. On All Hallows Eve, in 1970, he arranged for a "Witch-in" in New York City's Central Park. At first the

New York City Park Department refused to issue a permit. However, they changed their minds when Leo secured the services of the New York Civil Liberties Union and threatened a lawsuit on behalf of a minority religion whose rights were being violated. On Thursday, October 29, the permit was granted in a most cordial manner. Leo's sense of humor became apparent when the Park Department wanted to change the words "Witch-in." Leo refused, saying, "Since we will be in the sheep meadow in Central Park, and it once had sheep grazing in it, and since the symbolic God of the Witches is a goat, what could be more appropriate! Shall we call it a Goat-In?" Their jaws dropped, and he said, "I guess it was a good thing I didn't ask for a permission for a Goat-in!"

The Witch-in was attended by 1,000 persons, and was filmed and made into a documentary by Global Village. The Witch-in constituted the first civil rights victory for Witches. Witches and non-Witches held hands in the ever-widening circle and danced the Witches reel, while singing an old Wiccan tune, "London Bridge is Falling Down," with new words composed by a Connecticut Witch.

Witches meet in Central Park, Central Park, Central Park,
Witches meet in Central Park. For our Lady!

Leo always honored the women of the Craft, saying that there had to be balance between God and Goddess. Leo drafted a Witch Manifesto which called for a National Witch Day parade, the moral condemnation of the Catholic Church for its torture and murder of Witches during the Inquisition, a $500,000,000 lawsuit against the Church for damages and reparation to the descendants of victims to be paid by the Vatican, and a $100,000,000 suit against Salem, Massachusetts, for damages in the 1692 Witch Trials.

Leo foresaw that the Civil Rights Act of 1964 would enable the establishment of Wiccan temples and churches. His definition of a Witch was: "A wise practitioner of the craft, a nature worshipper, and a person who is in control of his or her life." To Leo, many people entered the craft with a great deal of hang-ups from their Judeo-Christian upbringing. The Sicilian tradition of the craft teaches that a wrong needs to be rectified in this life, and not left to karma in a future life. The Witch must not condone injustices. Leo's own philosophy, as outlined in his 1966 book *How to Prevent Psychic Blackmail*, is one of psychoselfism, and sensible selfishness versus senseless self-sacrifice.

In time, Leo founded the Witches Anti-Defamation League, dedicated to ensuring Witches' religious rights. By the late 1980s, chapters of the League had been established in every state in the U.S.A.

Other major publishing credits include *Witchcraft: The Old Religion; Black Magic; Satanism and Voodoo; Understanding the Tarot; It's Written in the Stars; It's Written in the Cards; Curses in Verses; Your Pen Personality;* and *The Hidden World of Hypnotism.*

Dr. Leo Louis Martello took a lot of important stands in the early days of the craft, and enabled those who came later to have it a little easier. However, Leo would now more than ever want us to continue creating an air of respect for the craft, never to allow our detractors to destroy our sacred faith. The craft is a sacred priest- and priestesshood. No matter how holy and sacred you try to appear—how many books you write, or lectures you give at festivals—if you are not sincere and respectful, then you have failed. You are not a Witch, and the God and Goddess see you down to your naked bones.

The following are words of Dr. Leo Louis Martello's from his book, *Witchcraft: The Old Religion.*

> In the Craft, there is no hard dogma. Hard drugs are forbidden. Mindless morons can't be a compliment to our Mother Goddess. Sex is sacred, not something to be exhibited at a peep show. Power is something personal, not to be used over others, which is contrary to Craft ethics. Those who think the Old Religion will make them masters over others are slaves to their own self delusions. A happy person is always a powerful person and is hated by those who aren't. A

happy person is in many ways selfish; in the Craft we must protect our best interests and ensure that the power that comes from joy remains constant, knowing that none of us are immune from the vicissitudes of life, but that our Old Religion will help us handle any adversity. The Craft has survived for thousands of years. After everything else has come and gone, it will remain. And one day, in the coming Age of Aquarius, there will once again be magnificent temples to the Goddess.

If you, as a Witch, allow wrongful acts in your midst and say nothing, you are as guilty as the perpetrator of the wrong Leo believed in justice, and he detested cowards.

He was the honorary father and elder of our coven. Our people miss him a great deal. Mere writing cannot tell how much we grieve for Leo. Within each and every one of us, he still lives. As Leo profoundly surmised: "The Craft is an underground spring which has existed for centuries and predates the Judeo-Christian and Muslim faiths, and occasionally rises to the surface in small streams and lakes. The modern craft movement reflects a worldwide rising of this underground spring coming with such force that it cannot be dammed by our enemies. The force behind this tidal wave is the murdered souls of the Witches condemned by the Inquisition! We are back and are going to stay to guide people to truly know what peace and respect of humanity is. Hail to our Goddess and God."

We remember Leo—your light will never be extinguished. Bless you for being a light unto the great light. May we meet again and walk the Elysian Fields with you. And may you return to help this mortal world when the need arises for the voice of justice to be heard.

Saluto, Papa!

WITCH VOW

BY LEO MARTELLO

Hear me, help me, Holy One,
My Witch life has just begun.
I dedicate myself to Thee;
My faith shall be fierce and free.

Make me worthy, make me wise,
Liberate me from all lies.
Guide me in thy Goddess light,
Illuminate each dark night.

I light the candle, I taste the wine,
I purify the air with incense fine.
I make the pentagram with my knife,
I declare my witchhood with my life.

I offer myself in naked truth.
Grant me wisdom and the joy of youth.
Upon thy altar my soul is bare,
I leave myself in thy loving care.

GAIANISM 101

BY ELIZABETH BARRETTE

Not everyone who follows a nature religion identifies with the word "Pagan." Some people feel it has negative connotations, while others feel it does not properly describes them. For those interested in Earth-based belief systems, there is another path.

Gaianism begins with the premise that the planet Earth is sacred and worthy of our respect because she gave birth to our species and she remains our only permanent home. This leads to two other core ideas. First, all other humans who live on this planet have something in common. And furthermore, we humans then had better take good care of our Earth, because we have nowhere else to go.

Does this mean need to believe in Gaia as a conscious, divine being? Actually, that part is optional. Some people find it comforting to conceive of a higher power watching over them, but others choose to do without this remnant of monotheism. In this religion, the choice is up to you. What counts in Gaianism is a willingness to act as though the Earth is holy. Essentially this means you commit to living a sustainable lifestyle, speak of her respectfully, and generally work to make the world a better place for all creatures.

One of the best things about Gaianism is that it's open to everybody. You can be Gaian and also be Pagan, Christian, Baha'i, atheistic, Buddhist, Wiccan, or any other tradition. Membership depends more on actions than beliefs or speeches. In fact, if you've been looking after the Earth then you may have been Gaian all along.

FOR FURTHER STUDY

You can learn more about this nascent tradition in such magazines as *PanGaia*. In particular, a regular column in *PanGaia* by Anne Newkirk Niven called "The Gospel According to Gaia: Spirituality as if It Really Mattered," gives a good sense of the basic ideas of this form of spiritual worship. (See recent issues of *PanGaia*, from issue 25 to the present).

HOUSE CLEANSING RITUAL

BY ANN MOURA

To purify a new house of unwanted energies you need a white candle, frankincense in a holder, a feather, spring water, a sprig of white heather or pine, and a small solar cross for each room. The cross should be equal-armed and made from palm strips or twigs. This cleansing ritual may be done when you feel that negative energies are building up in the house. It is particularly good to use at a new house.

At the eighth hour after sunrise or the third hour after sunset, during a waning Moon, light the candle and incense. One person then carries the candle into a room, circles the area widdershins (counterclockwise), and motions with the power hand towards the candlelight, saying: "I gather all negative energies, baleful and chaotic, to the light."

A second person with the incense enters the room, walking deosil (clockwise) around it and using the feather to waft the smoke into all corners, saying: "I purify this room with frankincense, that only joy and love enter and remain."

A third person enters and walks deosil around the room, sprinkling water with the sprig and saying: "With spring water is this room asperged and cleansed."

A fourth person holding the crosses enters, follows the incense around the room, and places a cross over the door of the room, saying: "This room is sealed. So mote it be!"

All proceed through the house. When finished, all exit the back door. The cross-bearer places one over the back door. The candle-bearer says: "This house is cleansed and purified, all baleful and chaotic energies I now release into the air."

Blow out the candle and return indoors, shutting the back door. Together, waft incense at the front door, sprinkle it with water, and place the last cross over the front door. Do not be surprised if a sudden wind picks up outside. The last time my family did this before moving into a new house, a sudden gust of wind buffeted the back of the house leaping over the roof to the front before being dispersed. So remember to keep the doors closed.

Know Yourself

By Estelle Daniels

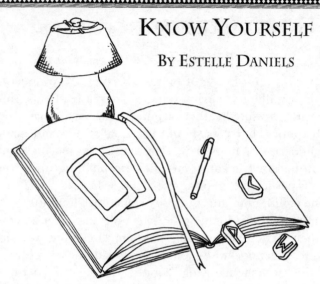

One goal of magic is to know yourself. In turn, the better you honestly know yourself, the more effective your magic can be.

One way to get to know yourself better is to take a personality inventory test. Not necessarily one which measures mental health, but one which measures character traits and preferences. The Kiersey Temperament sorter or the Meyers-Briggs personality test are among the best of these sorts of tests. These measure preferences, and can indicate how you tend to behave. In them, you are classified along four scales. From these four scales come sixteen personality types. Once you know your type, you can find many references to your type, and see how it fits into society. There are many websites on the Internet devoted to these topics.

Use what you have learned to determine one trait you want to change. Concentrate for a week on that negative trait, catching yourself, and trying to modify your behavior. Work on only one trait at a time, or you may be overwhelmed. But if you cultivate your awareness, you might find the problem may cure itself. Many of our negative traits are just patterns of habit. Becoming aware of them is half the battle.

It may be helpful to set aside fifteen to twenty in
each day, right before bedtime, to think over your day. Loo
for things you'd like to change, how you might you have handled yourself differently. In time, you will become more active
in dealing with your personality and its quirks.

Dream interpretation is an excellent path for self-improv-
ment. Write down your dreams in a journal. Many will deal
with how you handled yourself, and possibly what you might
have done better. Your higher mind is always watching and
judging you and your actions. You will know if you did something not be in your best interests for soul development.

If you have a dream with uncomfortable emotional over-
tones, it might be a warning about something you did, and a
caution to not repeat the behavior. A dream in which you are
deformed or crippled may be a strong commentary on your
actions. What you did crippled you in some way, or kept you
from your fullest potential. Your higher mind can be starkly
honest. Listen to it through your dreams.

Dialoguing with yourself can help work through difficulties.
If you are uncertain about how to conduct yourself in a situation, talk it out beforehand. Do it in your bedroom, or while
you are driving. Nobody else need hear, but just actually saying the words, rehearsing yourself through all the possible
scenarios, will help.

You can use divination too as a tool for self-exploration.
Ask a question several ways. In each answer you can find
insight into the possible consequences of your actions. Meditation is another path toward self-understanding. Calming the
mind and allowing your thoughts to flow freely can relieve
stress. Ask for insight and understanding of yourself.

Any or all of these techniques can be helpful for getting to
know yourself better. It may take time, but if you work at it a
bit each day the awareness will come. Being fully self-aware
and conscious about yourself and the world around you is
what makes for a successful magician. Good luck.

..L FOR
Loss

...ARDNER

...ng for a slimmer,
...er body—a body
that you can be proud of? If you
can imagine yourself in better
shape, you can manifest it
through magic.

This spell uses the power of
the Moon, of crystal, of candlelight, and of visualization to work
changes in your body image.

PREPARATION

Preparing for spell working is as important as the ritual itself.
Gather your materials with the intention that you are working on
a brand-new body image.

To begin, create a manifestation altar. This altar should be
separate from your meditation altar or other shrine to the Goddess. Whether it is placed on a dresser-top or in your magic room,
this altar is designated only for manifesting.

Use a silver cloth and place symbols of the Moon Goddess on
your altar. Obtain and cleanse a herkimer diamond and place
that on your altar as well. Herkimer diamonds are double-termi-
nated quartz crystals and are the ultimate stones for materializing
your desires. You'll need three tapers in black, red, and white to
represent the triple aspect of the Moon. Place a cauldron and
fourteen paper dolls on your altar. The paper dolls are cut out
from plain paper to represent you. They are merely symbols so
don't worry if you can't draw a perfect likeness of yourself.

Create a collage on poster-board or cardboard of pictures of
the body image you desire. Paste pictures of your face to the
images so you can better imagine the body you seek. Write words
on your collage such as "sleek" or "fit," whatever is meaningful for

you. Be sure that you also write the words of the Witches' pyramid on your collage: "know," "will," "dare," and "keep silent."

Imagination and will are copartners in workings of magic. Your imagination paints the image of your desire and your will gives the image power to manifest. Daring is the power to make changes in yourself and in your life. Silence keeps the spell focused on your goal. Meditate for a while on what these magical concepts mean to your spell-working.

The last step in the preparation is deciding on a healthy and reasonable diet and exercise program that you are willing to commit to. Remember that all acts of magic must be supported by physical effort. As Doreen Valiente once wrote: "There is a great difference between willing something and just weakly wishing it."

RITUAL

On the night of the Full Moon, bow to the Moon in reverence and chant: "Everything she touches, changes." If the Moon is visible, bathe your herkimer diamond in its light.

Go back to your altar and light the red candle. Holding your herkimer in your receptive hand, focus on the flame and believe in the possibility of your new body. Know that all acts of magic are possible on the Full Moon.

On the next night, repeat the ritual—bowing to the Moon, chanting, and capturing the moonlight in your herkimer diamond.

Go back to your altar, light the black candle, and place the diamond next to the burning candle. Hold one of your fourteen paper dolls in your dominant hand and gazing into the candle's flame, say: "What I see is glowing. What I rub is going."

Rub the paper doll over the parts of you that need reducing. Visualize the weight sliding off you easily. Feel the weight dropping from you. You want to eat less. You want to eat healthy foods. You enjoy being lean and fit.

Hold the paper doll to the burning candle, and drop it in your cauldron. As you watch the paper doll burning, visualize your metabolism speeding up, burning fat cells.

Repeat this ritual every night during the waning Moon. The Moon will rise later each successive night, so for most people it won't be practical to perform the outside portion of the spell. Be aware of the Moon and her power even if you can't see her. When the Moon becomes new and begins to wax again, light your white candle and visualize the new you. Prepare another set of fourteen paper dolls, and repeat the spell from the Full Moon through the waning Moon. Repeat this spell each waning Moon until you have achieved your desire.

Remember, if you wish to lose more than a few pounds, you need to give yourself time to manifest your new body. Make it happen. So mote it be.

FOR FURTHER STUDY

For crafting your own spells, I highly recommend all of Scott Cunningham's books. Cunningham's *The Complete Book of Incense, Oils and Brews* (Llewellyn Publications, 1989) provides a wealth of information about special incenses, inks, baths, and brews that you can make to help realize your goals. Cunningham's *Encyclopedia of Crystal, Gem and Metal Magic* (Llewellyn Publications, 1988) explains the magical properties and folklore of crystals. If I could recommend just one herbal, I would endorse Cunningham's *Encyclopedia of Magical Herbs* (Lewellyn Publications, 1985). Each of these books have tables of magical substitutions or magical intentions.

Also see:

Spinning Spells, Weaving Wonders. Patricia Telesco, Crossing Press, 1996. Explains how to craft spells and provides a wealth of information about magical symbols.

Natural Magic. Doreen Valiente. St. Martin's Press, 1975. Doreen Valiente continues to inspire me every time I read her books. This one is a serious treatise on magic and its workings.

Mayan Ballcourt Magic

By Bernyce Barlow

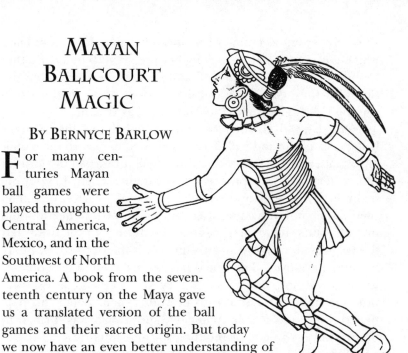

For many centuries Mayan ball games were played throughout Central America, Mexico, and in the Southwest of North America. A book from the seventeenth century on the Maya gave us a translated version of the ball games and their sacred origin. But today we now have an even better understanding of the mysteries of the games. Much of this new information comes from archaeological finds—vases, frescoes, statuary that depict the ball games and the ball courts. These artifacts span different centuries and have been very helpful in the studies of this subject.

Let us review the story of the ball games so we know why these ancient games were so important to the Native nations. It is a story of the gods and the mystical ways they played out good and evil, the underworld, middleworld, and life and death. It is told that the twin gods Hun-Hunahpu and Wuqub Hunapu were once playing a ballgame that was so noisy it disturbed the lords of the underworld. So the lords of death summoned the twins to the underworld to punish them for their disturbances, and they were forced to undergo many trials. Eventually, through tricks they lost the challenges and were put to death—the first born twin was beheaded, his head placed on a gourd tree as a warning to all others. Both twins' bodies were buried in the ball court as a further warning.

Xkikí was a daughter of an underworld lord and out of curiosity she went to see the skull hanging on the tree. The skull spoke to her and eventually convinced her to hold out her hand which it promptly spit in, making her pregnant. When her father found out he became enraged and ordered her death, but she fled with the help of the owl executioner to the middleworld where she birthed twins, Hun-Ahaw and Yax-Balam.

One day, with the help of a rat, the boys found their father's ball game regalia and ball. They proceeded to play and like their father made such a racket they once again disturbed the lords of the underworld who proceeded to summon them for punishment. But Hun-Ahaw and Yax-Balam knew of the tricks played on their father and won game after game. The lords of death would not allow this victory and planned the murder of the twins. But the twins made magical arrangements for their rebirth by jumping into a hot oven. The baked bones were ground into powder to be thrown into a river where they would emerge as fish who would eventually turn into strong young men. When this happened, there was a great rejoicing, and a plan was formed to destroy those who had played the ball game unfairly.

Hun-Ahaw and Yax-Balam went to the underworld disguised as dancers. As performers they entertained the lords of the underworld and managed to trick them into being sacrificed and then dismembered. The lords had agreed to this assuming they would be brought back to life. But the twins had lied and had no intention of bringing the lords back. And so the story reveals the importance of the ball game and the ball courts in Mexico and Central and North America. It is a game of victory of the living over the dead.

Many of the great ruins of Mexico still have the ball courts where the games were played. And like the story, the game was life or death. We know that the rules and the players differed from place to place and century to century. Some games were only played by the rulers and the elite, other games were played by captives, probably from neighboring provinces. The captives were sent in much like the gladiators of Rome for their final battle. In some games, players used their hands. In other games, the rules were much like soccer. Often, the captain of the winning team would present his head to the losing team. As odd as this sounds, it was a great honor to do this because the team would get a direct ticket to heaven instead of having to go through the thirteen different steps to reach heaven. Later after the Toltec reign, the head of the losing captain was put inside the ball. The game was played by the Aztec, Toltec, Teotihuacan, Olmec, Mixtec, Maya, Tajin, and later by Native Americans as it was brought into North America through the trade routes. There is a fine example of a ball court at the ruins of Wupatki in Arizona.

The costumes of the games also varied. One millennium after the Olmecs, stone yokes were adapted. These were called *yugos* and worn low around the waist. At the same time, large wooden balls were also employed as deflectors and worn high on the chest. There are vases from the eighth century that show ball game participants dressed in the same regalia as the deer dancers and hunters. Some vases from Aztec times showed helmeted and gloved players. Indeed, by the time the Spaniards came to Central America and Mexico, the ball games had gone through many transformations and regalia changes. The Spaniards were fascinated and horrified by the games; they even took an entire team back with them to Europe.

Although the ball games hold a great interest, the ball courts themselves are perhaps one of the greatest mysteries of our modern times. The ball court at Chichen Itza is 545 feet long, 225 feet wide with no vault and no break in the walls. The sky is the ceiling. The ends have been built with temple areas where the kings sat and watched the games. And its acoustics are remarkable. One can hear a whisper from across the court. It is said the Mayans especially were master scientists when it came to acoustics. In fact, many Mayan temples show the same characteristics.

So, next time you go to a soccer or football game, it may bring to mind the ancient games and players of the past, a time when the players were rulers and kings or captive gladiators fighting for honor before death. And although a victory in modern times brings a metal trophy, a blue ribbon, or Super Bowl ring, there was a time that victory was the ticket to heaven!

THE FOLK MAGIC OF HAIR

BY DAVID HARRINGTON

H air is a magical substance, springing from our heads, repository of our divine energy, home of what makes us human. In cultures worldwide, hair is a symbol of the individual, subject to suffering in negative spells, or potent as a blessing and talisman. Any time hair is tied or braided, a magical knot of protective energy is formed, keeping the person safe from harm.

In the Inca highlands, at one year of age, a child's family invites the villagers to the house. Everyone brings a gift, a blanket, a llama, gold jewelry, or other items. They place the offered gifts around the child. The child's hair is sectioned off and tied with colorful ribbons, often red in color. Throughout South America, and elsewhere, the color red is symbolic of life. Burials often include red pigment sprinkled over the body. The family takes a special pair of scissors—probably a modern version of the sacred obsidian knives used in the region—and at the point where the hair is tied off, they cut off the lock. This is then given to the visitors, who takes the tied lock home and keeps it in the house. In this way the child's life force is protected in many places, and also brings into the other houses some of the exuberant energy of the child, where it serves as a talisman of fertility for the keepers of the lock.

This magic behind this ceremony is universal. A remnant that survives in our own culture is the "Boy's First Haircut," which has unfortunately has been relieved of much of its original ritual significance. But this magic can be reclaimed easily and added to a child's first birthday party, or better yet, to a special celebration just for relatives. As hair is magically powerful, you don't want to give these locks to anyone you don't love and trust. And you probably won't want to shear your child's head so thoroughly as the highland villagers do, but little bows can be placed at the end of locks of hair, and trimmed, leaving a two-inch piece of hair bound with a ribbon. While red is traditional for this spell, other colors from our culture can be used, including the traditional pink for girls and blue for boys—or the longstanding compromise color yellow, which can be seen as a symbol of solar energy and the power of life.

Traditional worry dolls have found new life as a modern talisman for protecting the hair, and the person wearing it. These little dolls in the forms of men and women have been used for centuries. They are made of wire or clay, thread, and topped with a bit of black paint, often mixed with shiny metallic grains. The custom is for a child to tell these dolls his or her problems, one problem for each doll, then place them in a little box beside the bed at night before going to sleep. During the night the tiny dolls will work to solve the problems.

These popular little dolls are now being made into hair barrettes, where they serve a protective function and see a bit more of the physical world than from the traditional box beside the bed.

These, and other, hair ornaments are ordinarily reflective, distracting those who have the power of the evil eye. Instead of meeting the eyes of the individual, the malefic gaze is directed to the sparkling objects in the hair, and the evil effect is averted.

GODS OF THE BLACK LAND

BY JOHN MICHAEL GREER

For many centuries, it's been recognized in Western occult traditions that the art of magic had its origins in the spiritual traditions of the land that we call Egypt, "the Black Land," and with its ancient inhabitants called Khem. While other peoples also made major contributions to the rich tapestry of Western occult theory and practice, it's nonetheless true that much of the Western magical tradition had its roots on the banks of the Nile.

Understanding ancient Egyptian spirituality takes a certain amount of mental stretching for most people nowadays—even people who are part of today's Pagan renaissance. The common assumptions of modern Paganism don't fit Egyptian traditions well at all. If this isn't recognized, the result can be endless confusion. For example, if you asked an ancient Egyptian priestess about the Goddess, her first question would be, "Which one?" There are hundreds in Egyptian mythology, all different. If you went on to ask about the Earth Mother, the priestess might won-

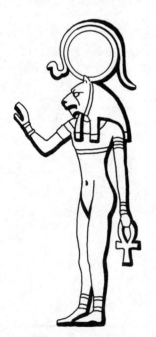

der why you didn't know the first thing about the gods, and patiently explain that the Earth was the god Geb, not a goddess at all.

In the lore of ancient Egypt, the Earth is a god and the sky is a goddess. The Moon is usually male, and the Sun is often female. Gods and goddesses fuse, blend, and spin off aspects of themselves with a freedom that leaves familiar categories in tatters. For example, Atum the creator manifests himself as the sun god Re, but Re is also the manifestation of Amun, "the Hidden One," the double-plumed god of Thebes. Meanwhile the Sun, which is Re, is also Horus, when it isn't the cat-goddess Bastet, or the lioness-headed Sekhmet, or the divine scarab beetle Khephera,

114

or any of several other gods and goddesses, and so on and so forth.

Some of this splendid confusion comes from differences between local religious traditions in different parts of Egypt. In Heliopolis, the most important religious center in Egypt, the first of the gods was Atum, the Creator, whose active manifestation was Re, the Sun, the king of the gods. Thebes, the capitol during the Middle and New Kingdom periods, had its own creator-god Amun, who also manifested as Re, whose wife was the vulture goddess Mut, and whose son was the Moon god Khons. In Esna, the ram-headed Khnum was the creator; he was a potter-god who fashioned the universe on his potter's wheel, and his wife was the frog goddess Heket, who breathed life into everything Khnum created. In the Old Kingdom capitol of Memphis, in turn, the creator was Ptah, the divine patron of craftsmen, while in Sais it was Neith, the androgynous archer-goddess of wisdom.

No matter what he (or she) was called, the creator had the help of Thoth, god of writing, knowledge, and the Moon, whose sacred animals were the ibis and the ape, and who served as scribe, adviser, and prime minister to Re. Four other deities who served the creator were Maat, the goddess of justice and rightness; Heka, the god of magic; Sia, the goddess of omniscient knowledge, and Hu, the god of the creative breath and voice. Also associated with the creator was Tatenen, the primal mound of earth that rose from the deeps at the beginning, who was also a god in his own right and was especially linked with Ptah.

Myths written down by priestly scribes helped sort out the relationships among this dizzying array of powers. According to the theology of Heliopolis, for instance, Atum dwelt alone on the primal mound Tatenen, and then created a group of serpent-gods, who helped him bring the universe into being. They then died and were mummified by Atum, becoming the first powers of the underworld.

Atum then masturbated into his hand, which gave birth to Shu, god of air, and Tefnut, goddess of moisture. Shu and Tefnut mated and engendered Geb, the god of the Earth, and Nut, the goddess of the sky. Meanwhile Atum took on a new form as Re, the Sun, and king of the gods. Nut became the wife of Re, but made love with her brother Geb, and gave birth to five children: Osiris, Isis, Aroueris, Nephthys, and Set.

Osiris married Isis and became king of Egypt, but he was slain by Set, resurrected by Isis, and then slain again and sent to the underworld to become king and judge of the dead. The myths, rituals, and traditions surrounding his life and death were central to much of ancient Egyptian spirituality. After his resurrection, Osiris mated with his sister-wife Isis, fathering Horus. Osiris also mated with Nephthys, Set's wife, fathering the jackal-headed Anubis, the Opener of the Ways, god of funeral rites and messenger of Osiris in the latter's role as lord of the underworld.

The falcon god Horus is among the most complex of Egyptian gods, and he had many different aspects—Harsiese, the infant suckled by Isis; Harpocrates, the child upon the lotus; Horus the Avenger, who slays Set; Horakhte, "Horus of the Two Horizons," who is the Sun and is identified with Re; and many more. Aroueris was a warrior god whose eyes are the Sun and the Moon; his relation to his nephew Horus the Younger is complex, and the two probably started out as the same very ancient solar god in Egyptian prehistory. The wife of Horus was Hathor, whose name literally means "House of Horus." She was originally the sky, but later became a cow-headed goddess of love, music, dance, and fertility.

Set, for his part, was not just the murderer of Osiris, but a powerful god in his own right, who stood guard on Re's boat to guard the Sun against the attacks of its monstrous enemies. A heavy drinker and a passionate lover of goddesses and gods alike, he was married to Nephthys but had no children.

There were many other gods and goddesses who had no relationship to the great family saga of Heliopolis. Sekhmet was a savage lioness-headed goddess of war and plague, who incarnated the killing heat of the desert sun. The cat-headed Bastet, patron of the city of Bubastis, was a solar goddess who protected pregnant women and infants and banished the powers of evil. Another solar deity was Khephera, "He who becomes," who took the form of the scarab beetle and was linked with the Sun at dawn.

Min was a fertility god whose immense erect penis was his most noticeable attribute. Bes, a minor god of the people who played no part in the priestly cult, was a grinning dwarf who served to drive away evil spirits, especially during childbirth. There were also countless minor deities whose names were simply "the god or goddess of such-and-such place."

The gods and goddesses of the Black Land offer an extraordinary richness of possibilities for the modern Pagan revival, as well as a useful corrective to attitudes that map one particular model of divinity onto all of Pagan spirituality. They are well worth our study, and our reverence.

For Further Study

Conceptions of God in Ancient Egypt. Erik Hornung, trans. John Baines Routledge & Kegan Paul, 1982.

Daily Life of the Egyptian Gods. Dimitry Meeks and Christine Favard-Meeks, trans. G. M. Goshgarian Cornell University Press, 1996.

The Mysteries of Isis. deTraci Regula. Llewellyn Publications, 1992.

Sacred Key to Ancient Egypt. Rosemary Clark. Llewellyn Worldwide, 2000.

Ritual Simplicity

By Cerridwen Iris Shea

I work in the theater, so I love props, and this carries over into my magical work. I love to make and use tools—scrying mirrors, oracles, a variety of gemstones, statues, scythes, and rattles. Seeing my chalices lined up in a row makes me happy. I have nearly thirty tarot decks, and I use all of them.

I store tools in boxes or cupboards when they are not in use. Still, often my altar resembles a rummage sale. Things accumulate here—gemstones, ribbons, workings and requests, spells-in-progress, and sometimes even lazy cats. At times, the mess can be overwhelming. I either need to redesign and enlarge my altar, or more regularly put my tools away.

In reality, though I regularly use all of my tools for various rituals, I don't actually need any of them. Tools are just tools, simple objects to help focus the magic. The real magic is inside and is infinite.

When I simply remove everything from the altar and do a ritual with an almost-blank stage, the magic is as pure as is possible. In these instances, I perform a ritual by placing five tarot cards in a medicine wheel to represent the four elements and spirit. Sometimes I use one candle, one small bowl of water, some salt in a clamshell, a stick of incense, and some sort of gift for the gods. Otherwise, I avoid all other tools—I don't use the athame, the wand, the sword, or the mirror. The magic comes simply from my myself. Instead of worrying about writing a twelve-page ritual with detailed correspondences, I cast a circle with my hands and simply sit and speak with the Divine. In these cases, the results are quicker and stronger than rituals with all the props.

Sometimes one gets so caught up in the stuff of magic, that one forgets the source of magic. Feng shui insists that clutter causes blocks in energy. Even if that clutter is magical clutter, it still can cause a block. When there is magical clutter, it can cause a loud disruption to the energy of your space. As I've learned through the years, taking time to put things away, clean up with reverence and joy, will add a great deal of pure magical energy to your practice.

Stripping away stuff is akin to stripping away words. And the least cluttered use of words is always the clearest. Designing, writing, rehearsing, and performing an elaborate ritual is lots of fun. However, if one is so caught up in the words, the gestures, and the "what comes next," one can disconnect from the power and the beauty of the energy. In other words, a simple ritual is best.

Here are some tips to provide you a ritual simplicity. Start with a bare working place. Focus on your purpose for the ritual. Use one representation for each element and one for spirit. Use your hands. Use your mind. Most importantly, use your heart. If you are out in nature, the representations will be all around you. If you choose, you can do your working with nothing but your own intentions and energy. You will be surprised how good this feels and may even decide that, in outdoor rituals, you no longer need to fill a cargo van with ritual tools. Notice that pure energy and power flows within yourself.

In the case of a group ritual, I have more of a problem connecting with the power, whether I am a guest or a leader. I find that if the ritual is simple, not only do newcomers tap into it much more quickly, but I can flow with the power and help direct it more clearly. And, I find that, even if I forget the carefully planned words, other words spring to mind quickly and smoothly. Especially in open ritual, the simpler the plan, the smoother the ceremony, and the more everyone gets out of it. I have been a guest at rituals where I felt more like an audience member than a participant. While I admire and appreciate the amount of work that goes into something like that, I do feel the elaborate ritual alienates guests and diffuses the energy.

When everyone is involved in a simple way, even if it is only lighting a candle or casting hand-to-hand instead of watching someone else cast the circle, I find the power and the cohesion in a ritual is much stronger.

And finally, never underestimate the power of laughter. It is the simplest expression of joy, and yet the most infectious energy you can bring to your ritual.

Props and tools are great, but make them a secondary element rather than the focal point of a simple ritual. Remember always, the magic is within.

FOR FURTHER STUDY

Magical Hearth: Home for the modern pagan. Janet Thompson. Samuel Weiser, 1995.

Move Your Stuff, Change Your Life: How to use feng shui to get love, money, respect, and happiness. Karen Rauch Carter. Simon and Schuster, 2000.

To Stir a Magick Cauldron. Silver RavenWolf. Llewellyn Publications, 1995.

A Witch Alone: Thirteen moons to master natural magic. Marian Green. Aquarian Press, 1991.

WATCH YOUR STEP!

BY MARGUERITE ELSBETH

The spiritual path is much more than a course of study. It is both a religion and a way of life that offers glimpses of enlightenment along with countless adventures leading to new heights of self-discovery.

However, a potentially dangerous aftermath often attends the beginning stages of magical attainment. Whether you are a long time seeker or a spiritual newcomer, and no matter what path you follow, there are pitfalls to beware of as you travel the road to realization.

PREACHING WHAT YOU PRACTICE

Newcomers to the spiritual path tend to become very excited when the doors of consciousness begin to open, and sometimes this leads to overenthusiastic sermonizing. This is especially true when desired life-changes start to occur at a rapid pace; the spiritual path you have chosen may suddenly seem nothing short of miraculous!

Working with any spiritual path is likely to boost your power-drive. This happens because any genuine mystical tradition will naturally awaken your chakras, the seven inner energy centers that have a direct influence on the body, mind, and emotions. When your chakras wake up, watch out! You will have more power than you ever dreamed possible, and still, you may want more.

The desire for raw, unadulterated power and control is an ethical no-no; furthermore, it breeds lust, greed, jealousy, and many other ills in the process. Seek empowerment instead, and find strength and courage to do something constructive.

Overall, be careful in this stage of your spiritual development. You should know that not everyone shares your enthusiasm. Just because you have switched to a vegetarian diet, for example, does not mean everyone you know will follow suit. Moreover, proselytizing with dogmatic zeal sounds judgmental, disapproving, and hypercritical. Yes, you have made positive changes, but no one is perfect, not even you. So, it is best to save your preaching for the equally passionate congregation.

METAPHYSICIAN, HEAL THYSELF

One of the first bits of knowledge gleaned on journeying the spiritual path is the realization that thoughts are things. You may seek to help others by discreetly thinking well of them, or you may be tempted to use your brand-new perception to mentally heal others "for their own good." If the latter occurs, resist the urge to send mental messages to the subconscious mind of another person, even though you have good intentions.

This goes for love too. Again, there are ethics involved when attempting to use mental abilities to formulate a romantic interest. Like attracts like, so if you are single and wish to be in partnership create a list of the qualities you desire in a partner and work to develop them in yourself. This way, you will attract the kind of person you want without interferring with his or her free will.

Eastern traditions are mystical in nature and focus upon emotional development. However, Western magical traditions lean toward the pursuit of intellectual knowledge, particularly in the early stages of the work. Still, a little knowledge can be a very dangerous thing when your emotional nature is undeveloped. Your emotions must flow in confluence with your mind, or very little changes on the spiritual levels. Lack of emotional growth puts you at the mercy of all your old, negative, instinctual habit patterns of anger, resentment, self-criticism, guilt, doubt, or shame.

This is especially so when participating in group-work, where each individual shares his or her experiences to create the collective whole. The group-mind, an organized body of people drawn together for a specific purpose, is ensouled by group-emotion, which is made vulnerable by chinks in the emotional armor of its members. However, by listening to your heart instead of your intellect when you embark on the spiritual path, you may weed out the outworn patterns that are a detriment to your self and others. Focus on your self first.

WHAT GOES UP MUST COME DOWN

Movement is life; to stand still is to cease living. Life is infinite, so there can be no final attainment, even in terms of your goals. You can never achieve the peak of perfection, because from that peak of perfection you must move to the next and higher mountain top. Consequently, rather than seeking spiritual, mental, emotional, or physical perfection, it is better to focus on moving upward and onward.

Still, there are valleys of sorrowful experience you must enter for every mountain you climb. This is when your memory of the mountain top will serve you well. When you are crestfallen, you can hold on to the inner core of peace and security you attained during a high that will enable you remain in synchronistic flow with the cosmos.

The greatest challenge of all, especially for neophytes, is formulating and living up to the ideal spiritual personality. If you are uncertain about the self you are trying to reinvent, or feel that you have accidentally taken a wrong turn on the spiritual path, use these guidelines to set your self in the right direction:

Develop the emotional qualities of your character as you increase the powers of your mind.

Eschew curiosity, ambition, and an overblown ego in favor of a big heart filled with empathy and compassion for the human condition shared by all.

Seek guidance and protection through those of likemind. Seek wisdom and depth through solitary dedication to the spiritual path.

Remember that no one human being or organization is pure and perfect. Gurus and groups may help to prepare you for initiation; they do not open your consciousness to a higher reality. True spiritual attainment comes through an intuitive connection to the cosmos. Therefore, trust and serve the Creator always.

FOR FURTHER STUDY

Care of the Soul: A guide for cultivating depth and sacredness in everyday life. Thomas Moore. Walker, 1993.

Magick for Beginners. J. H. Brennan. Llewellyn Publications, 1998.

Sane Occultism. Dion Fortune. Samuel Weiser, 1967.

Spring Resolution Ritual

By Laurel Nightspring

Here is a simple ritual to pack some added oomph into your New Year's resolutions. Perform it on the first New Moon of the new year, or adapt it to fit an event that suggests new beginnings and transition. You might also want to perform the ritual after a birthday or other major life-considering event.

Items Needed:

2   seasonal altar candles of any color

1   blue candle

2   silver candles

1   small white or silver birthday candle

1   small wooden box

    Various tokens representing resolutions

    A slip of good (parchment or drawing) paper

    A fountain pen

Decorate the box with drawings or pictures. Make it something that you'd like to look at and that has meaning to you. Whether you decorate it beforehand or make the decorating a part of the ritual, it will allow you to meditate more fully on the changes you want to make in your life.

Now, collect of small tokens to put in your box. These represent your resolution to focusing on your goals. Put some thought into what you'd like to use, as well as the types of resolutions you really want to make. Try to be realistic in what you really want to work towards in the coming year and in your ability to make your desires manifest.

Light all but the silver candles. Cast your circle, using whatever method feels the most comfortable. Invite the Moon and her powers in to your chambers, saying:

Lady Moon, dark Selene,
Please join in my task at hand.
May your presence add to my strength.
May you witness my determination.

Light silver candles, and bless and consecrate your box. Hold and name your tokens individually, charging each with your desire, intent, and purpose. Equate the name of the object with your purpose, linking it to a particular resolution. As you finish with each one, place it in the box.

Write your resolutions out on the paper. Make these positive statements of things you will do. Try to be specific. For example, don't simply say, "I will lose weight this year." Instead say, "I will lose fifteen pounds this year." This will also help increase your ability to make your resolutions manifest. Visualize the power in your script as your write. Be sure to write the date on your paper.

Finally, light the birthday candle, letting some wax drip near the top of the paper. Press your index finger into warm wax to better bind the resolutions to you. Roll the paper and secure it with a ring or a small length of colored floss. Place it in the box, adding the birthday candle. Close and charge the box. Place both of the silver candles on the box. Allow them to burn a little each day for seven days, until they are gone. Release the circle, you are done.

If you need some reinforcements, repeat the ritual again in six months, using new silver candles.

Magic and Healing among the Gladiators

By Nuala Drago

The lives of the gladiators were steeped in blood, which of course thrilled the populace of ancient Rome for more than seven hundred years. In a time when a human could be purchased for less than the cost of a nugget of amber, magic and ritual, combined with healing techniques, were a counterbalance to the harsh, violent world in which the gladiators were bought, sold, traded, and killed for the glory of a succession of emperor-gods.

The gladiatorial tradition began almost 2,300 years ago when the Roman Empire absorbed an Etruscan sacrificial funeral rite. In time, this combat to the death escalated into public spectacles in which tens of thousands of warriors brutally dismembered, flayed, decapitated, and disemboweled each other in a single day. These battles took place in huge arenas, such as the Flavian Amphitheater, before an audience that numbered up to fifty thousand. And, at the end of a day of fighting, the lucky ones lived to do it again.

Good gladiators, men, and less commonly, women, were in constant demand. A gladiator who was skilled enough to survive the games with courage and flair could attain great wealth, or perhaps win freedom. Not all gladiators were slaves, however. They came from diverse places and all walks of life. Many were prisoners of war or criminals, but a great number were volunteers who bound themselves to their profession through a guild or pledge of loyalty to their masters.

Winners in the arena were showered with gold, silver, jewelry, and expensive garments, and, because of their physical prowess, they were also showered with sexual favors from admiring fans. In spite of their popularity, gladiators were outcasts who lived apart from society in guilds or schools, through which their services could be purchased. Whatever far-off place had once been called home, whatever an individual's background, the gladiators melded together to form a brotherhood of the sword, an alliance of professional killers under the watchful eye of their favored deity—Mars, the god of war.

Feats of the gladiators so titillated the audiences that supernatural powers came to be attributed to some of them. Because of these beliefs, the market for weapons and body parts obtained from dead gladiators soon swelled. Pieces of flesh, fingers, toes, hair, clothing, and bones were all coveted for their magical potency. Priests, physicians, wizards, and soothsayers used them in rituals, fertility rites, spells of protection, and even incorporated them into medicines.

Dead or alive, the demand for gladiators escalated in time, along with the demand for greater spectacle and greater violence in the arenas. The pressure must have been overwhelming as gladiators struggled to balance their instincts for survival and for glory.

Out of a need to exert control over their own lives, and to maintain the focus necessary to survive, gladiators embraced sympathetic and representative magic, healing, meditation, and ceremonial sex—often blending the beliefs of their varying cultural backgrounds. Their goals were to please the gods enough to live another day.

Symbols and amulets representing supernatural powers were frequently incorporated into magical rites by gladiators. These afforded them additional strength and protected them when worn on the person, emblazoned on a shield, tattooed or branded on the flesh. The phallus was the most important of these symbols, particularly if fashioned of amber—the phallus signified life, and amber conferred rather powerful protection from evil. Many other natural shapes were also employed—hearts, skulls, effigies, crescents—according to their assigned properties. Amulets such as the *bulla* were also popular. This was a hollow sphere carved of bone, wood, or amber, or fashioned of metal or glass, which could then be inscribed with magic symbols and filled with the prescribed ingredients according to the desired effect.

Foods were also assigned magical properties, and physicians to the gladiators prescribed magical diets as part of the healing tradition. Apples, honey, and pomegranates, for example, were potent for fertility, longevity, and their association with the otherworld. Garlic was eaten for courage, while watercress was one of many aphrodisiacs. The physicians of the day, such as Galen who practiced over 1,800 years ago, understood the symbiosis between medicine and magic. And, although bloodletting was routine, they also practiced surgery and had at their disposal a vast pharmacopoeia. The most often-formulated treatment was the *theriac,* a combination of opiates and herbs. Opiates relieved pain and provided an anesthetic, while the herbs cleansed, promoted healing, and prevented infection.

Many of the botanicals that were employed magically by the gladiators and their physicians are still in use today, either by traditional or holistic healers. Digitalis was, and still is, used for heart conditions, quinine for malaria, and ginseng as a restorative. To staunch wounds and control bleeding, European chestnut, fenugreek, and garden loosetrife might have been employed, while certain members of the borage family were steeped in wine to heal damaged kidneys and treat urinary infections. Horehound and Roman chamomile were applied to animal and poisonous snake bites. Aloe was popular for all types of minor wounds, while comfrey, hounds-tongue, and sage were among the botanicals employed for broken bones and internal injuries.

Indeed, plants and herbs, accompanied by the appropriate ritual, provided a remedy for every physical ill—ranging from broken bones and severed limbs to warts and fistulas. These herbs helped to heal severed limbs, sprains, fractures, concussions, deep puncture wounds, gouged eyes, and all manner of ordinary distresses and afflictions such as nervous indigestion, internal parasites, skin eruptions, toothache, and fever. They also revived waning libidos. Such aphrodisiacs were considered by the gladiators one of the greatest gifts in their harsh world.

There is no doubt that the magic and healing techniques of the gladiators were inextricably intertwined. And, through them, the gladiators realized a truth that is as valid today as it was over 2,000 years ago. One must nurture and heal the spirit if one is to heal the body.

Their tradition allowed them to do this. Whether invoking the gods, calling upon healing spirits, swearing an oath, praying for victory, or cursing an enemy, the gladiators were alleviating their fear and suffering. Doing so gave them some perceived control over nature, their environment, and their own lives. This, in turn, instilled in them a sense of hope for the future. Truly an act of magic in such a violent world.

THE TRUE MEANING OF NIRVANA

BY KEN JOHNSON

Nirvana will blow you away, literally. The word *nirvana*, strictly translated, means "blown away," or (even better) "blown out."

So in real terms, contrary to popular belief, nirvana is not a place. It's not a condition of self-indulgent bliss, and soft music and sweet aromas won't get you there. It's not even a rock band.

Nirvana is a state of consciousness... but even that's not correct.

Nirvana is a state of "no consciousness."

THE BELIEFS OF THE BUDDHA

According to the Buddha, whom I am sure you remember, humans are all just packed full of stuff—food and clothing, ideas and emotions, friends and lovers, memories, physical aches and pains, worries about the mortgage, and so on. At present, for instance, I'm personally packed full of concerns about the pesky raccoon who keeps thinking my garden hose is his toy and biting it to pieces accordingly.

We're so packed full of stuff that we are always going around in circles. Everything is muddy and unclear.

The only way to deal with this, Buddha says, is to get empty... Blow all that extraneous stuff out of your brain and right of your life. Blow it away.

When you're empty, you're in nirvana. It's as simple as that.

CONDITIONED BEINGS

We are all conditioned. Everything we do is conditional. Nirvana is unconditional. Better than that, it's absolutely unconditioned. And when we're unconditioned, we are free.

Now if you're thinking that nirvana sounds suspiciously like the void (see page 53 in this edition of the *Magical*

Almanac for more information), you're right. In fact, the universe has its own nirvana, and that's the void.

A really cool piece of mysticism, right? But what does it have to do with magic?

Actually, quite a bit. Because some of the foremost magicians in the Western tradition have asserted that you can't really create magic unless you begin with emptiness. The Czech magus Franz Bardon placed emptiness at the beginning of his program for magical development, right in step one: First get empty, then you can make magic.

The founder of Chaos Magic, Austin Osman Spare, remarked that he did most of his best magical work while floating in absolute emptiness. (And of course they call it Chaos Magic because chaos is in the void, and the void is where all magic comes from, and the void is empty, and... well, you get the idea.)

So blow yourself away. Lay down your weary mind and get empty.

And then make your magic!

FOR FURTHER STUDY

Buddhism: Its essence and development. Edward Conze. Harper, 1959.

Initiation into Hermetics: a course of instruction in ten stages. Franz Bardon. English translation by A. Radspieler. Osiris-Verlag,1962.

The Tibetan Book of the Dead; or, The after-death experiences on the Bardo plane, according to Lama Kazi Dawa-Samdup's English rendering. W. Y. Evans-Wentz. Oxford University Press, 1927.

THE TREE OF HEALTH

BY DAVID CUMES

I f we define healing as the process of moving toward a greater
sense of wholeness and drawing
closer to our inner being or higher
self, then the Qabalistic "Tree of
Life," a model that represents polarity and balance, can assist us in our
quest to become healthy. We can
also extend the principles inherent
in the Tree of Life to a focused concept of a "Tree of Health."

TREE OF HEALTH

In order to understand the Tree of Health,
the basic idea of the Tree of Life needs to
be emphasized. Its central trunk embraces the concepts of will,
balance, and grace. In the Tree of Health, will comes from the
desire of a patient to be well. This will forces us to seek
balance, through which grace can enter at any time. All healing
occurs through these three essential properties on the central
limb of the tree.

According to the Qabala, we are all made in the image of
God. Since our inner healer also happens to be fashioned in the
image of God, it knows the alchemy required to create health out
of disease. It remains for us to maintain the equilibrium required
to allow healing to occur. In order to encourage this, some South
American shamans use a *mesa,* a table-like altar, as a tool for healing. Implicit in the mesa is the idea of balance or equilibrium. In
this practice, shamans see the dark, evil, or negative facets that
create illness on the left-hand side, and the light, positive, or healing attributes on the right. The shaman heals by staying in the
center of the mesa and balancing these opposites.

This universal principle of polarity balance can be extended
to a model of healing which is concordant not only with the idea

of the mesa, but also with the principles of the Tree of Life. By staying in the center of the Tree of Health, patients can attain balance, healing, and self-restoration. In order to maintain our equilibrium on the central trunk of the tree, some form of inner practice is crucial. This will enhance our life force, which in turn will enable the inner healer to do its job.

Still, to achieve healing, we need to discern the difference between curing a disease and healing the person. Whereas a person may be cured from cancer he may in fact not be healed. On the other hand a patient may not be cured of AIDS but may be healed from within. The polarities of the Tree of Health that a patient should develop are: on the left, restraint, resignation, inhibition, fear, guilt, denial, ignorance, lack of choice, and inaction; on the right, expansion, strength, hope, trust, faith, surrender, love, courage, knowledge, receptivity, and right action; and in the center, balance and equilibrium resulting in inner peace and harmony that supports the inner healer. Through the center, the patient's life force can assist the inner healer. Inner practices enhance the life force. Calling or naming our wish to be healed creates will, which with balance leads to healing. Grace may enter at any time, and its ultimate expression is spontaneous remission. When we find our center or we center ourselves, we are balanced in the core of a Tree of Health.

BELIEF AND HOPE

Belief and hope boost the effectiveness of the inner healer. This is also known as the "placebo response." The healer who is aware of the power of belief on the inner healer of the patient can put this effect to good use. Whereas placebo is almost a bad word to the Western doctor, it goes to the core of healing—in the relationship between the physician, the therapy, and the inner healer of the patient. Some doctors and healers exude a sense of unruffled calm, certainty, trust, composure, and confidence that augment the placebo effect. Shamans are masters at strengthening placebo.

The inner healer is activated within the belief system of the patient. At one level or another, the healer is also treating the patient's own specific consciousness and conviction. Ultimately this will translate into better alignment of the patient's energy

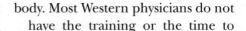

body. Most Western physicians do not have the training or the time to deal with illness in this way. Nevertheless, they need to pay attention to it. When healers disturb the belief system of the patient by the imposition of their own beliefs, they compromise the magical ability of the system to work. Faith or belief in the healer is critical and there must be a consistency between the patient's notion of healing and the doctor's approach.

When the oncologist tells the patient that he has a 50 percent chance that the drug or chemotherapy might not work, the power of hope has effectively been divided in half. For the treatment to work, both the patient and physician must believe in and be hopeful about its effectiveness. A Westerner may be satisfied with a written prescription and explanation as to how the medication is going to work. An aboriginal patient would trust a hands-on approach and the magic of the shaman's trance state.

Certain physicians are more influential than others even when the same treatment is administered. This occurs because of a special bond of belief, hope, and trust that arises between patient and healer. A lack of trust or belief in the physician could be harmful and even toxic to the patient's health. Patients who for financial or other reasons only have access to a fixed panel of doctors may have their own special needs compromised. This may not matter for the average medical problem but can become vital when managing difficult health challenges.

RESIGNATION VERSUS SURRENDER

Resignation, withdrawal, and hopelessness may be a manifestation of indifference, laziness, or passivity, all of which lead to inaction. Fear may play a part here.

Hopelessness and resignation are not the same as surrender, however. Surrender implies letting go and allowing a higher force to take over. Surrender is the ultimate expression of unconditional hope and belief—trust that whatever arises is for the best.

The patient feels gratitude and acceptance and is content to just be. Surrender is fearless and does not exclude the use of medical attention. Resignation implies desperation or depression, which is known to suppress the immune system. Passive resignation with an underlying hopelessness is not the same as the active and joyous acceptance of surrender. Surrender arises from a deep connection within and an acknowledgment of a higher power working to support the life force and strengthen the inner healer.

Surrender usually involves a certain humility and subordination of the ego. Therefore the boon that arises from surrender is affiliation with the higher self. Yoga and Buddhism teach that desirous attachment is one of the greatest obstacles on the enlightenment path. When we reach *keter,* the pinnacle of the Tree of Life, we experience the divine within and without, and we detach from everything. We just are; we attain pure being. If we lose the fear or the attachment we have to being cured, we may be healed and possibly even cured.

FEAR

There are two basic emotions: love and fear. Love is always good for healing. Fear is usually bad. Courage counteracts fear, and although bravery is usually part of one's makeup it can be nurtured and developed. As discussed above, fear is also part of resignation and hopelessness.

Disease creates fear, eliciting a response called the fight-or-flight reaction from the autonomic nervous system. This in turn elicits a response from the adrenal gland, which pours out hormones. If the reaction persists, the adrenaline overloads the cardiovascular system and taxes the immune system. Morbid fear can totally overwhelm the inner healer.

GUILT

Dread of the consequences of failure to heal causes feelings of inefficacy and paralysis. This generates guilt. Some patients for moral or religious reasons may feel they are not worthy of being well, and this will adversely affect their inner healer. Guilt may also be aggravated by a New Age misconception that not only has the patient caused the illness but he or she has the ability to correct it. When a cure does not occur, this guilt may lead to a sense of defeat. The physician can significantly aggravate the situation by giving gloomy or hopeless prognoses. Overall, guilt has no place if we desire to be well.

DENIAL

For some, denial can be a powerful coping mechanism. This seems a contradiction since denial is self-defeating when it comes to health. In the short term, however, denial may help the patient get over the terror of a medical crisis. The patient's subconscious may know that true knowledge of the predicament may be too much to handle at a critical time. Denial may be good in these circumstances, though not when it prevents the person from going to the hospital for treatment.

IGNORANCE

Ignorance, like denial, is also useful in certain predicaments, but probably not in the long term. For instance, South African physicians hardly ever tell their patients a diagnosis for their illness. In the United States, almost everyone is told their diagnosis; nevertheless, the results in the two systems are similar. Superficially, it would seem that ignorance of the condition might cause less fear and therefore a longer survival. However, it is likely that the patients knew at a subconscious level that they had cancer. If you added to this the physician's and the families' silent knowledge of the problem, and the projection of this awareness onto the patient, it is hardly surprising that the outcome was equivalent whether the patient was told or not.

TRUTH

There is something especially liberating about the truth. When a patient knows the truth about the nature of a disease, he or she knows the extent of the challenge. Just knowing a diagnosis can be reassuring and is therapy in itself. The inner healer can then come to grips with the challenge and do its job. On the other hand, confusion about a diagnosis and treatment can increase fear and inhibit the inner healer. Many patients are optimistic when they know what's wrong with them and can do something tangible about it. Denial may lead to a deluded sense of what is appropriate action, resulting in failure to properly contend with the problem. The patient has to be realistic about the undertaking or there will be a mismatch between the energy required for healing and the effort expended for the task. Denial may help us feel better temporarily, but in the long term truth is a more powerful agent. Truth is the antidote to denial and ignorance.

THE PROGNOSIS

Physicians, with their scientific training, feel obligated to tell patients the truth. They may quote statistics, such as, "You only have six months to live because you have stage X and grade Y of disease Z." This can be a powerful negative visualization, and even a type of voodoo curse or hex. Only exceptional patients can rise above such predictions.

American physicians are frequently motivated to tell the whole truth because of their own fear of the litigious nature of the society. There always seems to be a phantom attorney sitting on the patient's bed dictating the doctor's decisions. No medic wants to be sued for lack of full disclosure. "Informed consent" before invasive procedures requires listing all conceivable complications related to diagnosis and therapy.

This custom creates unnecessary fear and anxiety. The truth should be delivered in an informative, supportive, nurturing manner with due regard for a patient's sensitivities. There are different ways of telling the truth; the message does not have to be detached or cruel. Giving enough facts to inform, but not terrify, a patient is a vital clinical skill. The physician's fear of the legal system should not be transmuted into patient terror.

I try not to give my patient's statistics about their possible outcome. In the end it is arrogant to believe that in our limited capacity as healers we know the truth about the patient, the inner healer, God, and countless factors that cannot be measured.

I also believe that the raw truth may have a negative effect in healing. A balanced and hopeful look at the truth can be a grand transformational tool that induces the changes required for better health. A patient who is knowledgeable about his or her condition without being debilitated by fear can rise to the challenge. Knowledge of one's predicament can give a sense of control and lessen fear.

If we dwell on the concepts on the right side of the Tree of Health, we align with health. If we stress the dark aspects on the left, we do the opposite. We should strengthen and facilitate the positive conversation and beware of delving into negative dialogue.

In the end, if we stay centered we have the greatest likelihood for wholeness and health. A Tree of Health helps us remember the essential factors that influence the inner healer and reinforces the concept of balancing the opposites. This is the key to all healing.

FOR FURTHER STUDY

Anatomy of an Illness. Norman Cousins. Norton, 1995.

Healing Words. Larry Dossey, M. D. Harper, 1994.

The Holographic Universe. Michael Talbot. Harper Perennial, 1992.

Kabbalah: Tradition of hidden knowledge. Zev ben Shimon Halevi. Thames and Hudson, 1992.

Love and Survival. Dean Ornish. Harper Collins, 1998.

Spontaneous Remission: An annotated bibliography. Brendan O'Regan and Caryle Hirshberg. Institute of Noetic Sciences, 1993.

MAKING SPIRIT MASKS

BY LAUREN RAINE

M asks are truly magical tools. Finding a mask's hidden story and performing with its unique qualities can provide many powerful opportunities for personal insight and alchemical transformation.

We may well ask ourselves: Who are we beneath the many masks of our lives? What faces do we wear in the course of a day, a year, a lifetime? What are the mythic masks that inform our stories of who we are? Can we envision our "social masks," our "shadow masks," our archetypal masks, the deities within each of us? In all, masks can immerse us in the myths of our lives and can help us to find the unclaimed and abandoned aspects of ourselves that are crying for expression.

Masks can force our conscious selves to commune with hidden selves within the mask. Through our creative imaginations, through improvisational dialog, or within the sacred circle of ritual theater, we can get to know the spirit and characters we tend to repress. For example, creating and exaggerating the expression of our "social masks," through which we buffer our daily experience with the people we meet, can help us to loosen up and find humor in ourselves. By exaggerating the masks we wear in public, we find we have the freedom to take the weighty masks off, to dance more lightly within them. Making a mask of the "inner child," discovering what she or he has to say, can set free a playful vitality buried for too many years beneath the roles we have assumed as adults, as "professional people," as parents. Making the "mask of the shadow," meanwhile, can also be a profoundly revealing exercise, a ritual to name and acquaint ourselves with our internal demons.

Masks, animated by our vision and our bodies, become living metaphors, doorways into the house of our multi-dimensional selves. In tribal cultures around the world, masks are made and used with a great deal of ceremonial preparation, as they were intended to house the spirits of the gods and goddesses, or the ancestors or totem animals the tribe wishes to invoke. This same sense of the sacred can belong to a group that enters the magic circle with their masks. To wear the mask of the Green Man is to invite that great archetypal being into your own spirit, to make the mask of Gaia is to find her presence within ourselves.

SPIRIT MASK WORKSHOP

With your circle, be it a coven or a small group of friends, begin by choosing a mythic archetype that is important to you: an aspect of the Goddess, or of the God, an element, or perhaps a power animal guide.

Discuss the qualities of the sacred presence you wish to invoke. Do you need the fiery inspiration of Bridget? Have you journeyed your personal descent and rebirth this year? Would wearing the face of Inanna, the Sumerian goddess who made a journey into the underworld, help you to integrate your experience? Do you need to reclaim spring in your life by calling the joyful Green Man? Share what the mask would mean to you. When you go home, make an altar to the persona of the mask, and begin to incubate it by keeping a journal, gathering poems, collecting objects, remembering synchronicities, and inviting your dreams to inform your creative process.

When you gather with friends to make your masks, set aside an entire weekend. On the first day, share your writings and insights. Then, make plaster casts of each other's faces. Plaster-impregnated bandages can be purchased from an art supply store. Remember to apply Vaseline to your face, especially eyelashes, eyebrows, and hairline. When the mask is dry, cut away the eyeholes and the nostrils with an Exacto knife, and trim the sides. Build up the mask with more plaster bandage or papier-mâché if you wish. Attach objects, leaves, and seashells you've collected. Using acrylic paints, paint your mask, and don't worry if it is not perfect. It is more important that you imbue it with it with your unique vision. When finished, varnish each mask with an acrylic varnish or gel medium. Then place the mask in the center of your circle so you can contemplate them.

The next day, create a safe, sacred space in any way you wish: by casting a circle as a group, or by individually consecrating the space. Light votive candles to invite the spirits of the masks to enter. It is helpful to chose one member to facilitate, sensing and calling transition points. Begin your performance time by meditating on your mask.

Afterwards, play some evocative music, and do some muscle stretching together to relax your bodies and your minds. Separately, claim your own private place within the circle, and in the spot that belongs to you, explore the mask. Put it on, see how it wants to move. Let it move your body, and speak to you with your rhythms or an inner dialog. If there is exuberance, dance it. If there is sadness, investigate it. Allow yourself to make any sounds that seem necessary. You are in a completely safe space, free to allow yourself full expression.

When the facilitator senses it is appropriate, she or he can invite the group to rest in their places around the circle. As individuals feel the desire, they may enter the center of the circle and perform the mask. What does this being wish to say? How does it move? What story does it tell? How does it wish to interact with others, if it does?

Let it emerge in any fashion it wants to, and let the spirit of the mask come through you.

When the ritual performance is over, take off the masks and place them in the center. Thank the great beings embodied in the masks for joining your circle, and release them with gratitude to the other worlds. Place your hands on the ground, and send the energies you have held back down into the Earth. Release the circle, and then feast, drink, and share your insights and experiences. You are now a sacred performer.

For Further Study

Sacred Mask, Sacred Dance. Evan John Jones with Chas Clifton. Llewellyn Publications, 1997.

The Spiral Dance: A rebirth of the ancient religion of the great goddess. Starhawk. HarperSanFrancisco, 1999.

Seeing Earth Auras

By Mary Magpie

L ast weekend, I witnessed an amazing event. I was visiting my daughter at her new home. From her sitting room window I had a wonderful view of a rugged hill, and as the conversation buzzed comfortably around me I gazed out at it.

The hill was dotted with walkers, and as I strained my eyes to see the tiny figures more clearly I caught a flash of brilliant silver light surrounding the hill. When I focused on the light, it disappeared immediately, but when I turned my attention back to the walkers, it flashed into view again, even more richly colorful. Nearest the hill I could see golden yellow, firework-green, and a silver color shot through with gold. The brilliance extended and retreated, pulsing almost like disco lights. Having learned to see auras around people some years ago, I was fully aware of what I was witnessing. Indeed this was not my first sight of Earth aura, but it was the clearest I've ever seen.

After enjoying the spectacle for a few minutes I asked if anyone else noticed a brightness surrounding the hill. This is what amazed me most. There were five other people in the room and every one of them saw the aura quite clearly, describing exactly what I was seeing to a greater or lesser extent. Nobody had to make a great effort to see this aura; in fact at least two did not even accept that auras could be seen. They just looked up, and there it was.

If you would like to see Earth's aura for yourself, try looking at a hill against a light sky. Make sure the Sun is not in your field of vision, otherwise you risk damaging your eyesight and will not be able to see the more fleeting light of the aura. Don't focus directly on the outline of the hill, but on something actually on the skyline—a tree or a hiker. If you have no hills, wait for a really clear day and look towards the horizon, again away from the Sun. Allow your eyes to become slightly unfocussed and wait. If you are lucky you will see light emanating from the skyline. This is the aura. Write and tell me what you see in care of this publisher (the address is listed on the copywright page).

Magical Fish

By deTraci Regula

The magical and protective powers of plants and animals are well-known, but fish are the magical gems of the animal kingdom. These sparkling, flitting creatures draw positive magical influences into our lives and homes.

According to feng shui practitioners, fish balance energies and increase the flow of wealth. Fish ponds are recommended to keep positive influences from draining away from a house. The curved crescent shape of the swimming carp is considered fortunate. Some people place two fish in the central yin-yang roundel.

Zoroastrians use bowls of gold fish in New Year's ceremonies. Looking at the fish while the year changes is thought to bring good luck. They also represent the sign of Pisces—the last astrological period of the old year. After thirteen days, the fish are freed in rivers and streams, carrying with them any pain or bad energy.

The famous koi fish of Japan, called *nishikigoi*, or "colored carp," provide both beauty and magic. One variety, the red and white *kohaku*, have several evocative coloring patterns, including a red crown-shaped mark on the head symbolizing progress in a career. The *kuchibeni*, or "lipstick" marking, covers the fish lips with a deep crimson, symbolizing love or eroticism. The gold *yamabuki ogon* and the platinum *ogon* both represent wealth. The *kumon-ryu*, named for a dragon which transforms into a cloud, is a koi of transformation. A striking black and silver-white fish, its black patterns are mysteriously unstable, prone to emerge and vanish, so it is constantly in a state of change.

Even unliving representations of fish carry magic power. The silly cellophane "Fortune Telling Fish," which leaps and curls from the heat in the palm of the hand, is the watered-down modern version of ancient fish amulets worn to protect from drowning.

Fish for drawing abundance: Goldfish of all types, koi.

Fish for drawing love: Gouramis, pink or red fish, seahorses.

Fish for health: Any collection of fish will calm anxiety, lower blood pressure, induce relaxation. The radiant colors of fish can help treat various conditions. Seasonal depression: A tankful of gold, orange, and amber-colored fish will help replace the missing colors of summer sunlight. General healing: Turquoise fish and orange fish are good for general healing. Red varieties of fish are good for fever and inflammation. Blue fish are cooling and sedating; yellow fish are invigorating. Silver fish induce a meditative state. Brown fish are steadying and grounding.

Fish for protection: Siamese fighting fish, and other agressive species, help protect. But they also bring in energies of jealousy, passion, and violence. Dark-colored fish can also be protective. Fish that hide or conceal by changing color can symbolize defense and protection. Any bright, sparkling fish is protective in the same way as metallic amulets.

Labyrinths and Spirals

By Sedwin

The labyrinth appears in old legends and travel writings, in ancient art, on the floors and walls of churches, cut into turf, and built of low stone walls. In the last decade, the labyrinth has made a comeback as people have rediscovered its power and its mysteries.

What is a Labyrinth

Frequently, labyrinths are confused with mazes. In actuality, these two things are quite different. A maze is a puzzle with one real path leading through it, and many paths leading nowhere. A labyrinth has only one path that winds its way to the center—in order to leave, one must retrace the route.

The earliest mention of a labyrinth comes from Herodotus, the Greek historian, who referred to an enormous structure built in Egypt circa 2000 BC. It seems that this early labyrinth was a huge building, or series of connected buildings, with a myriad of confusing passageways. By the time Paul Lucas, a traveler from France, visited in 1700, very little remained of what had become known as the "Temple of the Labyrinth."

The most well-known legend of the labyrinth tells of the one King Minos of Crete built to constrain the minotaur. While the story describes the structure as being more like a maze, coins from ancient Crete display a one-path, seven-circuit labyrinth. Depictions of the Cretan labyrinth have also been found in the ruins of Pompeii and carved on a rock in Sardinia circa 2500 to 2000 BC.

The oldest known labyrinth design on a church floor dates to AD 400 in Orléansville, Algeria. It measured eight feet in diameter. By the twelfth century, variations began to appear on church floors in greater numbers throughout France. The largest is the eleven-circuit labyrinth of the cathedral in Chartres—it has a forty-two-foot diameter. Other cathedrals in France and Italy have two-foot wide labyrinths etched into their walls. Many of these have been worn down from people tracing over it with their fingers.

Typical church labyrinths differs from the Cretan labyrinth in that their path has a wide circle at its core, rather than a simple dead end. The labyrinth in Chartres, for instance, has a six-lobed rosette at its center.

During the time of Christian pilgrimages to the holy land, church labyrinths were referred to as "Chemin de Jerusalem." For people who could not afford, or were physically unable to take, a trip to the Middle East, the church labyrinth served as a way to take the spiritual journey.

The ancient Romans produced their version of the labyrinth in England in the form of "turf mazes." These were labyrinths cut approximately six inches into the ground, which worked very well in many parts of England where the thin layer of soil covers chalk or clay. These labyrinths were constructed for the children's game "Troy Town." According to the ancient Roman scholar Pliny, the game was so called because the seven circuits of the labyrinth resembled the seven defensive walls of the city of Troy.

The turf labyrinth form was more popular than the church labyrinth in England. Still, many of these turf labyrinths have been found near monastery ruins. A few of these date to between 1080 and 1220, the time of Saxon and Norman rule. Over the centuries, English labyrinths were also used for May Eve games. An English observer in 1866 noted that those who trod the labyrinth seemed to be under the "persuasion of something unseen and unknown."

A turf maze at Boughton Green in Northamptonshire called the Shepherd Ring has a spiral at its center. For centuries, beginning in 1353, walking this labyrinth was the main event of a three-day county fair. In Asenby, Yorkshire, a labyrinth was built on a rise called the Fairies' Hill. Up until the early part of the twentieth century, locals walked this labyrinth and paused at its center to "hear the fairies singing." Dr. Stukeley, an eighteenth-century antiquarian, noted that people who walked the labyrinth spoke of it "as if there was something extraordinary in the thing."

It is believed that the concept of the labyrinth was developed from the spiral—a fundamental natural form. To ancient people, the spiral was a sacred and powerful primal symbol of the Great Mother Goddess and her transformative powers. As a symbol representing energy and transformation, it was painted on cave walls in Spain circa 13,000–10,000 BC, on pottery throughout southeastern Europe circa 6300–3500 BC, and on the walls of the Tarxien temples of Malta circa 3000 BC. According to Professor Marija Gimbutas in *The Language of the Goddess*, symbols created from objects in the natural world function to open human awareness. The spiral visually portrayed life-force energy. As such, it is probably no accident that in our present-day culture the spiral has become a popular motif in jewelry and clothing, and in the labyrinth, as people unwittingly tap into the energy of this powerful symbol.

This may be a key to answering how labyrinths work. Though no one is certain how the winding path of the labyrinth creates psychological space for clarity, many have felt peaceful and focused as they thread the winding path. As a form of spiral, perhaps the labyrinth produces a vortex of transformative energy that allows us to connect with our deepest selves, the web of life, and the divine. Our very ancient ancestors seemed to have perceived this energy and knew that it was sacred.

If you have an opportunity to walk a labyrinth, walk the path and discover yourself.

For Further Study

Exploring the Labyrinth: A guide for healing and spiritual growth. Melissa Gayle West. Broadway Books, 2000.

Labyrinths in Culture and Society: Pathways to wisdom. Jacques Attali. Translated by Joseph Rowe. North Atlantic Books, 1999.

Mazes and Labyrinths: Their history and development. William Henry Matthews. Dover Publications, 1985.

Walking a Sacred Path: Rediscovering the labyrinth as a spiritual tool. Dr. Lauren Artress. Riverhead Books, 1995.

Maneki Neko:
The Fortune-Beckoning Cat

By S Y Zenith

The *maneki neko*, or "fortune-beckoning cat," is synonymous with Japanese culture and customs. People in Japan believe that cats possess the magical power to draw good fortune and money, especially to businesses and to the home. There are several Japanese legends about the origin of the maneki neko, passed down through the generations.

One of the most famous folktales of the fortune-beckoning cat occurs during the beginning of the Edo period in the seventeeth century. In a rundown temple in the western part of Tokyo lived a priest who kept a pet cat named Tama. Sometimes, the priest would voice complaints to Tama about the poor state of the temple and about their meager means. Nevertheless, the priest continued to shelter and feed Tama selflessly.

One day, Lord Naotaka Ii of the Hikone District near Kyoto was on his way home from a hunting trip when he was caught in a shower. While sheltering under a huge tree outside the temple, he noticed a cat beckoning to him at the gate. As soon as he

walked away from the tree, it was struck by a flash of lightning. Lord Naotaka was very grateful to Tama for saving his life.

Not long afterwards, Lord Naotaka decreed the temple to be the Ii family shrine, and in a gesture of gratitude, had it restored. He changed its name to Goutokuji. Backed by the powerful Ii clan, Goutokuji Temple became ever prosperous.

In the end, Tama had performed two wonderful feats. He saved Lord Naotaka's life, and he saved the temple from further ruin. When time came for Tama to make the transition to the next world, he was buried at Goutokuji's cat cemetery with full ceremony and respect. The term "maneki neko" was phrased in honor of his memory.

Today, figurines can be found of maneki neko all over Japan and in Asian stores worldwide. Many Japanese businesses and homes have at least one maneki neko to draw good fortune and happiness. It is one of the most famous lucky charms in Asia.

Typically, the maneki neko has either its right paw or left paw raised. It is believed that a maneki neko with the left paw raised beckons customers. Or when placed at home, it invites visitors. A maneki neko with its right paw raised draws money or good fortune. In general, the higher the paw is raised, the more the maneki neko beckons customers or fortune.

Maneki neko come in many colors—white, red, gold, pink, yellow, black, and gold. There are many ceramic artisans in Japan specialising in maneki neko. The most popular maneki neko is tri-colored. The white are also popular, as white is considered the color of purity. Black maneki nekos are believed to be talismans against stalkers and evil forces. The gold or yellow variety attracts money, and the pink draw love. Red maneki nekos exorcise evil spirits and illnesses. Sometimes the figurines come with inscriptions to draw success and achievement in life, exams, and other activities.

Place a maneki neko near the front entrance of your home or business and watch things go from good to better!

A SHORT MEDITATION ON THE ELEMENTS

BY TYGER'S EYE

The elements—earth, air, fire, and water—are a significant part of magical life. They are present in circles, rituals, and around us at all times. While it is ideal to know the elements well, we often become "out of tune" with them. The following are short meditations on the four elements. Read them, and let yourself experience the elements more regularly.

EARTH

For a meditation on the element of earth, walk outside and let your eyes fall upon a sea of greens and browns. Imagine the buildings disappearing—you are at the edge of a meadow surrounded by a thick forest of trees. Turn and walk towards the forest, feeling the stable earth beneath you. Reach out and put your palm on the trunk of a tree. Examine the bark, and feel a leaf between your fingertips. Kneel down and brush the grass with your hand. Dig your fingers into the soft soil. Pause to let the textures, smells, and sounds sink into your subconscious mind; then get up slowly. Look around you and see the buildings returning. Brush the soil from your hands, and return inside.

AIR

To experience the element of air, walk over to a window and open it to let in some fresh air. A gentle breeze flows in, carrying the sound of birds chirping and the scent of wild flowers. Close your eyes, and inhale the sweet fragrance. You can hear trees rustling, whispering the secrets of the universe. Listen. A sudden gust of wind brings you a scent of pine trees. The wind brushes your arms and face, and you feel your skin tingling. Smile as the breeze delivers its songs to you. Breathe in, and expand your stomach slowly. Let your breath out naturally. Gradually, you open your eyes. The wind has died down. Close the window gently and walk away.

FIRE

To meditate on fire, strike a match and watch the flame dance before touching it to the wick of the candle before you. Put out the match, and look back at the candle. It has grown into a bonfire, burning safely in a circle of stones. Take a few steps back, and sit on a log to enjoy the fire as it glows orange and red, radiating warmth in all directions. It crackles and snaps, climbing up towards the sky. Tiny sparks, like glowing particles of dust, escape into the air and disappear. Feel the warmth on your cheeks. Then, as quickly and silently as the fire has grown, it falls and sinks into the wood. You watch as a thin line of smoke rises up from a small pool of wax in a candleholder.

WATER

For a meditation on the element of water, wait for a rainy day. Go into your living room and sit on the couch. Close your eyes, and drift into a slumber to the sound of rain falling outside. Open your eyes again, and find yourself sitting at the bottom of a waterfall. The water gives off a low, continuous roar as it rushes over the top of the falls and tumbles into the river below. The uneven and rhythmic sound allows you to forget all of your worries. Step a bit closer, and let the soft mist of the water cool your cheeks. Slowly, walk down the river. Listen as the roar of the waterfall becomes a gurgling song as the water rolls over rocks and stones. A little further down, the rocks have spread out. Bend down, cup your hands, and have a taste of the water. It is fresh and clean, cool and nourishing. Dip your hands into the water again and feel it running over your skin. Splash the water over your face, then open your eyes to find yourself back at home, awakened by the rain outside.

GREEN IMAGERY ON THE MAJOR ARCANA

BY ANN MOURA

D ivination with the tarot invokes the arcane symbolic meanings of the cards. With green witchcraft, the approach to the tarot is based on Earth magic, nature, the elementals, and the Lord and the Lady of the Witch's world-view. The tarot may be interpreted using green imagery by relating the cards to the seasons, sabbats, esbats, fairy lore, herbs, woodland life, and Nature's abundance.

The tarot has major and minor arcanas. The major arcana includes archetypes of powers and fate, and the minor includes the mundane descriptives of daily events, and aspirations. The following is a suggested green interpretation of the major arcana, as related to card number and more common card-name (in parentheses). I consider the major arcana to be normally upright cards of power, and so only a few reversed possibilities are listed below.

The tarot is a tool of mediumship, or channeling, that brings the reader into contact with universal energy to address a particular question or problem or to offer guidance and comfort. As each card is understood in relation to the information sought, question asked, or the surrounding cards, not all the meanings provided here apply in any given throw. The list is intended only as a guideline, for the real unfolding comes from the psychic connection of the reader.

GREEN TAROT

0—The Green Man (The Fool): Awakening, fearlessness, quest begun, fertility, enthusiasm, an open mind, cycle renewal, innovation, fresh ideas, creativity, holidays. (In reverse, this could mean a time to rest and plan new goals)

1—The Witch (The Magician): Controlling own destiny, nature, communication skills, power to change, knowledge, the power of the craft.

2—The High Priestess (same): Discovery and use of hidden knowledge, insight, wisdom, understanding, innate wisdom, intuition.

3—Mother Earth (The Empress): Renewal of the Earth, folk magic, abundance, fruitfulness, fertility, pregnancy, fruition, nourishment, good health, communion with Nature.

4—The Horned God (The Emperor): Fertility, bringing ideas to life, accomplishment through leadership, personal power, husbandry, authority.

5—The High Priest (The Hierophant): Tradition, scholarship, mentoring, teaching natural magic, incorporating the Divine into all aspects of life, codifying and organizing spiritual insights, using ritual to guide intuitive power and magic.

6—The Lord and Lady of the Greenwood (The Lovers): Partnership, trust, commitment, loyalty, following the heart, new opportunities, growth, mutual compromise, respect, decision-making.

7—The Wagon (The Chariot): Balance, conquest, personal achievement, successful action, self-confidence, business travel, military service, moving.

8—The Crone (Strength): Unity of wisdom and action, overcoming obstacles, power used wisely, self-confidence, willpower, facing adversity with inner strength, fearlessness.

9—The Holly King (The Hermit): Wisdom gained over time, accumulated knowledge, creating one's own path, guidance, enlightenment, evolution, prudence, progress, growth.

10—The Wheel (The Wheel of Fortune): Universe in motion, improving fortunes, changes for the better, progress, fate, destiny, good luck, transitions.

11—The Standing Stone (Justice): Harmony, equilibrium, virtue, truth, impartiality, fairness.

12—The Oak King (The Hanged Man): Transition, patience, self-sacrifice for gain, weighing of options, meditation, inner peace. (In reverse, this could mean that a decision is made and action taken.)

14—The Lord of Shadows (Death): Transition and transformation, a turning point in life, rapid change, endings and beginnings, negative energies cleared away, optimism for the future, removal of opposition. (In reverse, this could mean a fear of change.)

14—The Sidhe (Temperance): Fusion, invigoration, blending ideas, ideas manifested, inspiration, physical and psychic realms in balance, patience, moderation, difficulties overcome, truce, reconciliation.

15—The Wild Hunt (The Devil): Uncontrolled forces, natural course of events, magical practice, unleashed potential, liberation, release from restrictions, natural attraction. (In reverse, this could mean bondage, uncertainties, inhibitions.)

16—The Tower (same): Abrupt change, sudden enlightenment, release from oppression, truth revealed, new freedom to act. (In reverse, this could mean healing has begun, or an inability to act ends.)

17—The Star (same): Opportunity, inspiration, bright prospects, manifesting one's dreams, recognition of others, wishes granted, hopes attained, peace.

18—The Moon (same): Heeding intuition, listening to instinct, visions, psychic dreams, magical education, imagination, introspection, journeying, understanding of the cycles of life, discovery of what is hidden, exposing deception and illusion, looking beneath facades for truth.

19—The Sun (same): Satisfaction, joy, harmony, achievement, accomplishment, friendship, revitalization, creative energy, mental and spiritual growth. (In reverse, this could mean burdens soon lifted, and efforts rewarded.)

20—The Harvest (Judgement): Rewards, accountability, potential fulfilled, good choices made, honest evaluation of efforts, awakening, renewed energy, restored health, new life, change for the better, spiritual rebirth.

21—The Earth (The World or The Universe): Wholeness, unity, conclusions, objectives attained, honors, perfection, completion, old cycle ending and new cycle begining, end of an era, success, advancement, joy.

FOR FURTHER STUDY

Green Witchcraft. Ann Moura. Llewellyn Publications, 1996.

Origins of Modern Witchcraft: Evolution of a world religion. Ann Moura. Llewellyn Publications, 2000.

The Universal Myths: Heroes, gods, tricksters, and others. Alexander Eliot. Meridian Books, 1990.

Empowering Your Works of Magic

By Raven Grimassi

M agic is more involved than the simple folk spells and charms. While placing a herb in one's shoe or the reciting a rhyme over a herbal blend can invoke the power of the mind, there exists a more reliable method to work magic, passed down to us through the centuries. These reliable techniques are based upon the metaphysical mechanism of nature. Seasoned practitioners of the craft refer to this as the magical formula.

The Magical Formula

The goal of the magic user is to perform spells and works of magic with consistent and reliable results. There are essentially five ingredients that comprise the art of creating successful works of magic. Each can be adapted or arranged according to your individual needs as long as you employ them together in working magic or casting spells.

These five components are:

1. Personal Will
2. Timing
3. Imagery
4. Direction
5. Balance

Personal Will

Personal will is the ability to focus the mind on a specifc goal. It can also be thought of as motivation, temptation, or persuasion.

The magic user must be sufficiently motivated in order to establish enough power to accomplish his or her goal in any work of magic. Unless you focus fully on the results and invest a substantial amount of energy in the desired outcome, you are unlikely to realize any reliable results. Therefore, the stronger your need or desire is, the more likely you will be able to raise the amount of energy required to manifest what you seek. However, desire or need is not enough by itself. The desire itself must be controlled, and the will must be focused only upon a detached view of the desired outcome of your spell or magical rite. That is, you must enflame your mind while at the same time separating yourself from the desired result. If you hold on to the desire, or obsess about the spell, you will only succeed in delaying the effect. This is because your conscious attachment to the outcome will draw energy back to you and away from the goal.

TIMING

In the performance of ritual, magic timing can mean success or failure. One must consider the phase and sign of the Moon, the hour of the day, and even the season of the year. The most succesful works of magic are those that work with the energies and power of nature.

Generally speaking, the best time to cast a spell or create a work of magic is when your target is most receptive. Receptivity is usually assured when the target is passive. People sleep, corporations close at night. In a sense, the best and most effective time to cast a spell is 4:00 am.

IMAGERY

The success of any work of magic depends upon images created and held by the mind. Most books on magic refer to this as the ability to visualize, and it is where your imagination is most important. At the same time, anything that serves to intensify your emotions will contribute to the success of your spell. Any drawing, statue, photo, scent, article of clothing, sound, or other sensory stimuli that helps to merge you with your desire will greatly add to your success.

Imagery is a constant reminder of what you wish to attract or accomplish. It acts as a homing device in representing the object, person, or situation for which the spell is intended. Imagery can be shaped and directed according to the will of the Wiccan without detracting from focusing the mind upon the spell's intent. This becomes the pattern or formula which leads to the realization of your desire. Surround yourself with images of your desire, and you will have more power to attract the thing you desire.

Direction

Once you have raised enough energy for a spell-working, you must still direct it towards your desire. Do not be anxious about the results as this will hold back the forces that you are drawing. You must release the spell in the proper direction, or you will draw the energy back to you before it can take effect. Perform your magic with the expectation that the spell will work. Then accept that it has worked and simply await its manifestation.

Do not reflect on the spell, wondering how things are going. Pondering only tends to ground the energy and draw the images and concepts back to you. Once the spell is cast, mentally detach yourself, and try to give the matter no more thought. Mark a seven-day period off on your calendar, and evaluate the situation seven days later.

Balance

The last aspect of magic to take into account is personal balance. In other words, you must always consider magic in terms of both need and consequences. If anger motivates your magical work, you may want to wait a few hours or sleep on it over night. While anger can be a useful propellant for a spell, it can also cloud the thinking and cause psychic repercussions. Bear in mind that any act of magic you perform will eventually affect you in mind, body, and spirit. If you harm people or misuse them through magic, there will be an unavoidable price to pay.

When considering a work of magic, make sure you have exhausted the normal means of dealing with something before you move to a magical solution. Magic should be the last resort.

Finally, make sure you are feeling well enough to work your magic. Magic requires a portion of your vital essence drawn from your aura. Replenish your workings with rest even if you do not feel tired. Health problems begin in the aura long before the body is aware of them. So be careful not to drain yourself through working magic, and be sure to cleanse yourself with incense smoke or salt water following any work of magic.

TALES OF WEST VIRGINIA BANSHEES

BY SUSAN SHEPPARD

Not all fairy tales have happy endings. Not all fairies bring goodness and light.

Among the Irish and Scottish people there is a spirit called the *banshee*. The banshee is an attendant death fairy, one who brings an omen of doom to those of Irish or Scottish blood. It is the banshee that announces the death of a family member, usually over bodies of water by *keening*, or raising a shrill cry for the dead. The banshee also travels to the homes of those about to die, sometimes mounted on a pale steed or riding a black funeral coach with two headless horses leading the way.

THE IRISH AND SCOTTISH BANSHEES

There are various descriptions of the banshee. The Irish banshee is called *bean sidhe*. Depending upon how you define the ancient tongue, bean sidhe can means "fairy woman" or "woman of the hills." The Irish banshee is often described as beautiful with streaming auburn hair. She wears a green woolen dress with gray cloak clasped about her shoulders. The only hint that this beautiful banshee is a messenger of doom is that her eyes are blood red from crying for her dead.

The Scottish banshee, or *bean nighe,* is more menacing. She dresses in grave clothes, her face covered by a veil. It is impossible to guess the banshee's age, but she typically appears as a crone.

The mid-Ohio Valley, which includes west-central West Virginia and southern Ohio, was settled mainly by people of Irish and Scottish blood. Stories of banshee spirits surely went underground as Irish and Scottish immigrants moved into the Ohio Valley, but her legend was not entirely forgotten.

BANSHEE LEGENDS

Let us now travel back to the shores of Scotland on a blustery winter day in 1590. A group of women, known as the Berwick Witches, summoned their powers at the ocean's edge. Meanwhile, over the icy waters of the North Sea, King James VI and his new bride Anne of Denmark nearly perished at sea when their boat was almost capsized.

Rumors circulated quickly, and the actions of the Berwick Witches caught James's attention, since he had always been fascinated by witchcraft. The Witches were captured and put on trial, and one of the Witches confessed under torture that she and others tried to murder James VI by casting evil spells. The woman also said that the Berwick Witches were in cahoots with the Earl of Boswell, first in line to the throne after King James's death. It was reported back to King James that a group of Scottish Witches had gathered at night near a castle in Edinburgh where they fashioned a waxen image, or "Witch's poppet," of the king. The group tossed the doll into a raging bonfire as the Witches chanted in unison to curse the life of King James.

More Witches were brought forth, interrogated by the king himself. It was alleged 200 Witches met at a church in North Berwick on All Hallows Eve to bring more evil against the king. Claims where made that the Devil presided over the meeting wearing a black mask and preaching obedience to him. For some inexplicable reason, at the trial one of the women gestured for the king to come closer. She whispered words King James had spoken to his wife on their wedding night. No one knew why the woman would do such a thing, or how she knew, but her actions sealed their doom. The Witches were later executed at Edinburgh's Castle Hill.

Did the Witches really try to kill the king, and did they have the power to do so? Most likely, they did not. But the story was enough to feed James's paranoia over witchcraft and the mysterious powers of women. Witchcraft has long had a stronghold in Scotland. Next to Germany, Scotland murdered more people during their Witch trials than any other country. Something about Scotland's remote forests, and those rolling, mystic, gloomy mountains, must be a breeding grounds for witchcraft.

North of Aberdeen in Scotland, there is a haunted place called the Forest of Marr. Marr is believed to be the area where some of the Scottish Witches of old escaped the anger and "justice" of King James. As they went underground, the Witches' occult powers grew. Local folklore claimed that ghosts of the executed Witches eventually became banshee spirits who roamed the countryside bringing doom to the clans who backed King James or were responsible for their persecution.

The Banshee of Marrtown

From the area around the Forest of Marr came a family named Marr, whose lives were marked for tragedy. Their trouble began after the family left Scotland to settle down in West Virginia.

Scottish immigrant Thomas Marr settled Marrtown, a small farming community southeast of Parkersburg, in 1836. He married a local woman named Mary Disosche.

Mary Marr was an autumn bride, considered to be an ill omen. In years to come, Mary would lose six of the eight children that she bore. Only two would carry on the Marr name.

Times were hard for Thomas and Mary Marr, but they did not lose their dream of a better life. They poured their energies into a simple tract of land that became their home, and soon built a picturesque white farmhouse against the shadowy woods thick with sumac, milkweed, and blackberry brambles.

The years of the Civil War, as for most, were not happy ones for the Marr Family. From their front window Thomas and Mary witnessed small clashes between Yankee and Confederate soldiers that turned into bloody battles. There were public hangings on nearby Fort Boreman Hill. As the war drew to a close, marauding soldiers from both sides stole freely from the Marrs, leaving them destitute.

After the Civil War, the Marr family's bad luck appeared to come to an end. Thomas landed a job as night watchman at the toll bridge that crossed over the Little Kanawha River leading into Marrtown. Mary stayed at home to tend the family and the farm. Still, there were ominous hints of what was about to unfold.

On several occasions, as Thomas traveled to and from his work, he saw a robed figure riding a white horse. Thomas claimed he came upon this rider nearly every night, yet he was not able to say much about the figure, as its face was always covered by a tattered hood. As he approached the shrouded figure, the white mare would rear, and horse and rider would disappear into the mists of morning.

On a cold February night in the year 1878, Mary sat by the front window waiting for Thomas to come home from his job. The middle-aged woman heard footsteps coming up the road, so she peered out the window. A white horse walked up to the front gate of the house and stopped. Sitting atop the horse was a rider whose face was covered by a ragged veil. Mary walked outside into the frigid night air. The rider remained silent.

As bitter winds gusted, Mary Marr pulled her woolen shawl close. She asked the rider what she wanted. There was no answer. Plumes of icy air billowed from the nostrils' of the white horse.

The decrepit rider sat stiffly in her saddle. Underneath the gauzy veil, Mary saw that a woman's eyes radiated an eerie red glow. After a few moments, the woman on the horse spoke. "I am here to tell you, Mary Marr, that Thomas Marr has just died. Say your prayers, Lady. I bid you well."

At that, the rider and horse turned abruptly and galloped away.

Mary collapsed onto the front stoop in tears. Within the hour, a man who worked with Thomas came to deliver the news.

No one knows for sure what happened to Thomas Marr that fated winter evening. Some say that while working at the toll bridge Thomas was shot by an assailant's bullet, then fell into the Little Kanawha River and drowned. Others claim that it was the cry of the banshee that startled Thomas into meeting his end in the river below. The truth is, Thomas Marr did die on February 5, 1878—the day the Marrtown banshee visited Mary Marr

Mary Marr lived to be ninety years old, an exception for the time. As Mary lay as a corpse in the parlor of her home many years after her husband's death, family members heard the rattling of chains in the attic. Others claimed to hear the shrieks of a woman. A few years after Mary died, one of the Marr children cut off his hand in a tragic accident. As family members sat up with the boy, they heard snarling sounds on the porch. When the women went outside, the stoop was covered with blood as if a terrible struggle had taken place.

What has become of the banshee of Marrtown? It is said she still rides, bringing dreaded omens to those of Scottish blood. You would be wise to avoid Marrtown on dark and moonless nights.

THE BANSHEE OF CENTER POINT

Though the wilderness is vanishing in the United States, West Virginia is still known as a wild and wonderful place. But the state's reputation for wildness may come from something other than open its lands. Early Native American tribes, such as the Shawnee, believed the area to be cursed by ghosts and strange beasts.

In West Virginia, there is a ghost town in a rural area called Center Point. It is typical of small mountain communities reclaimed by the woods—just a few modest white houses clinging to the hillsides, and a craggy brown creek that courses through lush foliage.

Life in Center Point was for a long time uneventful. That is, until the summer of 1918 when the black flu hit, and the world seemed to be coming to an end. At that time, a seven-year-old girl named Pearl White lived in Center Point. She loved to play in the woods, and she dreamed constantly of being able to flap her arms and fly away like a bird. There was plenty for Pearl to do. She was not worried about the black flu. Sickness was something that happened to older people.

At dusk, on a day in October of 1918, Pearl was staying with her grandmother at Center Point while relatives traveled to help others stricken with the black flu. Pearl's young, unmarried uncle had taken sick but appeared to be doing fine. He had remained in good spirits, sitting up and talking as the day wore on.

Soon evening drew in. Flickering stars studded the night sky. Pearl could almost count them as she dreamed still of flying. Pearl's grandmother took her granddaughter to the outhouse one more time before turning in for the night. Suddenly, they heard the sound of horses' hooves coming up the dirt road.

Grandmother's first thought was that perhaps it was the mailman paying a late visit. After all, the black flu had taken its toll on Center Point. Mail was arriving just about anytime of day or evening with bad news. They watched the rider and horse make their way toward the farmhouse.

The figure sat erect on the horse, shrouded in pale rags. The horse itself was white and ghostly. The rider looked to be an old woman, but the Pearl was not sure since her face was covered by a ragged veil. The decrepit hands at the reins appeared waxen, like those belonging to a corpse.

Pearl's grandmother recoiled, but Pearl raced without fear to meet the horse and rider. The Sun was gone, the world left in shadows. The rider tugged on the bridle, and the horse stopped. In later years, Pearl would say that she was so close to the banshee's horse that she could feel its hot breath on her face.

Yes, it was the banshee. Pearl and her relatives Scottish, and the banshee had come to bring them an ill-omen.

On that fated night in Center Point, the banshee spirit issued a warning. She pointed a bony finger at the old woman and child, and proclaimed: "One of yours is to die this very night." Then her keening cry split the night's stillness. The banshee and her horse instantly vanished.

Shaken and left in shadows, Pearl and her grandmother hugged each other. But there was no time to think about the frightening thing that had just happened to them. Already, they heard terrible sounds coming from the house—someone was struggling for air.

It was Pearl's uncle. The two ran inside just in time to realize that the young man's lungs had filled with fluid. Blood foamed from his nose and mouth. Within moments, Pearl's uncle had drowned in his own blood. After the final death rattle, Pearl and her grandmother heard the sounds of hooves beating the path through the forest.

Despite the evening when she witnessed her uncle's terrible death, Pearl White grew up and did learn to fly. She became a pioneer in the field of aviation and was the first woman to parachute out of a plane. Pearl was a member of the Barnstormers, and she performed airborne stunts all the way from the hills of West Virginia to the movie sets in California.

Pearl White feared very little. As a young woman she loved danger. At the age of sixteen she would strap herself to a plane, and perform feats for a terrified audience. Pilots would make loops and nosedives, and nothing seemed to phase this fearless woman. Nothing, that is except for the one thing every Scottish woman should fear the most.

In later years Pearl refused to sit outside in the evening on the front porch of her modest home on upper Juliana Street in Parkersburg. Something disturbed Pearl, despite her fearless ways. This was a woman who was not afraid to jump out of a plane or walk on the wing; the only thing Pearl White was ever afraid of was of meeting up with the banshee after dark.

THE COACH-A-BOWER OF MINERAL WELLS

The banshee has a power that she shares with Witches, and that is the power of *glamoury*. Glamoury is a Gaelic word that means "shape shifting."

Witches master glamoury by turning into birds, animals, or a more attractive or younger person. But in Ireland, Scotland, and

West Virginia the banshee sometimes takes on another form, one that is neither animal nor human.

Along Route 14, between the small communities of Mineral Wells and Elizabeth, the banshee assumes the disquieting form of a death omen. In Gaelic, it is called the *coiste-bodhar,* or the "coach-a-bower." It is a hearse with a coffin strapped to the top that is led by two white headless horses.

In Ireland and Scotland, the coach-a-bower precedes the visit of a banshee. In Ireland, it is best not to open your front door if you hear the coach-a-bower creaking past your home. In doing so, you may end up with a basin of blood thrown in your face.

In the quiet meadows and mossy woods of West Virginia, the coach-a-bower has been updated. It is an old black hearse that winds its way along the highway between Mineral Wells and Elizabeth.

The phantom hearse appeared to a woman in Mineral Springs who was a member of a spiritualist group before their meeting on the Full Moon. About a month after seeing the hearse, one of the members of the meeting circle, a woman of pure Scottish heritage, experienced a wrenching tragedy—a member of her family member was brutally murdered. No one else in the group had seen the hearse.

Was this the banshee's coach-a-bower foreshadowing another Scottish tragedy, or was it just a strange mix of coincidences as sometimes occur?

As with many mysteries, we will never know. The important lesson of course is to remember that every Scottish and Irish clan has its own banshee.

Luckily, I've not met my banshee yet.

Let us hope you won't meet yours anytime soon.

Almanac Section

Calendar

Time Changes

Full Moons

Sabbats

Lunar Phases

Moon Signs

World Holidays

Color of the Day

Incense of the Day

Almanac Listings

In these listings you will find the date, day, lunar phase, Moon sign, color and incense for the day, and festivals from around the world.

The Date

The date is used in numerological calculations that govern magical rites.

The Day

Each day is ruled by a planet that possesses specific magical influences:

MONDAY (MOON): Peace, sleep, healing, compassion, friends, psychic awareness, purification, and fertility.

TUESDAY (MARS): Passion, sex, courage, aggression, and protection.

WEDNESDAY (MERCURY): The conscious mind, study, travel, divination, and wisdom.

THURSDAY (JUPITER): Expansion, money, prosperity, and generosity.

FRIDAY (VENUS): Love, friendship, reconciliation, and beauty.

SATURDAY (SATURN): Longevity, exorcism, endings, homes, and houses.

SUNDAY (SUN): Healing, spirituality, success, strength, and protection.

The Lunar Phase

The lunar phase is important in determining the best times for magic.

THE WAXING MOON (from the New Moon to the Full) is the ideal time for magic to draw things toward you.

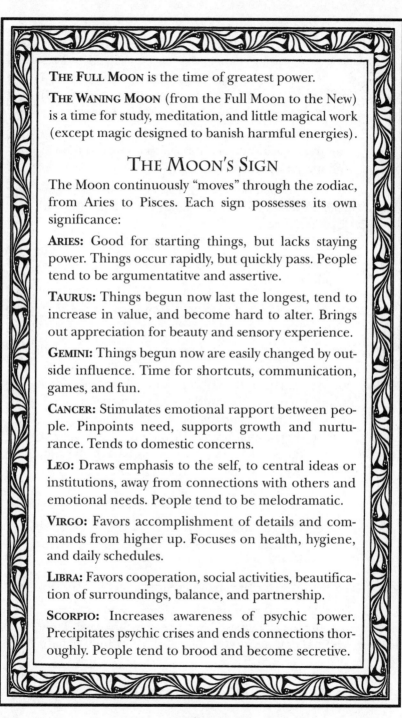

THE FULL MOON is the time of greatest power.

THE WANING MOON (from the Full Moon to the New) is a time for study, meditation, and little magical work (except magic designed to banish harmful energies).

THE MOON'S SIGN

The Moon continuously "moves" through the zodiac, from Aries to Pisces. Each sign possesses its own significance:

ARIES: Good for starting things, but lacks staying power. Things occur rapidly, but quickly pass. People tend to be argumentatitve and assertive.

TAURUS: Things begun now last the longest, tend to increase in value, and become hard to alter. Brings out appreciation for beauty and sensory experience.

GEMINI: Things begun now are easily changed by outside influence. Time for shortcuts, communication, games, and fun.

CANCER: Stimulates emotional rapport between people. Pinpoints need, supports growth and nurturance. Tends to domestic concerns.

LEO: Draws emphasis to the self, to central ideas or institutions, away from connections with others and emotional needs. People tend to be melodramatic.

VIRGO: Favors accomplishment of details and commands from higher up. Focuses on health, hygiene, and daily schedules.

LIBRA: Favors cooperation, social activities, beautification of surroundings, balance, and partnership.

SCORPIO: Increases awareness of psychic power. Precipitates psychic crises and ends connections thoroughly. People tend to brood and become secretive.

SAGITTARIUS: Encourages flights of imagination and confidence. This is an adventurous, philosophical, and athletic Moon sign. Favors expansion and growth.

CAPRICORN: Develops strong structure. Focus on traditions, responsibilities, and obligations. A good time to set boundaries and rules.

AQUARIUS: Rebellious energy. Time to break habits and make abrupt change. Personal freedom and individuality is the focus.

PISCES: The focus is on dreaming, nostalgia, intuition, and psychic impressions. A good time for spiritual or philanthropic activities.

COLOR AND INCENSE

The color and incense for the day are based on information from *Personal Alchemy* by Amber Wolfe, and relate to the planet that rules each day. This information can be taken into consideration along with other factors when planning works of magic or when blending magic into mundane life. Please note that the incense selections are not hard and fast. If you can not find or do not like the incense listed for the day, choose a similar scent that appeals to you.

FESTIVALS AND HOLIDAYS

Festivals are listed throughout the year. The exact dates of many of these ancient festivals are difficult to determine; prevailing data has been used.

TIME CHANGES

The times and dates of all astrological phenomena in this almanac are based on **Eastern Standard Time (EST).** They have NOT been adjusted for Daylight

Saving Time. If you live outside of EST, you will need to make the following changes:

PACIFIC STANDARD TIME: subtract three hours.

MOUNTAIN STANDARD TIME: subtract two hours.

CENTRAL STANDARD TIME: subtract one hour.

ALASKA/HAWAII: subtract five hours.

DAYLIGHT SAVING TIME: add an hour. Daylight saving time runs from April 7 to October 27, 2002.

2002 SABBATS AND FULL MOONS

January 28	Full Moon 5:50 PM
February 2	Imbolc
February 27	Full Moon 4:17 AM
March 20	Ostara (Spring Equinox)
March 28	Full Moon 1:25 PM
April 26	Full Moon 10:00 PM
May 1	Beltane
May 26	Full Moon 6:51 AM
June 21	Litha (Summer Solstice)
June 24	Full Moon 4:42 PM
July 24	Full Moon 4:07 AM
August 1	Lammas
August 22	Full Moon 5:29 PM
September 21	Full Moon 8:59 AM
September 22	Mabon (Fall Equinox)
October 21	Full Moon 2:20 AM
October 31	Samhain
November 19	Full Moon 8:34 PM
December 19	Full Moon 2:10 PM
December 21	Yule (Winter Solstice)

♑

1 **TUESDAY**
New Year's Day • Kwanzaa ends
Waning Moon
Moon Phase: Third Quarter
Color: Red

Moon Sign: Leo
Incense: Sage

2 **WEDNESDAY**
First Writing (Japanese)
Waning Moon
Moon Phase: Third Quarter
Color: Yellow

Moon Sign: Leo
Moon enters Virgo 6:34 pm
Incense: Sandalwood

3 **THURSDAY**
St. Genevieve's Day
Waning Moon
Moon Phase: Third Quarter
Color: Violet

Moon Sign: Virgo
Incense: Jasmine

4 **FRIDAY**
Frost Fairs on the Thames
Waning Moon
Moon Phase: Third Quarter
Color: White

Moon Sign: Virgo
Moon enters Libra 8:23 pm
Incense: Ylang ylang

☽ **SATURDAY**
Epiphany Eve
Waning Moon
Moon Phase: Fourth Quarter 10:55 pm
Color: Brown

Moon Sign: Libra
Incense: Pine

6 **SUNDAY**
Epiphany
Waning Moon
Moon Phase: Fourth Quarter
Color: Peach

Moon Sign: Libra
Moon enters Scorpio 11:41 pm
Incense: Parsley

7 **MONDAY**
Rizdvo (Ukrainian)
Waning Moon
Moon Phase: Fourth Quarter
Color: Silver

Moon Sign: Scorpio
Incense: Clove

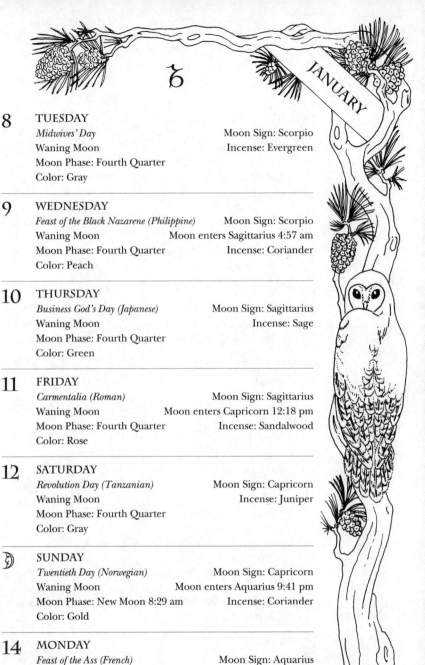

8 TUESDAY
Midwives' Day
Waning Moon
Moon Phase: Fourth Quarter
Color: Gray
Moon Sign: Scorpio
Incense: Evergreen

9 WEDNESDAY
Feast of the Black Nazarene (Philippine)
Waning Moon
Moon Phase: Fourth Quarter
Color: Peach
Moon Sign: Scorpio
Moon enters Sagittarius 4:57 am
Incense: Coriander

10 THURSDAY
Business God's Day (Japanese)
Waning Moon
Moon Phase: Fourth Quarter
Color: Green
Moon Sign: Sagittarius
Incense: Sage

11 FRIDAY
Carmentalia (Roman)
Waning Moon
Moon Phase: Fourth Quarter
Color: Rose
Moon Sign: Sagittarius
Moon enters Capricorn 12:18 pm
Incense: Sandalwood

12 SATURDAY
Revolution Day (Tanzanian)
Waning Moon
Moon Phase: Fourth Quarter
Color: Gray
Moon Sign: Capricorn
Incense: Juniper

☽ SUNDAY
Twentieth Day (Norwegian)
Waning Moon
Moon Phase: New Moon 8:29 am
Color: Gold
Moon Sign: Capricorn
Moon enters Aquarius 9:41 pm
Incense: Coriander

14 MONDAY
Feast of the Ass (French)
Waxing Moon
Moon Phase: First Quarter
Color: White
Moon Sign: Aquarius
Incense: Rose

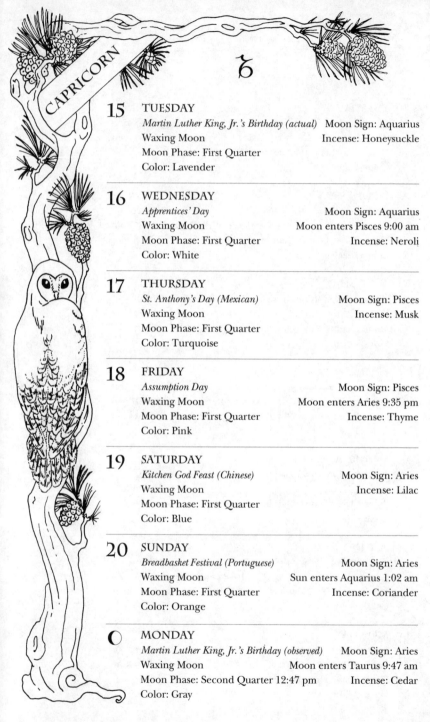

15 TUESDAY
Martin Luther King, Jr.'s Birthday (actual)   Moon Sign: Aquarius
Waxing Moon   Incense: Honeysuckle
Moon Phase: First Quarter
Color: Lavender

16 WEDNESDAY
Apprentices' Day   Moon Sign: Aquarius
Waxing Moon   Moon enters Pisces 9:00 am
Moon Phase: First Quarter   Incense: Neroli
Color: White

17 THURSDAY
St. Anthony's Day (Mexican)   Moon Sign: Pisces
Waxing Moon   Incense: Musk
Moon Phase: First Quarter
Color: Turquoise

18 FRIDAY
Assumption Day   Moon Sign: Pisces
Waxing Moon   Moon enters Aries 9:35 pm
Moon Phase: First Quarter   Incense: Thyme
Color: Pink

19 SATURDAY
Kitchen God Feast (Chinese)   Moon Sign: Aries
Waxing Moon   Incense: Lilac
Moon Phase: First Quarter
Color: Blue

20 SUNDAY
Breadbasket Festival (Portuguese)   Moon Sign: Aries
Waxing Moon   Sun enters Aquarius 1:02 am
Moon Phase: First Quarter   Incense: Coriander
Color: Orange

☾ MONDAY
Martin Luther King, Jr.'s Birthday (observed)   Moon Sign: Aries
Waxing Moon   Moon enters Taurus 9:47 am
Moon Phase: Second Quarter 12:47 pm   Incense: Cedar
Color: Gray

22 TUESDAY
St. Vincent's Day
Waxing Moon
Moon Phase: Second Quarter
Color: Black

Moon Sign: Taurus
Incense: Juniper

23 WEDNESDAY
St. Ildefonso's Day
Waxing Moon
Moon Phase: Second Quarter
Color: Brown

Moon Sign: Taurus
Moon enters Gemini 7:28 pm
Incense: Pine

24 THURSDAY
Alasitas Fair (Bolivian)
Waxing Moon
Moon Phase: Second Quarter
Color: White

Moon Sign: Gemini
Incense: Geranium

25 FRIDAY
Burns' Night (Scottish)
Waxing Moon
Moon Phase: Second Quarter
Color: Peach

Moon Sign: Gemini
Incense: Dill

26 SATURDAY
Republic Day (Indian)
Waxing Moon
Moon Phase: Second Quarter
Color: Indigo

Moon Sign: Gemini
Moon enters Cancer 1:17 am
Incense: Maple

27 SUNDAY
Vogelgruff (Swiss)
Waxing Moon
Moon Phase: Second Quarter
Color: Yellow

Moon Sign: Cancer
Incense: Basil

MONDAY
St. Charlemagne's Day
Waxing Moon
Moon Phase: Full Moon 5:50 pm
Color: Silver

Moon Sign: Cancer
Moon enters Leo 3:31 am
Incense: Clove

≈≈≈

29 TUESDAY
Australia Day   Moon Sign: Leo
Waning Moon   Incense: Poplar
Moon Phase: Third Quarter
Color: Gray

30 WEDNESDAY
Three Hierarchs' Day (Eastern Orthodox)   Moon Sign: Leo
Waning Moon   Moon enters Virgo 3:40 am
Moon Phase: Third Quarter   Incense: Maple
Color: Yellow

31 THURSDAY
Independence Day (Nauru)   Moon Sign: Virgo
Waning Moon   Incense: Carnation
Moon Phase: Third Quarter
Color: Violet

❦

SACRED BELLS

Many cultures have used bells or chimes as talismans of protection. An old bell custom from Brittany has its roots in the protective magic of that region's Celtic past. *Sacring* bells are still used in Breton churches to evoke the blessings and protection of the divine. These are small bells, similar to Christmas jingle bells, tied at intervals to the outer rim of a wooden wheel and placed near the entryway of a church or in a church yard. As the faithful file past, they give the wheel a few turns, releasing the musical magic of the bells. A remnant of this sacred bell tradition is present in household items such as doorbells and windchimes.

February

1 **FRIDAY**
St. Bridget's Day (Irish) — Moon Sign: Virgo
Waning Moon — Moon enters Libra 3:44 am
Moon Phase: Third Quarter — Incense: Rose
Color: White

2 **SATURDAY**
Imbolc • Groundhog Day — Moon Sign: Libra
Waning Moon — Incense: Patchouli
Moon Phase: Third Quarter
Color: Brown

3 **SUNDAY**
St. Blaise's Day — Moon Sign: Libra
Waning Moon — Moon enters Scorpio 5:35 am
Moon Phase: Third Quarter — Incense: Sage
Color: Peach

☽ **MONDAY**
Independence Day (Sri Lankan) — Moon Sign: Scorpio
Waning Moon — Incense: Chrysanthemum
Moon Phase: Fourth Quarter 8:33 am
Color: White

5 **TUESDAY**
Festival de la Alcaldesa (Italian) — Moon Sign: Scorpio
Waning Moon — Moon enters Sagittarius 10:21 am
Moon Phase: Fourth Quarter — Incense: Ginger
Color: Red

6 **WEDNESDAY**
Bob Marley's Birthday (Jamaican) — Moon Sign: Sagittarius
Waning Moon — Incense: Coriander
Moon Phase: Fourth Quarter
Color: Peach

7 **THURSDAY**
Full Moon Poya (Sri Lankan) — Moon Sign: Sagittarius
Waning Moon — Moon enters Capricorn 6:08 pm
Moon Phase: Fourth Quarter — Incense: Dill
Color: Green

8 FRIDAY
Mass for Broken Needles (Japanese)   Moon Sign: Capricorn
Waning Moon   Incense: Parsley
Moon Phase: Fourth Quarter
Color: Rose

9 SATURDAY
St. Marion's Day (Lebanese)   Moon Sign: Capricorn
Waning Moon   Incense: Cedar
Moon Phase: Fourth Quarter
Color: Gray

10 SUNDAY
Gasparilla Day   Moon Sign: Capricorn
Waning Moon   Moon enters Aquarius 4:15 am
Moon Phase: Fourth Quarter   Incense: Cinnamon
Color: Gold

11 MONDAY
Foundation Day (Japanese)   Moon Sign: Aquarius
Waning Moon   Incense: Lilac
Moon Phase: Fourth Quarter
Color: Lavender

☽ TUESDAY
Chinese New Year (horse) • *Mardi Gras*   Moon Sign: Aquarius
Waning Moon   Moon enters Pisces 3:53 pm
Moon Phase: New Moon 2:41 am   Incense: Gardenia
Color: White

13 WEDNESDAY
Ash Wednesday   Moon Sign: Pisces
Waxing Moon   Incense: Eucalyptus
Moon Phase: First Quarter
Color: Brown

14 THURSDAY
Valentine's Day   Moon Sign: Pisces
Waxing Moon   Incense: Evergreen
Moon Phase: First Quarter
Color: Turquoise

15 FRIDAY
Lupercalia (Roman)
Waxing Moon
Moon Phase: First Quarter
Color: Pink

Moon Sign: Pisces
Moon enters Aries 4:26 am
Incense: Ginger

16 SATURDAY
Maya Indian Lent (Mexican)
Waxing Moon
Moon Phase: First Quarter
Color: Blue

Moon Sign: Aries
Incense: Violet

17 SUNDAY
Quirinalia (Roman)
Waxing Moon
Moon Phase: First Quarter
Color: Orange

Moon Sign: Aries
Moon enters Taurus 4:58 pm
Incense: Parsley

18 MONDAY
Presidents' Day (observed)
Waxing Moon
Moon Phase: First Quarter
Color: Gray

Moon Sign: Taurus
Sun enters Pisces 3:13 pm
Incense: Maple

19 TUESDAY
Pero Palo's Trial (Spanish)
Waxing Moon
Moon Phase: First Quarter
Color: Black

Moon Sign: Taurus
Incense: Poplar

○ WEDNESDAY
Installation of the New Lama (Tibetan)
Waxing Moon
Moon Phase: Second Quarter 7:02 am
Color: Yellow

Moon Sign: Taurus
Moon enters Gemini 3:50 am
Incense: Cedar

21 THURSDAY
Feast of Lanterns (Chinese)
Waxing Moon
Moon Phase: Second Quarter
Color: White

Moon Sign: Gemini
Incense: Crysanthemum

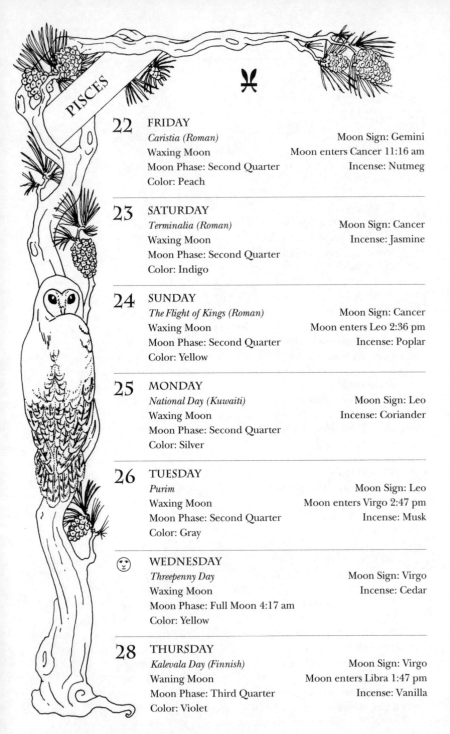

♓

22 FRIDAY
Caristia (Roman)
Waxing Moon
Moon Phase: Second Quarter
Color: Peach

Moon Sign: Gemini
Moon enters Cancer 11:16 am
Incense: Nutmeg

23 SATURDAY
Terminalia (Roman)
Waxing Moon
Moon Phase: Second Quarter
Color: Indigo

Moon Sign: Cancer
Incense: Jasmine

24 SUNDAY
The Flight of Kings (Roman)
Waxing Moon
Moon Phase: Second Quarter
Color: Yellow

Moon Sign: Cancer
Moon enters Leo 2:36 pm
Incense: Poplar

25 MONDAY
National Day (Kuwaiti)
Waxing Moon
Moon Phase: Second Quarter
Color: Silver

Moon Sign: Leo
Incense: Coriander

26 TUESDAY
Purim
Waxing Moon
Moon Phase: Second Quarter
Color: Gray

Moon Sign: Leo
Moon enters Virgo 2:47 pm
Incense: Musk

☺ **WEDNESDAY**
Threepenny Day
Waxing Moon
Moon Phase: Full Moon 4:17 am
Color: Yellow

Moon Sign: Virgo
Incense: Cedar

28 THURSDAY
Kalevala Day (Finnish)
Waning Moon
Moon Phase: Third Quarter
Color: Violet

Moon Sign: Virgo
Moon enters Libra 1:47 pm
Incense: Vanilla

1 FRIDAY
St. David's Day (Welsh)
Waning Moon
Moon Phase: Third Quarter
Color: White

Moon Sign: Libra
Incense: Chrysanthemum

2 SATURDAY
St. Chad's Day (English)
Waning Moon
Moon Phase: Third Quarter
Color: Brown

Moon Sign: Libra
Moon enters Scorpio 1:51 pm
Incense: Poplar

3 SUNDAY
Doll Festival (Japanese)
Waning Moon
Moon Phase: Third Quarter
Color: Peach

Moon Sign: Scorpio
Incense: Basil

4 MONDAY
St. Casimir's Day (Polish)
Waning Moon
Moon Phase: Third Quarter
Color: White

Moon Sign: Scorpio
Moon enters Sagittarius 4:55 pm
Incense: Myrrh

☽ TUESDAY
Isis Festival (Roman)
Waning Moon
Moon Phase: Fourth Quarter 8:25 pm
Color: Red

Moon Sign: Sagittarius
Incense: Clove

6 WEDNESDAY
Alamo Day
Waning Moon
Moon Phase: Fourth Quarter
Color: Peach

Moon Sign: Sagittarius
Moon enters Capricorn 11:48 pm
Incense: Dill

7 THURSDAY
Festival of Rama (Hindu)
Waning Moon
Moon Phase: Fourth Quarter
Color: Green

Moon Sign: Capricorn
Incense: Sandalwood

8 **FRIDAY**
International Women's Day — Moon Sign: Capricorn
Waning Moon — Incense: Clove
Moon Phase: Fourth Quarter
Color: Rose

9 **SATURDAY**
Forty Saints' Day (Romanian) — Moon Sign: Capricorn
Waning Moon — Moon enters Aquarius 9:56 am
Moon Phase: Fourth Quarter — Incense: Maple
Color: Gray

10 **SUNDAY**
Tibet Day — Moon Sign: Aquarius
Waning Moon — Incense: Nutmeg
Moon Phase: Fourth Quarter
Color: Gold

11 **MONDAY**
Feast of Gauri (Hindu) — Moon Sign: Aquarius
Waning Moon — Moon enters Pisces 9:55 pm
Moon Phase: Fourth Quarter — Incense: Lavender
Color: Lavender

12 **TUESDAY**
St. Gregory's Day — Moon Sign: Pisces
Waning Moon — Incense: Evergreen
Moon Phase: Fourth Quarter
Color: Black

☽ **WEDNESDAY**
Purification Feast (Balinese) — Moon Sign: Pisces
Waning Moon — Incense: Honeysuckle
Moon Phase: New Moon 9:03 pm
Color: White

14 **THURSDAY**
Mamuralia (Roman) — Moon Sign: Pisces
Waxing Moon — Moon enters Aries 10:34 am
Moon Phase: First Quarter — Incense: Pine
Color: Turquoise

15 FRIDAY
Islamic New Year　　　　　　　　Moon Sign: Aries
Waxing Moon　　　　　　　　　　Incense: Nutmeg
Moon Phase: First Quarter
Color: Pink

16 SATURDAY
St. Urho's Day (Finnish)　　　　　　Moon Sign: Aries
Waxing Moon　　　　　Moon enters Taurus 11:01 pm
Moon Phase: First Quarter　　　　　　Incense: Lavender
Color: Blue

17 SUNDAY
St. Patrick's Day　　　　　　　　Moon Sign: Taurus
Waxing Moon　　　　　　　　　　　Incense: Sage
Moon Phase: First Quarter
Color: Orange

18 MONDAY
Sheelah's Day (Irish)　　　　　　Moon Sign: Taurus
Waxing Moon　　　　　　　　　　　Incense: Pine
Moon Phase: First Quarter
Color: Gray

19 TUESDAY
St. Joseph's Day (Sicilian)　　　　　Moon Sign: Taurus
Waxing Moon　　　　Moon enters Gemini 10:20 am
Moon Phase: First Quarter　　　　　　Incense: Vanilla
Color: White

20 WEDNESDAY
Ostara • Spring Equinox • Int'l Astrology Day　　Moon Sign: Gemini
Waxing Moon　　　　　　Sun enters Aries 2:16 pm
Moon Phase: First Quarter　　　　　　Incense: Musk
Color: Brown

☽ THURSDAY
Juarez Day (Mexican)　　　　　　Moon Sign: Aries
Waxing Moon　　　　　Moon enters Cancer 7:06 pm
Moon Phase: Second Quarter 9:28 pm　　Incense: Gardenia
Color: Violet

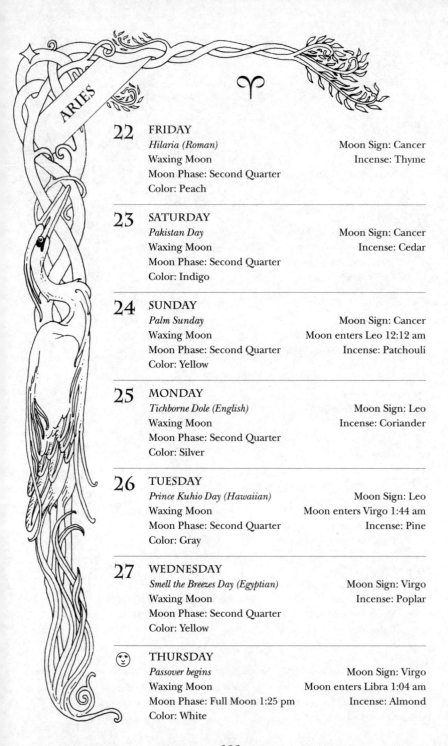

♈

22 FRIDAY
Hilaria (Roman)
Waxing Moon
Moon Phase: Second Quarter
Color: Peach

Moon Sign: Cancer
Incense: Thyme

23 SATURDAY
Pakistan Day
Waxing Moon
Moon Phase: Second Quarter
Color: Indigo

Moon Sign: Cancer
Incense: Cedar

24 SUNDAY
Palm Sunday
Waxing Moon
Moon Phase: Second Quarter
Color: Yellow

Moon Sign: Cancer
Moon enters Leo 12:12 am
Incense: Patchouli

25 MONDAY
Tichborne Dole (English)
Waxing Moon
Moon Phase: Second Quarter
Color: Silver

Moon Sign: Leo
Incense: Coriander

26 TUESDAY
Prince Kuhio Day (Hawaiian)
Waxing Moon
Moon Phase: Second Quarter
Color: Gray

Moon Sign: Leo
Moon enters Virgo 1:44 am
Incense: Pine

27 WEDNESDAY
Smell the Breezes Day (Egyptian)
Waxing Moon
Moon Phase: Second Quarter
Color: Yellow

Moon Sign: Virgo
Incense: Poplar

☺ **THURSDAY**
Passover begins
Waxing Moon
Moon Phase: Full Moon 1:25 pm
Color: White

Moon Sign: Virgo
Moon enters Libra 1:04 am
Incense: Almond

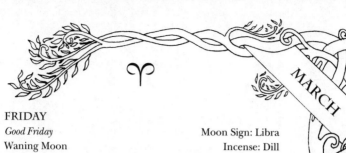

29 FRIDAY
Good Friday
Waning Moon
Moon Phase: Third Quarter
Color: Rose

Moon Sign: Libra
Incense: Dill

30 SATURDAY
Seward's Day (Alaskan)
Waning Moon
Moon Phase: Third Quarter
Color: Brown

Moon Sign: Libra
Moon enters Scorpio 12:21 am
Incense: Maple

31 SUNDAY
Easter
Waning Moon
Moon Phase: Third Quarter
Color: Peach

Moon Sign: Scorpio
Incense: Thyme

~✻~

OSTARA BROOM RITUAL

Mid-March, go to the drapery section of the department store and get two hooks (be sure your broom handle rests easily in them). Find a place on your wall and screw them in. Yes, this is a permanent thing, but you can display your broom all year long. Next stop: handi-craft store. Purchase plain Styrofoam eggs, ribbons, sequins, and so on—whatever you want to use to decorate your eggs. When finished, hang the eggs from ribbons on the horizontal handle of the broom. Or, you can make your broom into a bunny rabbit. The broom is a magical tool that will cleanse your home space with its magic.

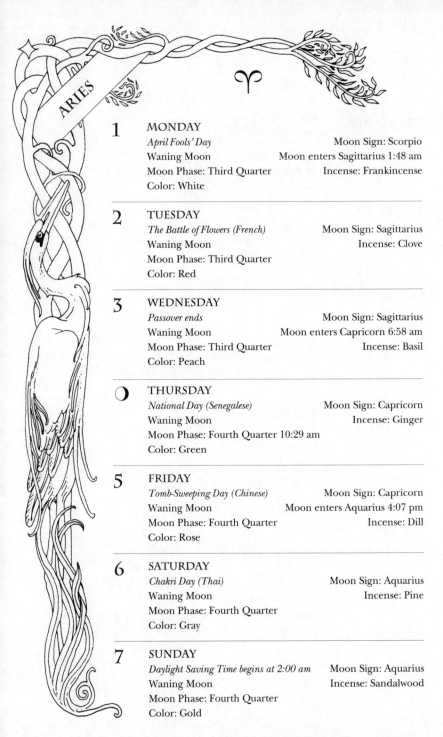

ARIES

♈

1 MONDAY
April Fools' Day   Moon Sign: Scorpio
Waning Moon   Moon enters Sagittarius 1:48 am
Moon Phase: Third Quarter   Incense: Frankincense
Color: White

2 TUESDAY
The Battle of Flowers (French)   Moon Sign: Sagittarius
Waning Moon   Incense: Clove
Moon Phase: Third Quarter
Color: Red

3 WEDNESDAY
Passover ends   Moon Sign: Sagittarius
Waning Moon   Moon enters Capricorn 6:58 am
Moon Phase: Third Quarter   Incense: Basil
Color: Peach

◑ THURSDAY
National Day (Senegalese)   Moon Sign: Capricorn
Waning Moon   Incense: Ginger
Moon Phase: Fourth Quarter 10:29 am
Color: Green

5 FRIDAY
Tomb-Sweeping Day (Chinese)   Moon Sign: Capricorn
Waning Moon   Moon enters Aquarius 4:07 pm
Moon Phase: Fourth Quarter   Incense: Dill
Color: Rose

6 SATURDAY
Chakri Day (Thai)   Moon Sign: Aquarius
Waning Moon   Incense: Pine
Moon Phase: Fourth Quarter
Color: Gray

7 SUNDAY
Daylight Saving Time begins at 2:00 am   Moon Sign: Aquarius
Waning Moon   Incense: Sandalwood
Moon Phase: Fourth Quarter
Color: Gold

8   MONDAY
Buddha's Birthday   Moon Sign: Aquarius
Waning Moon   Moon enters Pisces 3:57 am
Moon Phase: Fourth Quarter   Incense: Rose
Color: Lavender

9   TUESDAY
Valour Day (Philippine)   Moon Sign: Pisces
Waning Moon   Incense: Almond
Moon Phase: Fourth Quarter
Color: White

10   WEDNESDAY
The Tenth of April (British)   Moon Sign: Pisces
Waning Moon   Moon enters Aries 4:40 pm
Moon Phase: Fourth Quarter   Incense: Evergreen
Color: Brown

11   THURSDAY
Heroes' Day (Costa Rican)   Moon Sign: Aries
Waning Moon   Incense: Patchouli
Moon Phase: Fourth Quarter
Color: Turquoise

☽   FRIDAY
Cerealia (Roman)   Moon Sign: Aries
Waning Moon   Incense: Thyme
Moon Phase: New Moon 2:21 pm
Color: Pink

13   SATURDAY
Thai New Year   Moon Sign: Aries
Waxing Moon   Moon enters Taurus 4:55 am
Moon Phase: First Quarter   Incense: Peony
Color: Blue

14   SUNDAY
Sanno Festival (Japan)   Moon Sign: Taurus
Waxing Moon   Incense: Clove
Moon Phase: First Quarter
Color: Orange

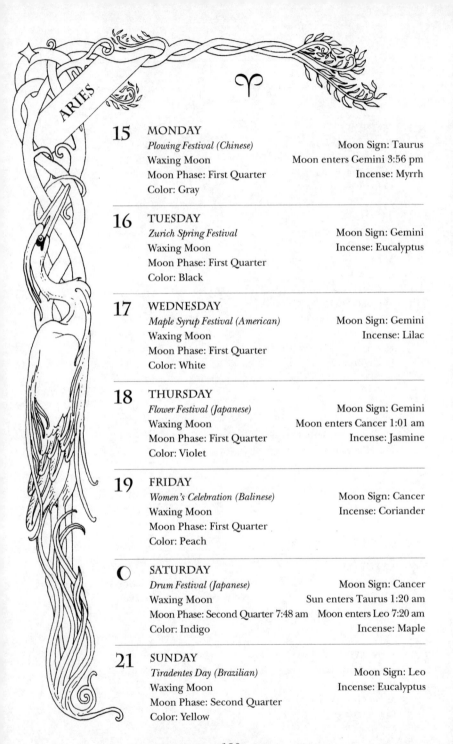

♈

15 MONDAY
Plowing Festival (Chinese)
Waxing Moon
Moon Phase: First Quarter
Color: Gray

Moon Sign: Taurus
Moon enters Gemini 3:56 pm
Incense: Myrrh

16 TUESDAY
Zurich Spring Festival
Waxing Moon
Moon Phase: First Quarter
Color: Black

Moon Sign: Gemini
Incense: Eucalyptus

17 WEDNESDAY
Maple Syrup Festival (American)
Waxing Moon
Moon Phase: First Quarter
Color: White

Moon Sign: Gemini
Incense: Lilac

18 THURSDAY
Flower Festival (Japanese)
Waxing Moon
Moon Phase: First Quarter
Color: Violet

Moon Sign: Gemini
Moon enters Cancer 1:01 am
Incense: Jasmine

19 FRIDAY
Women's Celebration (Balinese)
Waxing Moon
Moon Phase: First Quarter
Color: Peach

Moon Sign: Cancer
Incense: Coriander

☾ SATURDAY
Drum Festival (Japanese)
Waxing Moon
Moon Phase: Second Quarter 7:48 am
Color: Indigo

Moon Sign: Cancer
Sun enters Taurus 1:20 am
Moon enters Leo 7:20 am
Incense: Maple

21 SUNDAY
Tiradentes Day (Brazilian)
Waxing Moon
Moon Phase: Second Quarter
Color: Yellow

Moon Sign: Leo
Incense: Eucalyptus

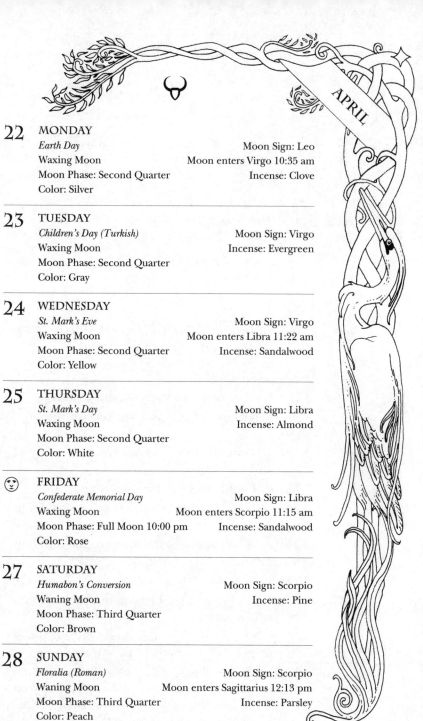

22 MONDAY
Earth Day
Waxing Moon
Moon Phase: Second Quarter
Color: Silver

Moon Sign: Leo
Moon enters Virgo 10:35 am
Incense: Clove

23 TUESDAY
Children's Day (Turkish)
Waxing Moon
Moon Phase: Second Quarter
Color: Gray

Moon Sign: Virgo
Incense: Evergreen

24 WEDNESDAY
St. Mark's Eve
Waxing Moon
Moon Phase: Second Quarter
Color: Yellow

Moon Sign: Virgo
Moon enters Libra 11:22 am
Incense: Sandalwood

25 THURSDAY
St. Mark's Day
Waxing Moon
Moon Phase: Second Quarter
Color: White

Moon Sign: Libra
Incense: Almond

FRIDAY
Confederate Memorial Day
Waxing Moon
Moon Phase: Full Moon 10:00 pm
Color: Rose

Moon Sign: Libra
Moon enters Scorpio 11:15 am
Incense: Sandalwood

27 SATURDAY
Humabon's Conversion
Waning Moon
Moon Phase: Third Quarter
Color: Brown

Moon Sign: Scorpio
Incense: Pine

28 SUNDAY
Floralia (Roman)
Waning Moon
Moon Phase: Third Quarter
Color: Peach

Moon Sign: Scorpio
Moon enters Sagittarius 12:13 pm
Incense: Parsley

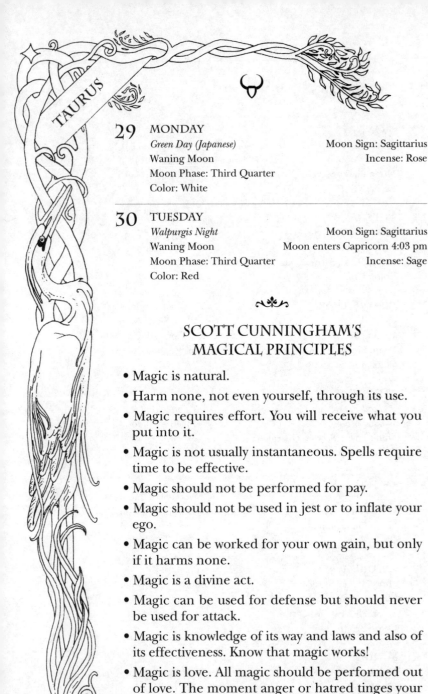

29 MONDAY
Green Day (Japanese)
Waning Moon
Moon Phase: Third Quarter
Color: White

Moon Sign: Sagittarius
Incense: Rose

30 TUESDAY
Walpurgis Night
Waning Moon
Moon Phase: Third Quarter
Color: Red

Moon Sign: Sagittarius
Moon enters Capricorn 4:03 pm
Incense: Sage

SCOTT CUNNINGHAM'S MAGICAL PRINCIPLES

- Magic is natural.
- Harm none, not even yourself, through its use.
- Magic requires effort. You will receive what you put into it.
- Magic is not usually instantaneous. Spells require time to be effective.
- Magic should not be performed for pay.
- Magic should not be used in jest or to inflate your ego.
- Magic can be worked for your own gain, but only if it harms none.
- Magic is a divine act.
- Magic can be used for defense but should never be used for attack.
- Magic is knowledge of its way and laws and also of its effectiveness. Know that magic works!
- Magic is love. All magic should be performed out of love. The moment anger or hatred tinges your magic you have crossed the border into a dangerous world, one that will ultimately consume you.

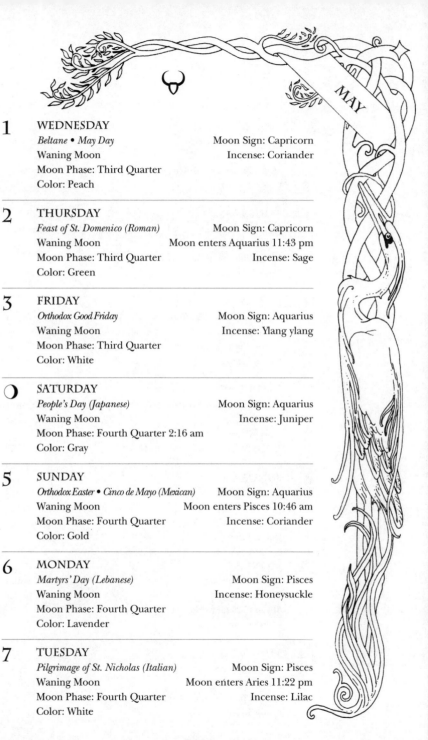

1 WEDNESDAY
Beltane • May Day
Waning Moon
Moon Phase: Third Quarter
Color: Peach

Moon Sign: Capricorn
Incense: Coriander

2 THURSDAY
Feast of St. Domenico (Roman)
Waning Moon
Moon Phase: Third Quarter
Color: Green

Moon Sign: Capricorn
Moon enters Aquarius 11:43 pm
Incense: Sage

3 FRIDAY
Orthodox Good Friday
Waning Moon
Moon Phase: Third Quarter
Color: White

Moon Sign: Aquarius
Incense: Ylang ylang

☽ SATURDAY
People's Day (Japanese)
Waning Moon
Moon Phase: Fourth Quarter 2:16 am
Color: Gray

Moon Sign: Aquarius
Incense: Juniper

5 SUNDAY
Orthodox Easter • Cinco de Mayo (Mexican)
Waning Moon
Moon Phase: Fourth Quarter
Color: Gold

Moon Sign: Aquarius
Moon enters Pisces 10:46 am
Incense: Coriander

6 MONDAY
Martyrs' Day (Lebanese)
Waning Moon
Moon Phase: Fourth Quarter
Color: Lavender

Moon Sign: Pisces
Incense: Honeysuckle

7 TUESDAY
Pilgrimage of St. Nicholas (Italian)
Waning Moon
Moon Phase: Fourth Quarter
Color: White

Moon Sign: Pisces
Moon enters Aries 11:22 pm
Incense: Lilac

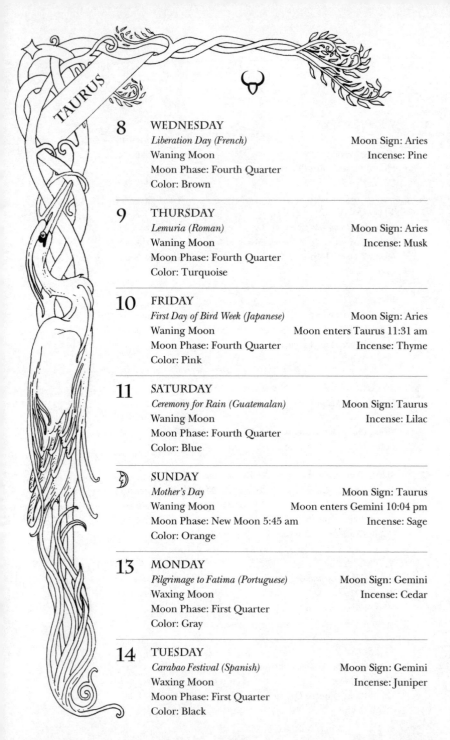

8 WEDNESDAY
Liberation Day (French)   Moon Sign: Aries
Waning Moon   Incense: Pine
Moon Phase: Fourth Quarter
Color: Brown

9 THURSDAY
Lemuria (Roman)   Moon Sign: Aries
Waning Moon   Incense: Musk
Moon Phase: Fourth Quarter
Color: Turquoise

10 FRIDAY
First Day of Bird Week (Japanese)   Moon Sign: Aries
Waning Moon   Moon enters Taurus 11:31 am
Moon Phase: Fourth Quarter   Incense: Thyme
Color: Pink

11 SATURDAY
Ceremony for Rain (Guatemalan)   Moon Sign: Taurus
Waning Moon   Incense: Lilac
Moon Phase: Fourth Quarter
Color: Blue

☽ SUNDAY
Mother's Day   Moon Sign: Taurus
Waning Moon   Moon enters Gemini 10:04 pm
Moon Phase: New Moon 5:45 am   Incense: Sage
Color: Orange

13 MONDAY
Pilgrimage to Fatima (Portuguese)   Moon Sign: Gemini
Waxing Moon   Incense: Cedar
Moon Phase: First Quarter
Color: Gray

14 TUESDAY
Carabao Festival (Spanish)   Moon Sign: Gemini
Waxing Moon   Incense: Juniper
Moon Phase: First Quarter
Color: Black

15 WEDNESDAY
Festival of St. Dympna (Belgian)   Moon Sign: Gemini
Waxing Moon   Moon enters Cancer 6:33 am
Moon Phase: First Quarter   Incense: Neroli
Color: White

16 THURSDAY
St. Honoratus' Day   Moon Sign: Cancer
Waxing Moon   Incense: Jasmine
Moon Phase: First Quarter
Color: Violet

17 FRIDAY
Shavuot   Moon Sign: Cancer
Waxing Moon   Moon enters Leo 12:52 pm
Moon Phase: First Quarter   Incense: Dill
Color: Peach

18 SATURDAY
Las Piedras Day (Uruguayan)   Moon Sign: Leo
Waxing Moon   Incense: Maple
Moon Phase: First Quarter
Color: Indigo

◖ SUNDAY
Pentecost   Moon Sign: Leo
Waxing Moon   Moon enters Virgo 5:01 pm
Moon Phase: Second Quarter 2:42 pm   Incense: Basil
Color: Yellow

20 MONDAY
Mecklenburg Independence Day   Moon Sign: Virgo
Waxing Moon   Incense: Myrrh
Moon Phase: Second Quarter
Color: Silver

21 TUESDAY
Victoria Day (Canadian)   Moon Sign: Virgo
Waxing Moon   Sun enters Gemini 12:29 am
Moon Phase: Second Quarter   Moon enters Libra 7:19 pm
Color: Gray   Incense: Poplar

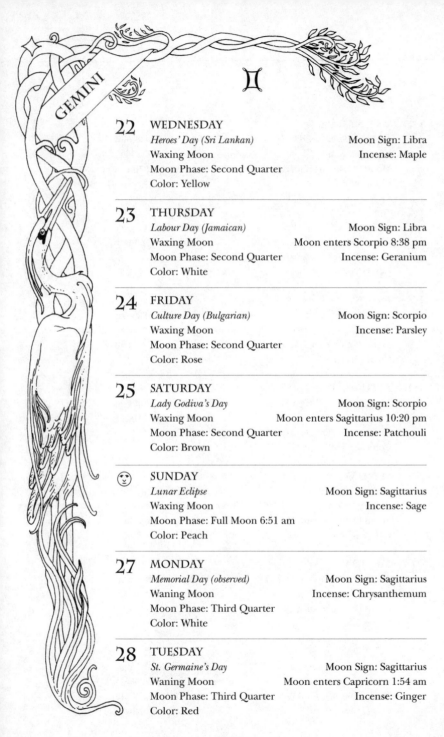

♊

22 **WEDNESDAY**
Heroes' Day (Sri Lankan)   Moon Sign: Libra
Waxing Moon   Incense: Maple
Moon Phase: Second Quarter
Color: Yellow

23 **THURSDAY**
Labour Day (Jamaican)   Moon Sign: Libra
Waxing Moon   Moon enters Scorpio 8:38 pm
Moon Phase: Second Quarter   Incense: Geranium
Color: White

24 **FRIDAY**
Culture Day (Bulgarian)   Moon Sign: Scorpio
Waxing Moon   Incense: Parsley
Moon Phase: Second Quarter
Color: Rose

25 **SATURDAY**
Lady Godiva's Day   Moon Sign: Scorpio
Waxing Moon   Moon enters Sagittarius 10:20 pm
Moon Phase: Second Quarter   Incense: Patchouli
Color: Brown

☺ **SUNDAY**
Lunar Eclipse   Moon Sign: Sagittarius
Waxing Moon   Incense: Sage
Moon Phase: Full Moon 6:51 am
Color: Peach

27 **MONDAY**
Memorial Day (observed)   Moon Sign: Sagittarius
Waning Moon   Incense: Chrysanthemum
Moon Phase: Third Quarter
Color: White

28 **TUESDAY**
St. Germaine's Day   Moon Sign: Sagittarius
Waning Moon   Moon enters Capricorn 1:54 am
Moon Phase: Third Quarter   Incense: Ginger
Color: Red

29 WEDNESDAY
Royal Oak Day (British)   Moon Sign: Capricorn
Waning Moon   Incense: Thyme
Moon Phase: Third Quarter
Color: Peach

30 THURSDAY
Memorial Day (actual)   Moon Sign: Capricorn
Waning Moon   Moon enters Aquarius 8:35 am
Moon Phase: Third Quarter   Incense: Dill
Color: Green

31 FRIDAY
Republic Day (South African)   Moon Sign: Aquarius
Waning Moon   Incense: Parsley
Moon Phase: Third Quarter
Color: Rose

MORE PROTECTIVE MAGIC

- WHEN SOMEONE TRIES TO READ YOUR THOUGHTS:

  If you believe that someone is trying to read your thoughts or otherwise intrude into your head, visualize it as being stuffed with thick mashed potatoes that make such penetration impossible.

- FOR MANY CIRCUMSTANCES:

  Taste salt, or throw it around you in a circle. (Carrying a small packet of salt from a restaurant facilitates this.)

  Cross your fingers. (This calls upon the force of the Sun.)

  Tighten your muscles and relax them while visualizing protection. (This sends out protective power.)

  Stand. (You're more in control when standing than when sitting or reclining.)

1 SATURDAY
National Day (Tunisian)
Waning Moon
Moon Phase: Third Quarter
Color: Gray

Moon Sign: Aquarius
Moon enters Pisces 6:37 pm
Incense: Cedar

☽ SUNDAY
Republic Day (Italian)
Waning Moon
Moon Phase: Fourth Quarter 7:05 pm
Color: Gold

Moon Sign: Pisces
Incense: Cinnamon

3 MONDAY
Memorial to Broken Dolls (Japan)
Waning Moon
Moon Phase: Fourth Quarter
Color: Lavender

Moon Sign: Pisces
Incense: Lilac

4 TUESDAY
Full Moon Day (Burmese)
Waning Moon
Moon Phase: Fourth Quarter
Color: White

Moon Sign: Pisces
Moon enters Aries 6:51 am
Incense: Gardenia

5 WEDNESDAY
Constitution Day (Danish)
Waning Moon
Moon Phase: Fourth Quarter
Color: Brown

Moon Sign: Aries
Incense: Eucalyptus

6 THURSDAY
Swedish Flag Day
Waning Moon
Moon Phase: Fourth Quarter
Color: Turquoise

Moon Sign: Aries
Moon enters Taurus 7:07 pm
Incense: Evergreen

7 FRIDAY
St. Robert of Newminster's Day
Waning Moon
Moon Phase: Fourth Quarter
Color: Pink

Moon Sign: Taurus
Incense: Ginger

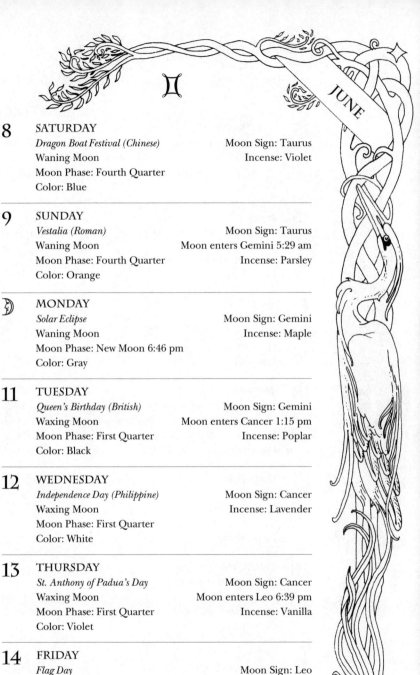

8 SATURDAY
Dragon Boat Festival (Chinese)   Moon Sign: Taurus
Waning Moon   Incense: Violet
Moon Phase: Fourth Quarter
Color: Blue

9 SUNDAY
Vestalia (Roman)   Moon Sign: Taurus
Waning Moon   Moon enters Gemini 5:29 am
Moon Phase: Fourth Quarter   Incense: Parsley
Color: Orange

MONDAY
Solar Eclipse   Moon Sign: Gemini
Waning Moon   Incense: Maple
Moon Phase: New Moon 6:46 pm
Color: Gray

11 TUESDAY
Queen's Birthday (British)   Moon Sign: Gemini
Waxing Moon   Moon enters Cancer 1:15 pm
Moon Phase: First Quarter   Incense: Poplar
Color: Black

12 WEDNESDAY
Independence Day (Philippine)   Moon Sign: Cancer
Waxing Moon   Incense: Lavender
Moon Phase: First Quarter
Color: White

13 THURSDAY
St. Anthony of Padua's Day   Moon Sign: Cancer
Waxing Moon   Moon enters Leo 6:39 pm
Moon Phase: First Quarter   Incense: Vanilla
Color: Violet

14 FRIDAY
Flag Day   Moon Sign: Leo
Waxing Moon   Incense: Nutmeg
Moon Phase: First Quarter
Color: Peach

♊

15 SATURDAY
Lantern Festival (Japanese)   Moon Sign: Leo
Waxing Moon   Moon enters Virgo 10:23 pm
Moon Phase: First Quarter   Incense: Jasmine
Color: Indigo

16 SUNDAY
Father's Day • Bloomsday (Irish)   Moon Sign: Virgo
Waxing Moon   Incense: Poplar
Moon Phase: First Quarter
Color: Yellow

☾ MONDAY
Bunker Hill Day   Moon Sign: Virgo
Waxing Moon   Incense: Nutmeg
Moon Phase: Second Quarter 7:29 pm
Color: Silver

18 TUESDAY
Independence Day (Egyptian)   Moon Sign: Virgo
Waxing Moon   Moon enters Libra 1:11 am
Moon Phase: Second Quarter   Incense: Musk
Color: Gray

19 WEDNESDAY
Juneteenth   Moon Sign: Libra
Waxing Moon   Incense: Cedar
Moon Phase: Second Quarter
Color: Yellow

20 THURSDAY
Flag Day (Argentinian)   Moon Sign: Libra
Waxing Moon   Moon enters Scorpio 3:42 am
Moon Phase: Second Quarter   Incense: Chrysanthemum
Color: White

21 FRIDAY
Litha • Summer Solstice   Moon Sign: Scorpio
Waxing Moon   Sun enters Cancer 8:24 am
Moon Phase: Second Quarter   Incense: Clove
Color: Rose

JUNE

♋

22 SATURDAY
Rose Festival (British)　　　　　　Moon Sign: Scorpio
Waxing Moon　　　Moon enters Sagittarius 6:42 am
Moon Phase: Second Quarter　　　　　Incense: Poplar
Color: Brown

23 SUNDAY
St. John's Eve　　　　　　Moon Sign: Sagittarius
Waxing Moon　　　　　　　　　　Incense: Basil
Moon Phase: Second Quarter
Color: Peach

☻ MONDAY
Lunar Eclipse　　　　　　Moon Sign: Sagittarius
Waxing Moon　　　Moon enters Capricorn 11:01 am
Moon Phase: Full Moon 4:42 pm　　　Incense: Myrrh
Color: White

25 TUESDAY
Fiesta of Santa Orosia (Spanish)　　Moon Sign: Capricorn
Waning Moon　　　　　　　　　　Incense: Clove
Moon Phase: Third Quarter
Color: Red

26 WEDNESDAY
Pied Piper Day (German)　　　　Moon Sign: Capricorn
Waning Moon　　　Moon enters Aquarius 5:36 pm
Moon Phase: Third Quarter　　　　　Incense: Dill
Color: Peach

27 THURSDAY
Day of the Seven Sleepers (Islamic)　Moon Sign: Aquarius
Waning Moon　　　　　　Incense: Sandalwood
Moon Phase: Third Quarter
Color: Green

28 FRIDAY
Paul Bunyan Day　　　　　　Moon Sign: Aquarius
Waning Moon　　　　　Incense: Chrysanthemum
Moon Phase: Third Quarter
Color: White

CANCER

♋

29 SATURDAY
Saints Peter's and Paul's Day　　　Moon Sign: Aquarius
Waning Moon　　　Moon enters Pisces 3:00 am
Moon Phase: Third Quarter　　　Incense: Maple
Color: Gray

30 SUNDAY
The Burning of the Three Firs (French)　　　Moon Sign: Pisces
Waning Moon　　　Incense: Nutmeg
Moon Phase: Third Quarter
Color: Gold

꙳✤꙳

AT THE CROSSROADS

Throughout old Europe, the crossroad was considered a magical place. It had its own deities, guardians, magical associations, and folklore. The most obvious reason for these assocations is the shape of the crossroad itself—that of an equal-armed cross, sometimes known as a "Sun wheel" in Europe. The Sun wheel is a symbol of perfect balance whose four end points represent the two equinoxes and solstices of the solar year.

Because of the protection symbolism of the crossroad, rites to evoke its protective powers have been held at many an isolated crossing. If you want to garner for yourself some added magical protection, take a small offering such as a coin, stone, or piece of bread, and carry it to a secluded crossroad. Go to the center of the intersection and turn to the four cardinal points (north, east, south, and west), offering your blessing. Afterward, take the offering to any corner which calls your attention and set it down. Stand and make the sign of the equal-armed cross to all four of the cardinal points. Stay still for a moment. When you feel your offering has been accepted, thank the deity of the crossroads and leave. You will have the protection of the crossroad for the next lunar month.

1   MONDAY
Passion Play at Oberammergau   Moon Sign: Pisces
Waning Moon   Moon enters Aries 2:49 pm
Moon Phase: Third Quarter   Incense: Rose
Color: Lavender

2   TUESDAY
Heroes' Day (Zambian)   Moon Sign: Aries
Waning Moon   Incense: Almond
Moon Phase: Fourth Quarter 12:19 pm
Color: White

3   WEDNESDAY
Indian Sun Dance (Native American)   Moon Sign: Aries
Waning Moon   Incense: Basil
Moon Phase: Fourth Quarter
Color: Peach

4   THURSDAY
Independence Day   Moon Sign: Aries
Waning Moon   Moon enters Taurus 3:16 am
Moon Phase: Fourth Quarter   Incense: Ginger
Color: Green

5   FRIDAY
Tynwald (Nordic)   Moon Sign: Taurus
Waning Moon   Incense: Dill
Moon Phase: Fourth Quarter
Color: Rose

6   SATURDAY
Khao Phansa Day (Thai)   Moon Sign: Taurus
Waning Moon   Moon enters Gemini 2:01 pm
Moon Phase: Fourth Quarter   Incense: Pine
Color: Gray

7   SUNDAY
Weaver's Festival (Japanese)   Moon Sign: Gemini
Waning Moon   Incense: Sandalwood
Moon Phase: Fourth Quarter
Color: Gold

8 MONDAY
St. Elizabeth's Day (Portuguese)   Moon Sign: Gemini
Waning Moon   Moon enters Cancer 9:36 pm
Moon Phase: Fourth Quarter   Incense: Daffodil
Color: Gray

9 TUESDAY
Battle of Sempach Day   Moon Sign: Cancer
Waning Moon   Incense: Gardenia
Moon Phase: Fourth Quarter
Color: White

☽ WEDNESDAY
Lady Godiva Day (English)   Moon Sign: Cancer
Waning Moon   Incense: Evergreen
Moon Phase: New Moon 5:26 am
Color: Brown

11 THURSDAY
Revolution Day (Mongolian)   Moon Sign: Cancer
Waxing Moon   Moon enters Leo 2:08 am
Moon Phase: First Quarter   Incense: Patchouli
Color: Turquoise

12 FRIDAY
Lobster Carnival (Nova Scotian)   Moon Sign: Leo
Waxing Moon   Incense: Basil
Moon Phase: First Quarter
Color: Pink

13 SATURDAY
Festival of the Three Cows   Moon Sign: Leo
Waxing Moon   Moon enters Virgo 4:41 am
Moon Phase: First Quarter   Incense: Lavender
Color: Blue

14 SUNDAY
Bastille Day (French)   Moon Sign: Virgo
Waxing Moon   Incense: Clove
Moon Phase: First Quarter
Color: Orange

♋

15 MONDAY
St. Swithin's Day   Moon Sign: Virgo
Waxing Moon   Moon enters Libra 6:39 am
Moon Phase: First Quarter   Incense: Frankincense
Color: White

○ TUESDAY
Our Lady of Carmel   Moon Sign: Libra
Waxing Moon   Incense: Evergreen
Moon Phase: Second Quarter 11:47 pm
Color: Black

17 WEDNESDAY
Rivera Day (Puerto Rican)   Moon Sign: Libra
Waxing Moon   Moon enters Scorpio 9:13 am
Moon Phase: Second Quarter   Incense: Cedar
Color: Yellow

18 THURSDAY
Gion Matsuri Festival (Japanese)   Moon Sign: Scorpio
Waxing Moon   Incense: Carnation
Moon Phase: Second Quarter
Color: White

19 FRIDAY
Flitch Day (English)   Moon Sign: Scorpio
Waxing Moon   Moon enters Sagittarius 1:02 pm
Moon Phase: Second Quarter   Incense: Coriander
Color: Peach

20 SATURDAY
Binding of Wreaths (Lithuanian)   Moon Sign: Sagittarius
Waxing Moon   Incense: Violet
Moon Phase: Second Quarter
Color: Indigo

21 SUNDAY
National Day (Belgian)   Moon Sign: Sagittarius
Waxing Moon   Moon enters Capricorn 6:26 pm
Moon Phase: Second Quarter   Incense: Eucalyptus
Color: Yellow

22 MONDAY
St. Mary Magdalene's Day
Waxing Moon
Moon Phase: Second Quarter
Color: Silver

Moon Sign: Capricorn
Sun enters Leo 7:15 pm
Incense: Clove

23 TUESDAY
Mysteries of Santa Cristina (Italian)
Waxing Moon
Moon Phase: Second Quarter
Color: Gray

Moon Sign: Capricorn
Incense: Evergreen

WEDNESDAY
Pioneer Day (Mormon)
Waxing Moon
Moon Phase: Full Moon 4:07 am
Color: Yellow

Moon Sign: Capricorn
Moon enters Aquarius 1:40 am
Incense: Sandalwood

25 THURSDAY
St. James' Day
Waning Moon
Moon Phase: Third Quarter
Color: Violet

Moon Sign: Aquarius
Incense: Jasmine

26 FRIDAY
St. Anne's Day
Waning Moon
Moon Phase: Third Quarter
Color: White

Moon Sign: Aquarius
Moon enters Pisces 11:04 am
Incense: Ylang ylang

27 SATURDAY
Sleepyhead Day (Finnish)
Waning Moon
Moon Phase: Third Quarter
Color: Brown

Moon Sign: Pisces
Incense: Pine

28 SUNDAY
Independence Day (Peruvian)
Waning Moon
Moon Phase: Third Quarter
Color: Peach

Moon Sign: Pisces
Moon enters Aries 10:39 pm
Incense: Parsley

29 MONDAY
Pardon of the Birds (French)
Waning Moon
Moon Phase: Third Quarter
Color: White

Moon Sign: Aries
Incense: Rose

30 TUESDAY
Micmac Festival of St. Ann
Waning Moon
Moon Phase: Third Quarter
Color: Red

Moon Sign: Aries
Incense: Sage

31 WEDNESDAY
Weighing of the Aga Khan
Waning Moon
Moon Phase: Third Quarter
Color: Peach

Moon Sign: Aries
Moon enters Taurus 11:17 am
Incense: Coriander

CREATE A TALKING STICK

Talking sticks have been used in Native American councils for generations. The purpose of the stick is to allow each person to state what is on his or her mind without being interrupted. To create a stick, useful in resolving conflict within your family, you may choose a part of a living tree based on the following associations:

Apple	*Honor*
Aspen	*Clarity*
Birch	*Truth*
Cedar	*Cleansing*
Cherry	*Higher Emotions*
Elm	*Wisdom*
Hazel	*Abundance*
Maple	*Gentleness*
Olive	*Peace*
Palm	*Renewal*
Redwood	*Truth*
Reed	*Harmony*
Yew	*Immortality*

LEO ♌

THURSDAY ☽
Lammas
Waning Moon
Moon Phase: Fourth Quarter 5:22 am
Color: Green
Moon Sign: Taurus
Incense: Sage

2 **FRIDAY**
Porcingula (Native American)
Waning Moon
Moon Phase: Fourth Quarter
Color: Rose
Moon Sign: Taurus
Moon enters Gemini 10:46 pm
Incense: Sandalwood

3 **SATURDAY**
Drimes (Greek)
Waning Moon
Moon Phase: Fourth Quarter
Color: Gray
Moon Sign: Gemini
Incense: Juniper

4 **SUNDAY**
Cook Islands Constitution Celebrations
Waning Moon
Moon Phase: Fourth Quarter
Color: Gold
Moon Sign: Gemini
Incense: Coriander

5 **MONDAY**
Benediction of the Sea (French)
Waning Moon
Moon Phase: Fourth Quarter
Color: Lavender
Moon Sign: Gemini
Moon enters Cancer 7:02 am
Incense: Honeysuckle

6 **TUESDAY**
Hiroshima Peace Ceremony
Waning Moon
Moon Phase: Fourth Quarter
Color: White
Moon Sign: Cancer
Incense: Lilac

7 **WEDNESDAY**
Republic Day (Ivory Coast)
Waning Moon
Moon Phase: Fourth Quarter
Color: Brown
Moon Sign: Cancer
Moon enters Leo 11:27 am
Incense: Pine

☽ **THURSDAY**
Dog Days (Japanese)
Waning Moon
Moon Phase: New Moon 2:15 pm
Color: Turquoise

Moon Sign: Leo
Incense: Musk

9 FRIDAY
Nagasaki Peace Ceremony
Waxing Moon
Moon Phase: First Quarter
Color: Pink

Moon Sign: Leo
Moon enters Virgo 1:03 pm
Incense: Thyme

10 SATURDAY
St. Lawrence's Day
Waxing Moon
Moon Phase: First Quarter
Color: Blue

Moon Sign: Virgo
Incense: Lilac

11 SUNDAY
Puck Fair (Irish)
Waxing Moon
Moon Phase: First Quarter
Color: Orange

Moon Sign: Virgo
Moon enters Libra 1:38 pm
Incense: Clove

12 MONDAY
Fiesta of Santa Clara
Waxing Moon
Moon Phase: First Quarter
Color: Gray

Moon Sign: Libra
Incense: Cedar

13 TUESDAY
Women's Day (Tunisian)
Waxing Moon
Moon Phase: First Quarter
Color: Black

Moon Sign: Libra
Moon enters Scorpio 3:01 pm
Incense: Juniper

14 WEDNESDAY
Festival at Sassari
Waxing Moon
Moon Phase: First Quarter
Color: White

Moon Sign: Scorpio
Incense: Neroli

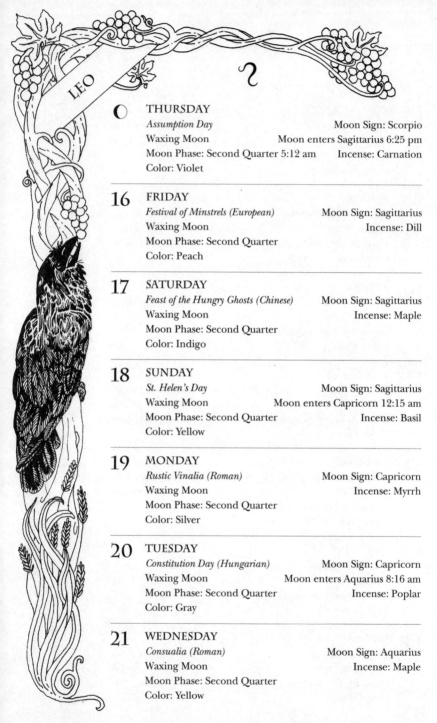

LEO ♌

☽ THURSDAY
Assumption Day   Moon Sign: Scorpio
Waxing Moon   Moon enters Sagittarius 6:25 pm
Moon Phase: Second Quarter 5:12 am   Incense: Carnation
Color: Violet

16 FRIDAY
Festival of Minstrels (European)   Moon Sign: Sagittarius
Waxing Moon   Incense: Dill
Moon Phase: Second Quarter
Color: Peach

17 SATURDAY
Feast of the Hungry Ghosts (Chinese)   Moon Sign: Sagittarius
Waxing Moon   Incense: Maple
Moon Phase: Second Quarter
Color: Indigo

18 SUNDAY
St. Helen's Day   Moon Sign: Sagittarius
Waxing Moon   Moon enters Capricorn 12:15 am
Moon Phase: Second Quarter   Incense: Basil
Color: Yellow

19 MONDAY
Rustic Vinalia (Roman)   Moon Sign: Capricorn
Waxing Moon   Incense: Myrrh
Moon Phase: Second Quarter
Color: Silver

20 TUESDAY
Constitution Day (Hungarian)   Moon Sign: Capricorn
Waxing Moon   Moon enters Aquarius 8:16 am
Moon Phase: Second Quarter   Incense: Poplar
Color: Gray

21 WEDNESDAY
Consualia (Roman)   Moon Sign: Aquarius
Waxing Moon   Incense: Maple
Moon Phase: Second Quarter
Color: Yellow

☺ **THURSDAY**
Feast of the Queenship of Mary (British)   Moon Sign: Aquarius
Waxing Moon   Moon enters Pisces 6:11 pm
Moon Phase: Full Moon 5:29 pm   Incense: Dill
Color: Green

23 FRIDAY
National Day (Romanian)   Moon Sign: Pisces
Waning Moon   Sun enters Virgo 2:17 am
Moon Phase: Third Quarter   Incense: Parsley
Color: Green

24 SATURDAY
St. Bartholomew's Day   Moon Sign: Pisces
Waning Moon   Incense: Cedar
Moon Phase: Third Quarter
Color: Gray

25 SUNDAY
Feast of the Green Corn (Native American)   Moon Sign: Pisces
Waning Moon   Moon enters Aries 5:48 am
Moon Phase: Third Quarter   Incense: Cinnamon
Color: Gold

26 MONDAY
Pardon of the Sea (French)   Moon Sign: Aries
Waning Moon   Incense: Lilac
Moon Phase: Third Quarter
Color: Lavender

27 TUESDAY
Summer Break (British)   Moon Sign: Aries
Waning Moon   Moon enters Taurus 6:32 pm
Moon Phase: Third Quarter   Incense: Ginger
Color: Red

28 WEDNESDAY
St. Augustine's Day   Moon Sign: Taurus
Waning Moon   Incense: Thyme
Moon Phase: Third Quarter
Color: Peach

♍

29 THURSDAY
St. John's Beheading   Moon Sign: Taurus
Waning Moon   Incense: Evergreen
Moon Phase: Third Quarter
Color: Turquoise

☽ FRIDAY
St. Rose of Lima Day (Peruvian)   Moon Sign: Taurus
Waning Moon   Moon enters Gemini 6:45 am
Moon Phase: Fourth Quarter 9:31 pm   Incense: Ginger
Color: Pink

31 SATURDAY
Unto These Hills Pageant (Cherokee)   Moon Sign: Gemini
Waning Moon   Incense: Violet
Moon Phase: Fourth Quarter
Color: Blue

❧

ANCIENT HERBAL SPELLS

• Place thorny rose branches on the front doorstep to keep evil far from your abode.

• Consuming a bit of wild thyme before retiring will grant the diner a sleep free from nightmares.

• Keep money with cedar chips in a small box to attract yet more money.

• To discover the future, take two acorns. Name one "yes," the other "no." Place them in a basin of water and ask your question. The acorn that floats toward you indicates the answer.

• Gather the first anemone flower to bloom in spring and carry it with you as a charm against sickness.

• To keep evil spirits from the house, hang dried seaweed in the kitchen.

1 SUNDAY
New Year's Day (Greek)
Waning Moon
Moon Phase: Fourth Quarter
Color: Orange

Moon Sign: Gemini
Moon enters Cancer 4:14 pm
Incense: Parsley

2 MONDAY
Labor Day
Waning Moon
Moon Phase: Fourth Quarter
Color: Gray

Moon Sign: Cancer
Incense: Maple

3 TUESDAY
Founder's Day (San Marino)
Waning Moon
Moon Phase: Fourth Quarter
Color: Black

Moon Sign: Cancer
Moon enters Leo 9:36 pm
Incense: Poplar

4 WEDNESDAY
Los Angeles' Birthday
Waning Moon
Moon Phase: Fourth Quarter
Color: Brown

Moon Sign: Leo
Incense: Eucalyptus

5 THURSDAY
Roman Circus
Waning Moon
Moon Phase: Fourth Quarter
Color: White

Moon Sign: Leo
Moon enters Virgo 11:16 pm
Incense: Chrysanthemum

☽ FRIDAY
Virgin of the Remedies (Mexican)
Waning Moon
Moon Phase: New Moon 10:10 pm
Color: Peach

Moon Sign: Virgo
Incense: Nutmeg

7 SATURDAY
Rosh Hashanah
Waxing Moon
Moon Phase: First Quarter
Color: Indigo

Moon Sign: Virgo
Moon enters Libra 10:57 pm
Incense: Jasmine

VIRGO ♍

8 SUNDAY
Birthday of the Virgin Mary
Waxing Moon
Moon Phase: First Quarter
Color: Yellow

Moon Sign: Libra
Incense: Poplar

9 MONDAY
Chrysanthemum Festival (Japanese)
Waxing Moon
Moon Phase: First Quarter
Color: Silver

Moon Sign: Libra
Moon enters Scorpio 10:48 pm
Incense: Nutmeg

10 TUESDAY
Festival of the Poets (Japanese)
Waxing Moon
Moon Phase: First Quarter
Color: White

Moon Sign: Scorpio
Incense: Vanilla

11 WEDNESDAY
Coptic New Year
Waxing Moon
Moon Phase: First Quarter
Color: Yellow

Moon Sign: Scorpio
Incense: Cedar

12 THURSDAY
National Day (Ethiopian)
Waxing Moon
Moon Phase: First Quarter
Color: Green

Moon Sign: Scorpio
Moon enters Sagittarius 12:44 am
Incense: Sandalwood

☾ FRIDAY
The Gods' Banquet (Roman)
Waxing Moon
Moon Phase: Second Quarter 1:08 pm
Color: White

Moon Sign: Sagittarius
Incense: Chrysanthemum

14 SATURDAY
Holy Cross Day
Waxing Moon
Moon Phase: Second Quarter
Color: Brown

Moon Sign: Sagittarius
Moon enters Capricorn 5:47 am
Incense: Poplar

♍

15 SUNDAY
Birthday of the Moon (Chinese)
Waxing Moon
Moon Phase: Second Quarter
Color: Peach

Moon Sign: Capricorn
Incense: Basil

16 MONDAY
Yom Kippur
Waxing Moon
Moon Phase: Second Quarter
Color: White

Moon Sign: Capricorn
Moon enters Aquarius 1:54 pm
Incense: Myrrh

17 TUESDAY
Von Steuben's Day
Waxing Moon
Moon Phase: Second Quarter
Color: Red

Moon Sign: Aquarius
Incense: Clove

18 WEDNESDAY
Dr. Johnson's Birthday
Waxing Moon
Moon Phase: Second Quarter
Color: Peach

Moon Sign: Aquarius
Incense: Dill

19 THURSDAY
St. Januarius' Day (Italian)
Waxing Moon
Moon Phase: Second Quarter
Color: White

Moon Sign: Aquarius
Moon enters Pisces 12:18 am
Incense: Carnation

20 FRIDAY
St. Eustace's Day
Waxing Moon
Moon Phase: Second Quarter
Color: Rose

Moon Sign: Pisces
Incense: Sandalwood

☺ SATURDAY
Sukkot begins
Waxing Moon
Moon Phase: Full Moon 8:59 am
Color: Gray

Moon Sign: Pisces
Moon enters Aries 12:11 pm
Incense: Maple

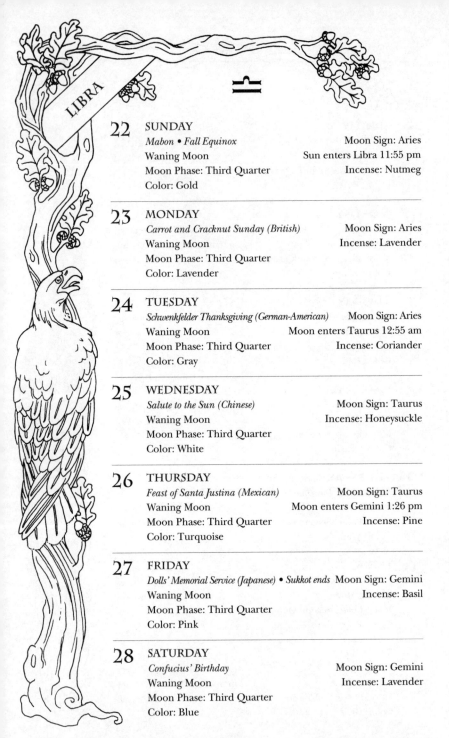

LIBRA ♎

22 SUNDAY
Mabon • Fall Equinox
Waning Moon
Moon Phase: Third Quarter
Color: Gold

Moon Sign: Aries
Sun enters Libra 11:55 pm
Incense: Nutmeg

23 MONDAY
Carrot and Cracknut Sunday (British)
Waning Moon
Moon Phase: Third Quarter
Color: Lavender

Moon Sign: Aries
Incense: Lavender

24 TUESDAY
Schwenkfelder Thanksgiving (German-American)
Waning Moon
Moon Phase: Third Quarter
Color: Gray

Moon Sign: Aries
Moon enters Taurus 12:55 am
Incense: Coriander

25 WEDNESDAY
Salute to the Sun (Chinese)
Waning Moon
Moon Phase: Third Quarter
Color: White

Moon Sign: Taurus
Incense: Honeysuckle

26 THURSDAY
Feast of Santa Justina (Mexican)
Waning Moon
Moon Phase: Third Quarter
Color: Turquoise

Moon Sign: Taurus
Moon enters Gemini 1:26 pm
Incense: Pine

27 FRIDAY
Dolls' Memorial Service (Japanese) • Sukkot ends
Waning Moon
Moon Phase: Third Quarter
Color: Pink

Moon Sign: Gemini
Incense: Basil

28 SATURDAY
Confucius' Birthday
Waning Moon
Moon Phase: Third Quarter
Color: Blue

Moon Sign: Gemini
Incense: Lavender

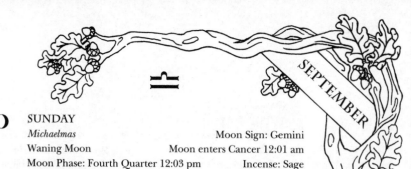

SUNDAY
Michaelmas
Waning Moon
Moon Phase: Fourth Quarter 12:03 pm
Color: Orange

Moon Sign: Gemini
Moon enters Cancer 12:01 am
Incense: Sage

30 MONDAY
St. Jerome's Day
Waning Moon
Moon Phase: Fourth Quarter
Color: Gray

Moon Sign: Cancer
Incense: Pine

YOUR MAGICAL JEWELS

Precious gems are treasured for their beauty, but there is more to gemstones than meets the eye. They have very real power to affect our moods and general health in subtle unseen ways. Every atom of the universe is in constant motion, and everything in existence vibrates to its own unique rhythm. The rate of vibration varies from one substance to another. Hard objects have regular vibrations, and soft objects irregular. Gems and crystals are very hard, and their atoms vibrate at a very predictable rate—so predictable that we can use quartz crystals to regulate our timepieces. We can also regulate the atoms in our own bodies just by using a gem.

For this, do not buy a new jewel. Rather, gems are more powerful when received as a gift or inheritance. If you have one, wash it, dry it in sunlight, then wear it and feel your outlook becoming more positive as harmony flows into your life. A good way of selecting the best stone for you is to allow your intuition to make the choice. Just use the gem you feel drawn to. This might be different according to your mood or circumstances. Follow your instincts and you will feel the magic.

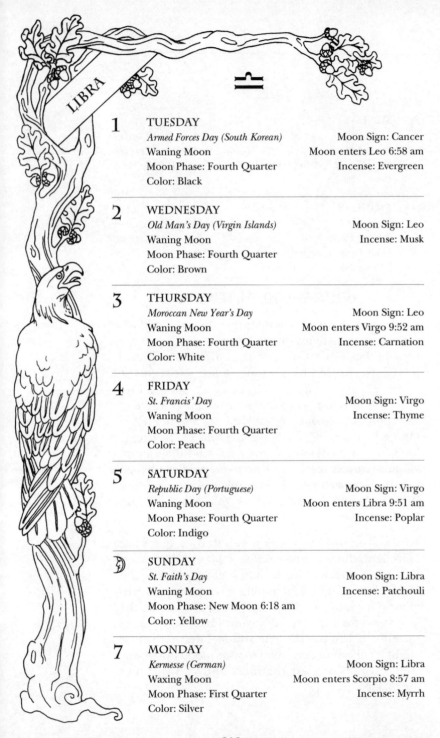

LIBRA ♎

1 TUESDAY
Armed Forces Day (South Korean)
Waning Moon
Moon Phase: Fourth Quarter
Color: Black

Moon Sign: Cancer
Moon enters Leo 6:58 am
Incense: Evergreen

2 WEDNESDAY
Old Man's Day (Virgin Islands)
Waning Moon
Moon Phase: Fourth Quarter
Color: Brown

Moon Sign: Leo
Incense: Musk

3 THURSDAY
Moroccan New Year's Day
Waning Moon
Moon Phase: Fourth Quarter
Color: White

Moon Sign: Leo
Moon enters Virgo 9:52 am
Incense: Carnation

4 FRIDAY
St. Francis' Day
Waning Moon
Moon Phase: Fourth Quarter
Color: Peach

Moon Sign: Virgo
Incense: Thyme

5 SATURDAY
Republic Day (Portuguese)
Waning Moon
Moon Phase: Fourth Quarter
Color: Indigo

Moon Sign: Virgo
Moon enters Libra 9:51 am
Incense: Poplar

☽ SUNDAY
St. Faith's Day
Waning Moon
Moon Phase: New Moon 6:18 am
Color: Yellow

Moon Sign: Libra
Incense: Patchouli

7 MONDAY
Kermesse (German)
Waxing Moon
Moon Phase: First Quarter
Color: Silver

Moon Sign: Libra
Moon enters Scorpio 8:57 am
Incense: Myrrh

8 TUESDAY

Okunchi (Japanese)
Waxing Moon
Moon Phase: First Quarter
Color: Gray

Moon Sign: Scorpio
Incense: Pine

9 WEDNESDAY

Alphabet Day (South Korean)
Waxing Moon
Moon Phase: First Quarter
Color: Yellow

Moon Sign: Scorpio
Moon enters Sagittarius 9:21 am
Incense: Poplar

10 THURSDAY

Health Day (Japanese)
Waxing Moon
Moon Phase: First Quarter
Color: Violet

Moon Sign: Sagittarius
Incense: Gardenia

11 FRIDAY

Medetrinalia (Roman)
Waxing Moon
Moon Phase: First Quarter
Color: White

Moon Sign: Sagittarius
Moon enters Capricorn 12:45 pm
Incense: Violet

12 SATURDAY

National Day (Spanish)
Waxing Moon
Moon Phase: First Quarter
Color: Brown

Moon Sign: Capricorn
Incense: Musk

◖ SUNDAY

Floating of the Lamps (Thai)
Waxing Moon
Moon Phase: Second Quarter 12:33 am
Color: Peach

Moon Sign: Capricorn
Moon enters Aquarius 7:51 pm
Incense: Coriander

14 MONDAY

Columbus Day (observed)
Waxing Moon
Moon Phase: Second Quarter
Color: White

Moon Sign: Aquarius
Incense: Frankincense

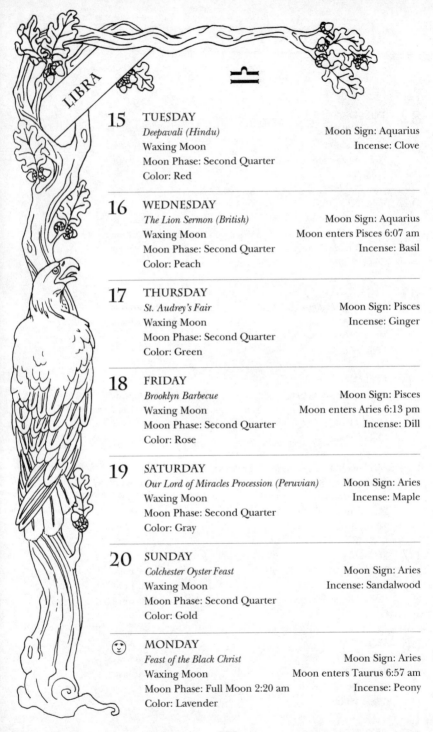

LIBRA

♎

15 TUESDAY
Deepavali (Hindu)
Waxing Moon
Moon Phase: Second Quarter
Color: Red

Moon Sign: Aquarius
Incense: Clove

16 WEDNESDAY
The Lion Sermon (British)
Waxing Moon
Moon Phase: Second Quarter
Color: Peach

Moon Sign: Aquarius
Moon enters Pisces 6:07 am
Incense: Basil

17 THURSDAY
St. Audrey's Fair
Waxing Moon
Moon Phase: Second Quarter
Color: Green

Moon Sign: Pisces
Incense: Ginger

18 FRIDAY
Brooklyn Barbecue
Waxing Moon
Moon Phase: Second Quarter
Color: Rose

Moon Sign: Pisces
Moon enters Aries 6:13 pm
Incense: Dill

19 SATURDAY
Our Lord of Miracles Procession (Peruvian)
Waxing Moon
Moon Phase: Second Quarter
Color: Gray

Moon Sign: Aries
Incense: Maple

20 SUNDAY
Colchester Oyster Feast
Waxing Moon
Moon Phase: Second Quarter
Color: Gold

Moon Sign: Aries
Incense: Sandalwood

☻ **MONDAY**
Feast of the Black Christ
Waxing Moon
Moon Phase: Full Moon 2:20 am
Color: Lavender

Moon Sign: Aries
Moon enters Taurus 6:57 am
Incense: Peony

220

22 TUESDAY
Goddess of Mercy Day (Chinese)
Waning Moon
Moon Phase: Third Quarter
Color: White

Moon Sign: Taurus
Incense: Almond

23 WEDNESDAY
Revolution Day (Hungarian)
Waning Moon
Moon Phase: Third Quarter
Color: Brown

Moon Sign: Taurus
Sun enters Scorpio 9:18 am
Moon enters Gemini 7:17 pm
Incense: Evergreen

24 THURSDAY
United Nations Day
Waning Moon
Moon Phase: Third Quarter
Color: White

Moon Sign: Gemini
Incense: Almond

25 FRIDAY
St. Crispin's Day
Waning Moon
Moon Phase: Third Quarter
Color: Pink

Moon Sign: Gemini
Incense: Basil

26 SATURDAY
National Day (Austrian)
Waning Moon
Moon Phase: Third Quarter
Color: Blue

Moon Sign: Gemini
Moon enters Cancer 6:10 am
Incense: Peony

27 SUNDAY
Daylight Saving Time ends at 2:00 am
Waning Moon
Moon Phase: Third Quarter
Color: Orange

Moon Sign: Cancer
Incense: Clove

28 MONDAY
Ochi Day (Greek)
Waning Moon
Moon Phase: Third Quarter
Color: Gray

Moon Sign: Cancer
Moon enters Leo 2:20 pm
Incense: Daffodil

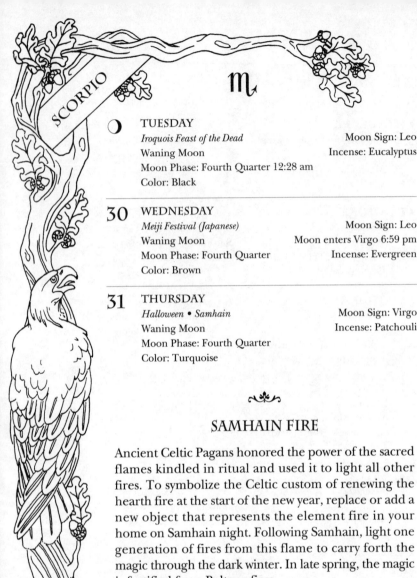

♏

TUESDAY
Iroquois Feast of the Dead
Moon Sign: Leo
Waning Moon
Incense: Eucalyptus
Moon Phase: Fourth Quarter 12:28 am
Color: Black

30 WEDNESDAY
Meiji Festival (Japanese)
Moon Sign: Leo
Waning Moon
Moon enters Virgo 6:59 pm
Moon Phase: Fourth Quarter
Incense: Evergreen
Color: Brown

31 THURSDAY
Halloween • Samhain
Moon Sign: Virgo
Waning Moon
Incense: Patchouli
Moon Phase: Fourth Quarter
Color: Turquoise

❧✥☙

SAMHAIN FIRE

Ancient Celtic Pagans honored the power of the sacred
flames kindled in ritual and used it to light all other
fires. To symbolize the Celtic custom of renewing the
hearth fire at the start of the new year, replace or add a
new object that represents the element fire in your
home on Samhain night. Following Samhain, light one
generation of fires from this flame to carry forth the
magic through the dark winter. In late spring, the magic
is fortified from Beltane fires.

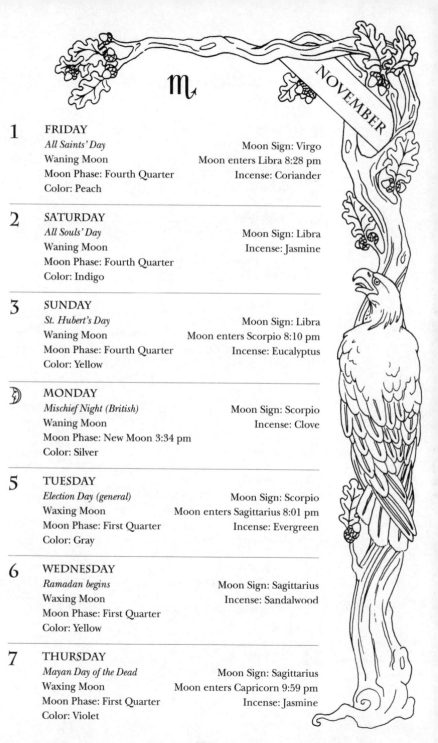

♏

1 FRIDAY
All Saints' Day
Waning Moon
Moon Phase: Fourth Quarter
Color: Peach

Moon Sign: Virgo
Moon enters Libra 8:28 pm
Incense: Coriander

2 SATURDAY
All Souls' Day
Waning Moon
Moon Phase: Fourth Quarter
Color: Indigo

Moon Sign: Libra
Incense: Jasmine

3 SUNDAY
St. Hubert's Day
Waning Moon
Moon Phase: Fourth Quarter
Color: Yellow

Moon Sign: Libra
Moon enters Scorpio 8:10 pm
Incense: Eucalyptus

MONDAY
Mischief Night (British)
Waning Moon
Moon Phase: New Moon 3:34 pm
Color: Silver

Moon Sign: Scorpio
Incense: Clove

5 TUESDAY
Election Day (general)
Waxing Moon
Moon Phase: First Quarter
Color: Gray

Moon Sign: Scorpio
Moon enters Sagittarius 8:01 pm
Incense: Evergreen

6 WEDNESDAY
Ramadan begins
Waxing Moon
Moon Phase: First Quarter
Color: Yellow

Moon Sign: Sagittarius
Incense: Sandalwood

7 THURSDAY
Mayan Day of the Dead
Waxing Moon
Moon Phase: First Quarter
Color: Violet

Moon Sign: Sagittarius
Moon enters Capricorn 9:59 pm
Incense: Jasmine

8 FRIDAY
Queen's Birthday (Nepalese)
Waxing Moon
Moon Phase: First Quarter
Color: White

Moon Sign: Capricorn
Incense: Ylang ylang

---

9 SATURDAY
Lord Mayor's Day (English)
Waxing Moon
Moon Phase: First Quarter
Color: Brown

Moon Sign: Capricorn
Incense: Pine

---

10 SUNDAY
Martin Luther's Birthday
Waxing Moon
Moon Phase: First Quarter
Color: Peach

Moon Sign: Capricorn
Moon enters Aquarius 3:27 am
Incense: Parsley

☾ MONDAY
Veterans Day
Waxing Moon
Moon Phase: Second Quarter 3:52 pm
Color: White

Moon Sign: Aquarius
Incense: Rose

---

12 TUESDAY
Tesuque Feast Day (Native American)
Waxing Moon
Moon Phase: Second Quarter
Color: Red

Moon Sign: Aquarius
Moon enters Pisces 12:42 pm
Incense: Sage

---

13 WEDNESDAY
Festival of Jupiter (Roman)
Waxing Moon
Moon Phase: Second Quarter
Color: Peach

Moon Sign: Pisces
Incense: Coriander

---

14 THURSDAY
The Little Carnival (Greek)
Waxing Moon
Moon Phase: Second Quarter
Color: Green

Moon Sign: Pisces
Incense: Sage

♏ ♐

15 FRIDAY
St. Leopold's Day   Moon Sign: Pisces
Waxing Moon   Moon enters Aries 12:38 am
Moon Phase: Second Quarter   Incense: Sandalwood
Color: Rose

16 SATURDAY
St. Margaret of Scotland's Day   Moon Sign: Aries
Waxing Moon   Incense: Juniper
Moon Phase: Second Quarter
Color: Gray

17 SUNDAY
Queen Elizabeth's Day   Moon Sign: Aries
Waxing Moon   Moon enters Taurus 1:23 pm
Moon Phase: Second Quarter   Incense: Coriander
Color: Gold

18 MONDAY
St. Plato's Day   Moon Sign: Taurus
Waxing Moon   Incense: Honeysuckle
Moon Phase: Second Quarter
Color: Lavender

☺ TUESDAY
Lunar Eclipse   Moon Sign: Taurus
Waxing Moon   Incense: Lilac
Moon Phase: Full Moon 8:34 pm
Color: White

20 WEDNESDAY
Revolution Day (Mexican)   Moon Sign: Taurus
Waning Moon   Moon enters Gemini 1:25 am
Moon Phase: Third Quarter   Incense: Pine
Color: Brown

21 THURSDAY
Repentance Day (German)   Moon Sign: Gemini
Waning Moon   Incense: Musk
Moon Phase: Third Quarter
Color: Turquoise

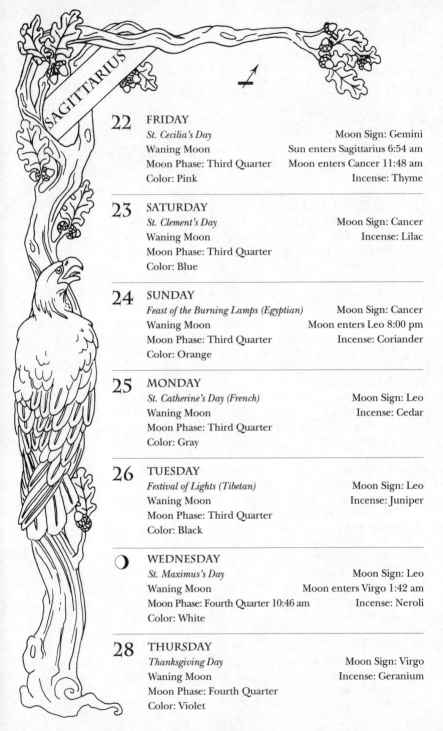

22 FRIDAY
St. Cecilia's Day — Moon Sign: Gemini
Waning Moon — Sun enters Sagittarius 6:54 am
Moon Phase: Third Quarter — Moon enters Cancer 11:48 am
Color: Pink — Incense: Thyme

23 SATURDAY
St. Clement's Day — Moon Sign: Cancer
Waning Moon — Incense: Lilac
Moon Phase: Third Quarter
Color: Blue

24 SUNDAY
Feast of the Burning Lamps (Egyptian) — Moon Sign: Cancer
Waning Moon — Moon enters Leo 8:00 pm
Moon Phase: Third Quarter — Incense: Coriander
Color: Orange

25 MONDAY
St. Catherine's Day (French) — Moon Sign: Leo
Waning Moon — Incense: Cedar
Moon Phase: Third Quarter
Color: Gray

26 TUESDAY
Festival of Lights (Tibetan) — Moon Sign: Leo
Waning Moon — Incense: Juniper
Moon Phase: Third Quarter
Color: Black

○ WEDNESDAY
St. Maximus's Day — Moon Sign: Leo
Waning Moon — Moon enters Virgo 1:42 am
Moon Phase: Fourth Quarter 10:46 am — Incense: Neroli
Color: White

28 THURSDAY
Thanksgiving Day — Moon Sign: Virgo
Waning Moon — Incense: Geranium
Moon Phase: Fourth Quarter
Color: Violet

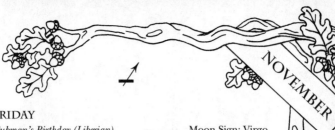

29 **FRIDAY**
Tubman's Birthday (Liberian)   Moon Sign: Virgo
Waning Moon   Moon enters Libra 4:54 am
Moon Phase: Fourth Quarter   Incense: Dill
Color: Peach

30 **SATURDAY**
Hanukkah begins   Moon Sign: Libra
Waning Moon   Incense: Maple
Moon Phase: Fourth Quarter
Color: Indigo

THE LORE OF MONEY

*Here are some delightful "old wisdoms," lore,
and spells concerning cash:*

- Always keep a few coins in your home when leaving for a journey. To do otherwise bodes ill.

- If you drop any money in the home, say: "Money on the floor, money at the door." Step on the money and pick it up; more will come to you.

- Finding money is fortunate, but to keep such money invites misfortune. Spend it as quickly as possible, and tell no one of its origin.

- Never leave the house without at least one coin in your pocket or handbag. The best charm of all is a bent coin or a coin pierced with a hole. These coins are both "lucky" and protective.

- If you fold your bills, fold them toward you to indicate that money will come to you. Folding money away from you will result in its absence.

- To ensure that you will always have money and friends, tie a string into a circle and keep it in your pocket, wallet, or purse.

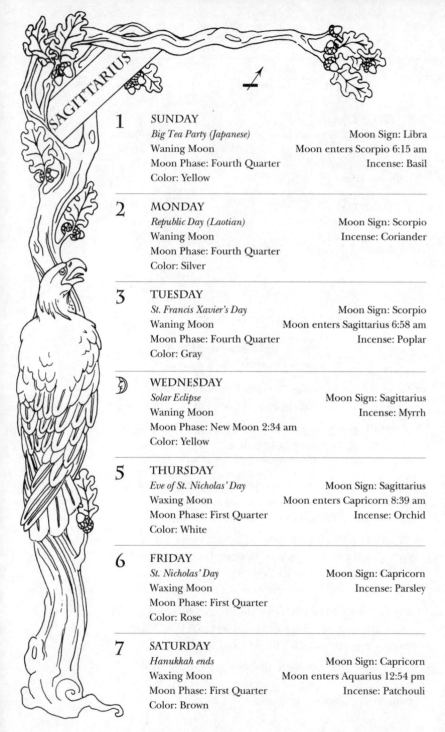

1 SUNDAY
Big Tea Party (Japanese)
Waning Moon
Moon Phase: Fourth Quarter
Color: Yellow

Moon Sign: Libra
Moon enters Scorpio 6:15 am
Incense: Basil

2 MONDAY
Republic Day (Laotian)
Waning Moon
Moon Phase: Fourth Quarter
Color: Silver

Moon Sign: Scorpio
Incense: Coriander

3 TUESDAY
St. Francis Xavier's Day
Waning Moon
Moon Phase: Fourth Quarter
Color: Gray

Moon Sign: Scorpio
Moon enters Sagittarius 6:58 am
Incense: Poplar

4 WEDNESDAY
Solar Eclipse
Waning Moon
Moon Phase: New Moon 2:34 am
Color: Yellow

Moon Sign: Sagittarius
Incense: Myrrh

5 THURSDAY
Eve of St. Nicholas' Day
Waxing Moon
Moon Phase: First Quarter
Color: White

Moon Sign: Sagittarius
Moon enters Capricorn 8:39 am
Incense: Orchid

6 FRIDAY
St. Nicholas' Day
Waxing Moon
Moon Phase: First Quarter
Color: Rose

Moon Sign: Capricorn
Incense: Parsley

7 SATURDAY
Hanukkah ends
Waxing Moon
Moon Phase: First Quarter
Color: Brown

Moon Sign: Capricorn
Moon enters Aquarius 12:54 pm
Incense: Patchouli

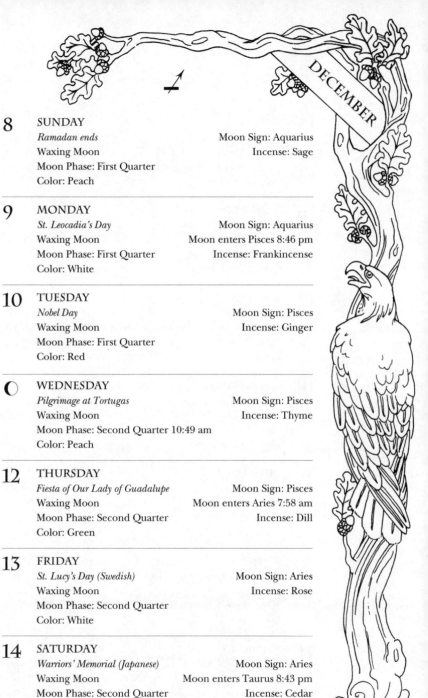

8 SUNDAY
Ramadan ends
Waxing Moon
Moon Phase: First Quarter
Color: Peach

Moon Sign: Aquarius
Incense: Sage

9 MONDAY
St. Leocadia's Day
Waxing Moon
Moon Phase: First Quarter
Color: White

Moon Sign: Aquarius
Moon enters Pisces 8:46 pm
Incense: Frankincense

10 TUESDAY
Nobel Day
Waxing Moon
Moon Phase: First Quarter
Color: Red

Moon Sign: Pisces
Incense: Ginger

☽ WEDNESDAY
Pilgrimage at Tortugas
Waxing Moon
Moon Phase: Second Quarter 10:49 am
Color: Peach

Moon Sign: Pisces
Incense: Thyme

12 THURSDAY
Fiesta of Our Lady of Guadalupe
Waxing Moon
Moon Phase: Second Quarter
Color: Green

Moon Sign: Pisces
Moon enters Aries 7:58 am
Incense: Dill

13 FRIDAY
St. Lucy's Day (Swedish)
Waxing Moon
Moon Phase: Second Quarter
Color: White

Moon Sign: Aries
Incense: Rose

14 SATURDAY
Warriors' Memorial (Japanese)
Waxing Moon
Moon Phase: Second Quarter
Color: Gray

Moon Sign: Aries
Moon enters Taurus 8:43 pm
Incense: Cedar

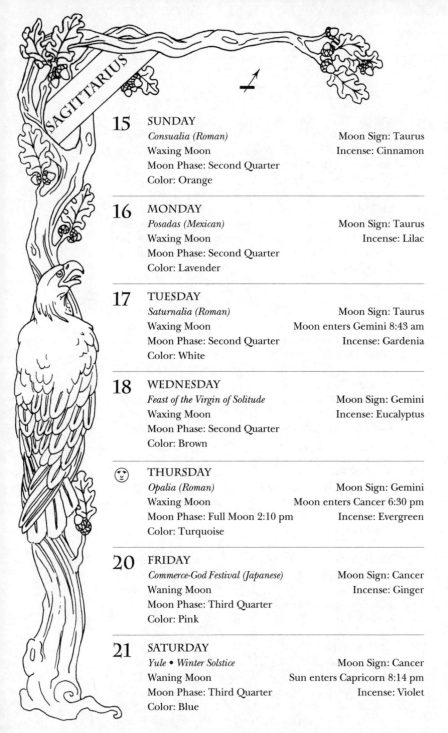

15 SUNDAY
Consualia (Roman)
Waxing Moon
Moon Phase: Second Quarter
Color: Orange

Moon Sign: Taurus
Incense: Cinnamon

16 MONDAY
Posadas (Mexican)
Waxing Moon
Moon Phase: Second Quarter
Color: Lavender

Moon Sign: Taurus
Incense: Lilac

17 TUESDAY
Saturnalia (Roman)
Waxing Moon
Moon Phase: Second Quarter
Color: White

Moon Sign: Taurus
Moon enters Gemini 8:43 am
Incense: Gardenia

18 WEDNESDAY
Feast of the Virgin of Solitude
Waxing Moon
Moon Phase: Second Quarter
Color: Brown

Moon Sign: Gemini
Incense: Eucalyptus

THURSDAY
Opalia (Roman)
Waxing Moon
Moon Phase: Full Moon 2:10 pm
Color: Turquoise

Moon Sign: Gemini
Moon enters Cancer 6:30 pm
Incense: Evergreen

20 FRIDAY
Commerce-God Festival (Japanese)
Waning Moon
Moon Phase: Third Quarter
Color: Pink

Moon Sign: Cancer
Incense: Ginger

21 SATURDAY
Yule • Winter Solstice
Waning Moon
Moon Phase: Third Quarter
Color: Blue

Moon Sign: Cancer
Sun enters Capricorn 8:14 pm
Incense: Violet

230

♑

22   SUNDAY
Fiesta of Santo Tomas (Guatemalan)   Moon Sign: Cancer
Waning Moon   Moon enters Leo 1:48 am
Moon Phase: Third Quarter   Incense: Parsley
Color: Orange

23   MONDAY
Larentalia (Roman)   Moon Sign: Leo
Waning Moon   Incense: Daffodil
Moon Phase: Third Quarter
Color: Gray

24   TUESDAY
Christmas Eve   Moon Sign: Leo
Waning Moon   Moon enters Virgo 7:05 am
Moon Phase: Third Quarter   Incense: Poplar
Color: Black

25   WEDNESDAY
Christmas Day   Moon Sign: Virgo
Waning Moon   Incense: Eucalyptus
Moon Phase: Third Quarter
Color: Brown

○   THURSDAY
Kwanzaa begins   Moon Sign: Virgo
Waning Moon   Moon enters Libra 10:53 am
Moon Phase: Fourth Quarter 7:31 pm   Incense: Carnation
Color: White

27   FRIDAY
Feast of St. John the Evangelist   Moon Sign: Libra
Waning Moon   Incense: Nutmeg
Moon Phase: Fourth Quarter
Color: Peach

28   SATURDAY
Holy Innocents' Day   Moon Sign: Libra
Waning Moon   Moon enters Scorpio 1:41 pm
Moon Phase: Fourth Quarter   Incense: Jasmine
Color: Indigo

♑

29 SUNDAY

St. Thomas à Becket
Waning Moon
Moon Phase: Fourth Quarter
Color: Yellow

Moon Sign: Scorpio
Incense: Poplar

30 MONDAY

Republic Day (Madagascar)
Waning Moon
Moon Phase: Fourth Quarter
Color: Silver

Moon Sign: Scorpio
Moon enters Sagittarius 4:01 pm
Incense: Nutmeg

31 TUESDAY

New Year's Eve
Waning Moon
Moon Phase: Fourth Quarter
Color: Gray

Moon Sign: Sagittarius
Incense: Pine

~❦~

GIFT SHOWER SPELL

Who doesn't like to be showered with gifts? This is a
luxurious spell that will help bring you everything your
heart desires. To start, you'll need a gold-colored
candle, a sweet fragrant oil (rose or jasmine, for
example), white sugar, and a string of pearls. Roll the
candle in the oil and sugar and allow it to dry hard.
Place it in a candleholder and wind the string of pearls
around the bottom of the candle. As you light it, say to
your admirer, "I am special and deserving. Show your
love for me in ways to see." Then sit and visualize your
admirer presenting you with gifts, and you opening
them with glee.

PICKLED WATERMELON RINDS

BY CHANDRA BEAL

Pickled watermelon rind is an old-fashioned summer favorite and the perfect weekend project. You can serve these sweet rinds just like any other pickle.

¼ cup pickling or non-iodized salt

8 cups cold water (or more to cover rinds)

4 quarts 1-inch cubes of pared watermelon rind

1 piece of gingerroot

3 sticks cinnamon, broken

2 tbsp whole cloves

8 cups cider vinegar

9 cups sugar

Cheesecloth

To pare the rind, use a sharp vegetable peeler. Watermelon rinds are very tough, so be certain that no green skin is remaining. Dissolve the salt in cold water and pour over the watermelon rinds in a Dutch oven. Let it stand in a cool place for eight hours.

Drain the rinds, then cover with fresh cold water. Heat to boiling and cook until tender, about 10–15 minutes. Drain again. Tie the spices in a cheesecloth bag and heat with vinegar and sugar to boiling. Cook five minutes, then reduce heat and add rinds. Simmer uncovered for 1 hour. Remove the cheesecloth bag. When the rinds are ready, immediately pack the mixture into hot clean canning jars, leaving ¼-inch headspace. Wipe the rims of the jars, seal, and process in a boiling water bath for 10 minutes. Let the jars cool, then test the seal. They can be enjoyed for a couple weeks if kept in the fridge. The recipe makes 7 or 8 pints.

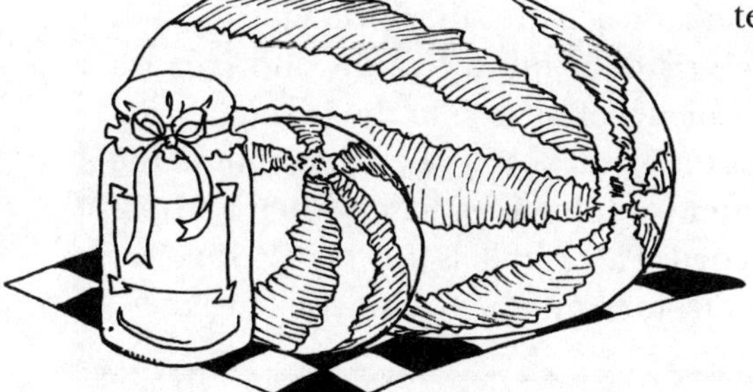

EXERCISE AND MAGIC

BY DIANA RAJCHEL

M ost people know about the physical benefits of exercise. It feels great and promotes overall well-being. But recent studies also suggest that people who exercise regularly think better and more clearly than those who do not.

In fact, the benefits of exercise might at last be a reason for us bookish occultists to set down our dusty tomes and go for a walk. To be sure, the necessity of physical activity has not been totally ignored in esoteric studies. Many occult texts do suggest that dietary and physical adjustments will produce better results. Yet most texts only mention this idea but once, and few point to exercise as part of an integrative practice.

The esoteric integrative approach to exercise suggests that keeping the body in optimal aesthetic condition allows the mind and body to work together. This union of the physical and nonphysical self allows the spirit to part temporarily from the body—encouraging for such work as astral projection and shamanic trance work—while the body cushions both the physical and spiritual stress of the activity. As a person exercises, he or she has increasing awareness of where the aura and the body meet and develops control and strength over this area.

Exercising releases chemicals within the brain and body. These chemicals, called endorphins, can produce a "high," much like that produced in ecstatic meditation. Endorphins enhance the performance of the body and serve to increase your ability to think and concentrate. With regular exercise, you will gain stamina useful in difficult ritual processes. An occultist needs to think in a better-than-average manner. Practicing the arcane arts demands a healthy and creative mind. A fit body sends plenty of oxygen to the brain.

Exercise also helps the astral body to better anchor in the physical body during times of illness, precisely when a strong astral body is most needed. This parallels the increased power of the immune system from exercise. To some extent, these magical benefits will occur naturally in an exercise process. Meditation and visualization act as "weights" to increase resistance and to further condition the astral body.

The process of exercise also enhances the physical aura—the stronger the body, the stronger the aura. A strong aura can aid in both channeling large amounts of energy, and is particularly useful in drawing-down rituals. A strong aura can also aid in shielding and in other protective measures.

The method of exercise you choose does not matter so long as it serves as a consistent and safe method for staying in shape. The variety of exercise methods that incorporate a spiritual approach are broad enough that any seeker should be able to choose a method best suited to his or her lifestyle.

Mainstream methods of exercise such as aerobics, weight-lifting, swimming, or jogging can be used along with a meditative state to enhance the effectiveness of the workout. As always, use common sense—jogging into oncoming traffic while "tranced out" will likely impede your spiritual growth if you get hit by a car. Also, choose a program you enjoy. Sticking to an exercise program is much easier if it's fun for you. Varying your training methods, otherwise known as cross-training, can help maintain interest and benefit with a more versatile approach to health.

For the time-impaired, exercise that can enhance meditation and occult ability is still available. Several companies produce videotapes focusing on a martial art or meditative exercise. The twenty-minute yoga series, for example, offers reasonably thorough workouts in less than half an hour. It is possible to work out to one of these tapes and still have time to perform all the other necessary tasks in a day.

A series of visualizations used while engaging in exercise enhance the physical process and adapt the auric body to the desired physical appearance. The following visualizations are meant to help engage the brain in reaching the goals set for the body.

To lose weight, visualize the excess of fat melting and moving into the aura. In its astral state, fat will strengthen

:tive shields and cushion against invasive emotions from ᵤₕₑᵣₛ. Plus, you'll feel great when you are lighter.

To build muscle, see slivers of light slipping into the muscles and becoming part of the muscular structure. As the light visualization builds, so the muscle builds.

To increase flexibility, visualize the aura extending only slightly beyond the maximum stretching point. Visualize the body reaching to that stretching point.

To increase stamina, see a well of motion forming in the solar plexus that builds for every movement made. Periodically test the well by visualizing energy from it going to moving body parts when tired.

Visualizations should help encourage the body to demonstrate the new physical abilities desired and reduce monotony in workouts. At the same time, the esoteric skills of visualization and meditation are developed in an integrative status with the body.

Do not feel discouraged if your body does not change much despite your increased activity. Many people who exercise regularly still appear overweight or perceive themselves as imperfect. The benefits will eventually become apparent to you, even if you do not detect outward changes in clothing size or arbitrary standards of beauty. As stamina builds along with the immune system, and as you gain self-confidence, rituals will go more smoothly, and the feeling of exhaustion at the end of even minor rituals will lessen. By maintaining the physical body, your appearance will soon start to match the healthy soul—the real goal of any magic practitioner.

FOR FURTHER STUDY

Whole Body Healing. Carl Lowe and James W. Nechas. Rodale Press, 1983.

YOGURT

THE ANCIENT MAGICAL FOOD

BY JIM WEAVER

Before the Parthenon was built on its overlook above ancient Athens, and before the great pyramids towered above the sand dunes of Egypt, yogurt was already one of the world's most ancient foods. Since before recorded history, yogurt was believed to be a magical and healing food. In fact, along with grains, yogurt is one of the foods which literally helped fuel the growth of human civilization.

As is the case with most foods dating far back into antiquity, the exact time and place yogurt originated is lost forever in the mists of centuries. Most likely, yogurt's origin took place in ancient Mesopotamia (present-day Iraq), sometime after plants, goats, and sheep were domesticated. Therefore, some authorities date yogurt's beginning to as early as 5000 BC.

Since there was no refrigeration back then, goat's milk that was probably stored in gourds or goatskin bags would have naturally fermented in Mesopotamia's warm climate. This fermentation process gave us the creamy semisolid dairy product we now call yogurt. And luckily, some brave soul we'll never be able to identify decided to sample this food, and then shared it with his or her fellow villagers. Due to yogurt's seemingly miraculous occurrence, the ancients believed yogurt was a divine gift of the gods and goddesses.

From Mesopotamia, the idea to use yogurt as both a food and a magical healing substance spread to all areas of the ancient world. As time passed, yogurt became one of the most basic and most respected foods of Eastern Europe and the Middle East.

Middle Easterners have an almost mystical attachment to yogurt, and few households are without a constant supply of fresh homemade yogurt. To do this, a few tablespoons of yogurt must be ever set aside to serve as the "starter" for the next batch.

In rural areas of the Near East, it is the custom that if a family should move a great distance, to ensure the new home would have yogurt, the wife will spread a small amount of her current yogurt supply on a clean cloth, let it dry, then fold it and pack it with loving care along with the family's treasured possessions. Upon arrival in the new house, the dried yogurt culture (starter) is scraped from the cloth and into warm milk. In this way, the new home, as well as its attendant guardian "house spirit," has its first batch of yogurt.

To people interested in magic, the home preparation of yogurt is rewarding because in some ways it parallels magical rituals—you start with a goal, follow a ritual, and the result of changing milk into yogurt gives you the same satisfaction spell-casting does when it physically manifests your desire into your life. Since yogurt has been made in the same way for centuries, it also links us with our Pagan roots.

To make yogurt, you don't need any fancy equipment. The following recipe is the way I've made it for years. Just be aware that when you make yogurt, you're dealing with active yogurt cultures, which can be unpredictable at times; your yogurt may not set up correctly at first. I urge you to keep trying—you will get the magic right after a time or two.

HOMEMADE YOGURT

1	quart milk
2	tbsp prepared yogurt

In a saucepan, bring the milk to a boil, and as soon as the froth rises remove the pan from the heat and let cool to lukewarm. Cool milk just enough so you can dip your finger in it and count to ten. With a spoon, beat the 2 tablespoons of yogurt starter in a small bowl until smooth. Blend a few tablespoons of the warm milk into the starter, then pour the starter mixture back into the pan of warm milk; stir to spread the yogurt bacteria. Now, simply spoon the milk mixture into small glasses or custard cups; cover each with foil. Place glasses or cups close together in a draft-free place in your kitchen and cover with 2 kitchen towels. Leave them undisturbed for 8 hours or overnight. Refrigerate immediately after it firms. It will keep for one week in the refrigerator. Yield: 4 cups of yogurt.

Use your yogurt plain as a healthy snack or to replace sour cream in baking. Sprinkled with sugar or blended with fruit, yogurt becomes a simple dessert.

Modern science has proven the ancients were correct—yogurt is indeed a healthy and nourishing food. Yogurt is easier to digest than milk, and its good bacteria helps to maintain a healthy digestive system. For magical people, yogurt is a food of the Goddess and is ruled by the Moon. Traditionally, yogurt was used for healing skin ailments, so it is happens to be ideal for use in beauty spells. The following spell is the perfect way to relax after a hectic day.

Yogurt Facial Spell

Gather 1 tablespoon cold plain yogurt, a light blue candle, and some gardenia incense. Light the candle and the incense; rinse your face with warm water and dry. As you pat on the yogurt speak this charm:

Wholesome food of the Ancient Ones,
Ease my tension until it's gone.
Nourish my spirit and my skin,
Make my face smooth and fresh again.
Blessed be.

Now kick back and relax, or soak in the tub. Leave the yogurt on your face for about ten minutes, then rinse with cool water and dry. You'll be refreshed.

Extra tip: This spell also works well for a mild case of sunburn.

Finally, remember this: Each time you use yogurt, either as a food or in a ritual, you are connecting with magical wisdom passed down to us from great ancient civilizations. This is magic for the ages.

MIDSUMMER FAIRY CONTACT

BY ANNA FRANKLIN

Midsummer Eve is, along with Halloween and May Eve, one of the three great fairy festivals. All sorts of enchantments are in the air on this day. Spirits and fairies, who are abroad until St. Peter's Day on June 29, suddenly find themselves moving among human-kind again, frolicking around the Midsummer bonfires and playing all sorts of tricks—ranging from small pranks to horrible curses and even death for those that offend them. It is also at this time that male fairies most often steal away human women to become their brides.

Traditionally, therefore, the best time to see fairies is on Midsummer Eve. Wreaths of eerie mist often surround fairy mounds, fairy rings, stone circles, and other magical places. Should you find a gap in the mist you will be able to pass through into the otherworld. In fact, on this night the fairy mounds open, and numerous fairy denizens may be seen feasting inside. To find the entrance to a fairy hill you should walk nine times around it. Sometimes a procession of lights can be seen moving from one hill to another, and this is the fairies moving house or visiting their neighbors. They use well-trodden paths running in straight lines between the mounds. Any building on one of these fairy ways will meet with disturbances.

It was on Midsummer Eve that St. Levan saw the fairy gardens near Logan Rock in Cornwall, as he wrote long ago:

When I have been to sea close under the cliffs, of a fine summer's night, I have heard the sweetest music, and seen hundreds of little lights moving about amongst what looked like flowers. Ay! And they are flowers too, for you may smell the sweet scent far out at sea. Indeed, I have heard many of the old men say that they have smelt the sweet perfume and heard the fairy music from the fairy gardens of the castle when more than a mile from the shore.

Those who have seen the gardens in the Midsummer moon-light say they are covered with flowers of every color, all more brilliant than any mortal flower.

Fairy kingdoms exist in another dimension from that of humankind. Still, there is a square of turf in Wales where, if you trip over it, you will get a single glimpse of fairies, though the spot can never be found twice.

Fairies can become visible or invisible at will, or be visible to one person while being invisible to another, though sometimes they can be spied at their revels unawares. You must gaze steadily to see fairies, for if you blink they will disappear. They are most often seen at noon, midnight, or twilight.

If you want to see fairies then you will need the aid of certain magical herbs such as thyme and primrose. The sight can also be opened by a four-leaf clover, as the milkmaid discovered when she accidentally picked a four-leaf clover with the grass she used to soften the weight of the pail on her head. Imagine her surprise when she looked at her cow and she saw dozens of fairies milking it. An old recipe for a potion to enable you to see fairies ran thus:

Take a pint of Sallet oil and put it in a glasse, first washing it with rose water. Then put thereto the budds of hollyhocke, of mary-golde, of young hazle and the topps of wild thyme. Take the grasse of a fairy throne; then all these put into the glasse—dissolve three dayes in the sunne, and keep it for thy use.

You may note that the recipe includes wild thyme. If you can find a bed of wild thyme, know that the King of the Fairies will dance there with his followers at midnight on Midsummer Eve. Wild thyme is an ingredient of many magical potions, dating from around 1600, which allow those who take them to see fairies. One simple charm is to make a brew of wild thyme tops gathered near the side of a fairy hill and grass from a fairy throne, and anoint your eyes with it. Take care though, wild thyme is unlucky if brought indoors.

A simpler spell involves gathering fern seeds at midnight on Midsummer Eve and rubbing them on your eyelids. The fairy folk are also particularly fond of rosemary. The incense attracts them. Pour a libation of rosemary infusion on a fairy-haunted spot to please them.

The Good Folk often inhabit woody dells, concealing themselves among the flowers of the foxglove. Growing foxgloves in your garden will attract fairies, so if you want to keep fairies away, you should weed these plants out. Like other fairy flowers, it is unlucky to take them indoors.

In Brittany the rite of sounding the basins, or *senin ar cíhirinou*, is undertaken at Midsummer to conjure up the wildfolk. For this, pebbles and coins were placed into a copper basin and shaken.

PROTECTION FROM MISCHIEVOUS FAIRIES

While you might like to meet some happy and friendly fairies, there are others who like to play cruel and evil malicious tricks on humans at Midsummer. Their favorite prank is to lead travelers away from their path; this is called being *pixy-led*. Other fairies try to frighten people, steal away young girls for brides, shoot harmful elf-bolts at those who intrude on fairy territory, or even lay dreadful curses that bring illness and death. It may be necessary to take precautions against the attentions of such creatures.

According to Irish lore these fairies try to pass around the *baal* fires in a whirlwind in order to extinguish them, but may be kept off by throwing fire at them.

Humans can protect themselves from fairies by leaping through the fire. Cattle too are protected from the attentions of evil spirits by driving them through the embers of the baal fire.

Other charms against fairies: Cross a stream of running water. Carry a little bit of rue in your pocket. If fairies are troubling you or if you are being pixy-led, turn your clothes inside out to confuse them long enough to allow you to make your escape. If a friend has been dragged into a fairy ring, toss one of your gloves inside and the revelers will disperse. To keep fairies out of your bedroom scatter flax on the floor.

Fairies are terrified of iron and they will vanish immediately on being shown any form of the metal. Keep a knife or a nail in your pocket and under your pillow at night. A *hag stone,* or naturally holed stone, hung up by the door or in the byre will keep bad fairies away. A rowan cross-tied with red thread will offer protection when hung in a high place in the house or byre. The besom placed beside the hearth will prevent fairies coming down the chimney. A *witch bottle,* or a bottle containing sharp objects such as nails and pins, ashes, salt and rowan wood, can be buried before the doorstep for protection

If oatmeal is sprinkled on clothes or carried in the pocket no bad fairy will approach. St. John's wort prevents fairies from carrying off people while they sleep. A mulberry tree in your garden will keep away evil fairies. At the dangerous time of Midsummer, you should dance around the mulberry tree counterclockwise for protection. This is likely the origin of the rhyme "Here we go round the mulberry bush."

Good fairies start to come out around the Vernal Equinox, and are very animated by Beltane, or May Day, and at the peak of their activities by Midsummer. By Halloween, most of the good fairies have disappeared from sight. Bad fairies, such as goblins, rule the winter period.

MIDSUMMER MAGIC AND DIVINATION

BY ANNA FRANKLIN

Midsummer is a day of very potent magic, a time when the otherworld is close, and it is possible to see into the future.

In the past, a wide variety of Midsummer divination techniques were employed by country people. In fact, many of these techniques are employed even today—farmers view the weather on the solstice as a potential indicator of the bounty of the harvest. Rains on this day indicate a poor and wet grain harvest, but a large crop of apples and pears.

MIDSUMMER LOVE DIVINATION

In bygone days, young girls would take the opportunity on the Summer Solstice to perform various acts of divination, usually to discover whom they would marry. You might like to try some of these yourself—after all, you don't have to be a young girl to be interested in potential lovers. But be forewarned, some of these techniques are pretty scary, designed to conjure up an apparition of the lover rather than a rosy-cheeked warm-blooded person.

At midnight on St. John's Eve, walk seven times sunwise around a church, scattering hempseed and saying, "Hempseed I sow. Hempseed I sow. Let the one that is my true love come after me and mow." When you've completed the circuits, look over your left shoulder to see your true love coming after you—with a scythe in hand.

On Midsummer Eve, meanwhile, take off your shift and wash it, then turn it inside out and hang it over the back of a chair near the fire. Do it all in silence, and you will see your future husband at midnight, intent on turning the shift right side out.

You can also test on Midsummer Eve whether a partner returns your love. Follow this ancient Roman method of divination: Eat an apple and save back one pip, which you will address with your lover's name. Flick the pip from your finger with your thumb nail—if it hits the ceiling then your love is returned.

Daisies are associated with faithful love and are sacred to the love goddesses Venus, Aphrodite, and Freya. Their folk name "measure of love" comes from the following charm. To find out whether someone loves you, take a daisy and pull off the petals one by one, saying alternately after each: "He loves me. He loves me not." The final petal will give you the answer.

To discover when you will marry, find a meadow or lawn where daisies grow. Close your eyes and pull up a handful of grass. The number of daisies in the handful is the number of unmarried years remaining to you.

One Welsh method of divination called *ffatio* involves washing clothes at midnight in a well while chanting: *Sawl ddaw I gyd-fydio, doed I gyd-ffatio* ("He who would my partner be, let him come and wash with me"). The lover will then appear to help with the laundry. Finally, to find your husband, fast on Midsummer Eve till midnight, then spread a supper of bread, cheese, and ale on a clean cloth. Leave the front door wide open. Your future husband will enter the room, drink a glass of ale, bow, and leave.

Or it might be a burglar, you never know.

CYBERSPACE AND THE ASTRAL PLANE

By Marguerite Elsbeth

Cyberspace and the Internet, also known as the world wide web, are technological doorways to an otherworldly dimension reminiscent of the astral plane. Think of it this way, when we go online we bridge the gap between earth time and virtual reality.

VIRTUAL REALITY

In general, we experience earth time on the physical plane. Here, we see, hear, touch, taste, and smell a variety of animate and inanimate forms in the world around us.

This linear way of thinking allows us to grasp the totality of the cosmos with our minds. The mind, or our consciousness, is what holds earth-forms in place even though everything vibrates on a molecular level. Consciousness causes this vibratory motion to appear static to the naked eye, granting us the ability to perceive thoughts, feelings, and impressions.

The universe exists as a result of oscillating sound and light waves, which manifest as electromagnetic energy. Electromagnetism, or spiritual light, is the indefinable energy that underlies the physical forces of electricity, magnetism, heat, and visible light. The physical world is the visible manifestation of electro-

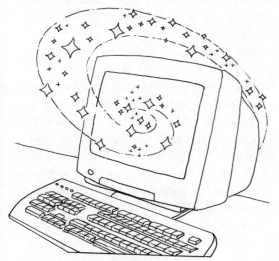

magnetic energy, and is the real controlling factor of our vitality and life force. This subtle energy radiates to all dimensions of space and beyond. Therefore, we are able to link up with the entire world when we connect to the Internet.

When we enter the virtual reality of cyberspace, we journey into a state of being that exists in essence or effect, yet is not truly actual or real. It is much like certain people we encounter throughout the day—we have met them and may recall their inherent essence or power, yet still they are virtual strangers. Likewise, cyberspace provides a point of virtual focus waiting for resolution according to our innate perceptions and outward inclinations.

LOST IN CYBERSPACE

The world wide web is the great unknown—a foreign land of mysteries without conscious limitations. Similarly, the astral plane is a dimension of mind, with many interesting inhabitants and a variety of gateways into other worlds. Just as the elemental planes provide substance for the natural world, so the astral plane is a place of potential ideas, offering the substance through which our thoughts take physical form. Cyberspace and the astral plane are templates for what is manifested in the physical world; yet, they are realms wherein we may freely function without the body.

Subtle experiences come through cyberspace and the astral plane, because both places are amphitheaters for our emotions, desires, and imaginations. Cyberspace and the astral plane are nonphysical places; whatever we choose to imagine or reinvent about ourselves can be true here. Hence, they are also worlds of illusion wherein invisible forces abound. Therefore, the kind of person we really are makes all the difference, because in cyberspace, like attracts like.

When we journey to the astral plane in dreams or through astral projection, we do so in our subtle bodies, which envelop our physical bodies as radiant energy fields of multicolored light. Although we are awake in the physical body while traveling through cyberspace, the experience is much the same as journeying in the astral double. The astral double contains a matrix of the physical body that normally is tied to the solar plexus (located above the navel) by a silvery cord. Just as when the cord to your computer is cut or damaged, causing your system will shut down, so can your physical, emotional, mental, and spiritual bodies may be harmed if the cord connecting your astral body, or in this case, your cyberbody, to your physical body is severed or damaged by an unknown force.

CYBER SAFETY

Once we are logged on to the Internet, we project a mindful, bodiless form-wave across the galactic universe. Everyone exists everywhere in cyberspace, shape-shifting to suit his or her need. Together or alone, we surf the web, journeying to educational, informative, or magical realms. Exchanging ideas and opinions on message boards or in chat rooms, we make friends, find lovers, and may even discover a marriage partner or life-mate.

However, like the possible dangers inherent in astral projection, there are times when we may bring the attention of the more challenging elements of the virtual world. This occurs when our penchant for adventure leads us out of our depth, or when we inadvertently reveal our emotional vulnerabilities to someone who has no conscience, personal ethics, moral scruples, or civility. These days, you may even become the victim of cyberterrorism, stalking, sex-offense, crime, e-mail abuse, or an Internet flame war. If this happens, you may find yourself under cyber attack, with symptoms such as heart palpitations, cold sweats, hot flashes, numbness, shock, anger, sadness, fear, panic, dissociation, and even feelings of impending doom or death.

These cybersafety tips can help you keep your cyber body out of harm's way:

Sprinkle sea salt around your computer monitor and tower. Place a halite crystal near your workspace.

Set your desktop wallpaper to display a graphic image of your favorite sacred place or totem animal, or place a stuffed animal representing your totem on top of your CPU.

"Purify" your computer's system. Use Reiki or other alternative healing techniques to remove bad vibes. Get rid of useless junk files stored on your computer's hard drive.

ALTERNATIVE SABBAT CELEBRATIONS

BY ESTELLE DANIELS

The eight sabbat celebrations all have their traditions. The Yule log is burned on the Winter Solstice to symbolize the warmth of nature in a cold and dead part of the year. Eggs are painted on Ostara to celebrate nature's rebirth.

That is to say, the sabbats are based upon an agrarian model, and nature worship is inherent in the dance of the seasons. But the modern world is ironically, for the most part, an indoor world.

This is the impetus for creating a series of alternative sabbat celebrations which have to do with being outdoors and working with the seasons. The following suggestions are based upon a four-season year. Some localities have years with just three, or even two seasons, and growing and planting occurs at different times. Adapt your outdoor sabbat celebrations, then, to the individual climate of your locality.

SAMHAIN

Samhain is the season of the root harvest, and also of the hunting season. For this sabbat, consider taking up hunting—you can use a camera if you'd rather not carry an actual gun. Just getting out into the woods in the fall and observing how nature is getting ready to bed down for the winter can give you a good Samhain feeling. Once you are outdoors, watch the sights and listen to the sounds. This is the time that birds migrate. Make a point of learning which birds go and which stay. Afterwards, make up a thick stew with veggies (and meat, if you eat it). This is good and warming way to celebrate winter root crops.

YULE

Yule is the dark time of the year. As mentioned, sitting vigil on the longest night with a Yule fire is one way to celebrate this sabbat. Fire is a sacred thing, and necessary for life. But modern society has tamed fire, so it's no longer the big deal it once was. A good alternative Yule celebration involves getting up before dawn after the longest night of the year, and gathering at a place with a good eastern view to greet the Sun as it comes up. Some ancient societies felt that this Sun greeting was crucial to ensure its constant return. Alternatively, go ice skating, skiing, or sledding outdoors on this day, and enjoy what the season has to offer. Then come in and drink warm cider, celebrating the fruits of an earlier season, and appreciating the comforts of central heating.

IMBOLC

Imbolc is the traditional time for working on the tools necessary for for the coming year. Clean out your chests and closets, and sift through your Books of Shadows and other tools. Review and reorganize your magical stuff. Imbolc is also usually the coldest time of the year in northern climes. Go outside and watch the stillness of the world now. If the Sun is out, it will be strong enough to melt ice and snow even if the temperature is below freezing. How does the old snow look, compared to when it was new? If you get one of those rare warm days, a winter thaw, go outside and enjoy the Sun and warmth. Feel the Sun growing stronger, the days longer, and realize that spring and summer aren't far behind. Cook a meal using dried ingredients. In the past, this is the time people ate from their stores and reserves.

Ostara

Ostara is the Spring Equinox. If you can feel the spring's arrival, go outside and see how things are changing. Are the buds swelling on the trees? Are there flowers poking out of the snow? Watch the animals, are they more active after the winter. Are they mating? Building nests? Are fish running in your area? Watch the birds migrating back from the south, closing the cycle of the year.

Beltane

Beltane is when spring has arrived. The plants and trees are now in flower, so it's a perfect time to go out. Look at the new plants, and at how the old plants are putting on new growth. Check what survived, and what did not, over the winter. Have a picnic outside, if it's warm enough. Go to a farmers market and get some first fruit: asparagus, strawberries—whatever grows first in your area. Eating foods in season in your locality is one way to keep your body in tune with nature. Make yourself a spring salad or tonic. Has fishing season started? Try going fishing. You can cook up what you catch, or just catch and release.

Midsummer

Midsummer is when the crops are in and fruit is more abundant. The first hay is usually ready. An outdoor picnic and walk is always fun. A trip to the swimming hole is fun too. On the longest day of the year, put a stick in the ground and see how short the shadow is at noon. Examine the Sun. It is most closely overhead at noon in Midsummer in the northern hemisphere. You can stay up for the shortest night, having a party or just enjoying the warm weather. Go berry picking at a pick-your-own place. Eat some as you pick, and try to store some for the coming winter.

LAMMAS

Lammas is the first harvest and the height of summer. Crops are becoming ripe at the hottest time of the year. Camping is always fun now. Swimming cools your body naturally. This is the time for picnics and games. Ancient peoples celebrated these times with games and contests, which tested the people in preparation for the coming hard months.

MABON

Mabon is the main harvest. Go apple picking. Visit the farmers market and see the bounty available in your area. Make a meal with only fresh foods harvested in your area. Give thanks for the bounty that is all around. Go outside and see how life is adapting and storing up resources for the winter to come. This is the main canning and preserving season. Try putting up something from your local food market.

ISIS IN RUSSIA

BY deTRACI REGULA

Behind the former Iron Curtain may seem an odd place to search for Isis, the Egyptian and Greco-Roman goddess of mystery, magic, and motherhood. But Isis was never a "stay-at-home" kind of goddess. Instead, she traveled mythologically outside Egypt every chance she could, and some of her journeys led her to Russia and the nations once part of, or dominated by, the former Soviet Union.

It's not certain when Isis or her followers first reached the cold north, but her influence is felt in many unexpected northern places. Some Swedish authors, writing in the 1600s, claimed that Isis originated in the far north, and that her name, Isis, was derived from Eis, or Ice, an expansion of her role as a goddess of water and moisture. They saw the depictions of Isis on Roman coinage as showing her standing on an ice floe, when in fact these "ice floes" were more likely primitive depictions of a boat.

Isis is connected with Russia through Helena Petrovna Blavatsky's work, *Isis Unveiled*. Blavatsky's works established theosophy throughout the world and indirectly influenced many representations of Isis. In her book, Blavatsky treats Isis more as a symbol of divine wisdom than as a specific divinity. She notes that a theosophical theater was named for Isis, and that dramatic recreations of Isian rites were presented in many places after a craze for all things Egyptian flared up even before the opening of Tut's tomb in the 1920s. In all, however, Blavatsky's influence was much greater outside of Russia than it was within.

Russian folklorist Alexander Asov believes that the Russian divinity Asova was in fact Isis, and points to the Egyptian form of her name, Ast. If this is so, Isis once again is associated with the "throne," since a sanctuary to the god Welas and Asova stood on top of the Borovickiy knoll where the Kremlin now stands.

In modern times, Isis has slipped into many unlikely spots in Russia. The *blini,* a quintessentially Russian pancake eaten during Shrovetide, is believed by some authorities on Russian culture to have developed from cakes baked for Isis festivals. The shipyard fortress known as the Admiralty in St. Petersburg depicts Isis not once, but twice, rendering homage or asking her blessing as the goddess of navigation, along with Urania, patroness of astronomy who was often combined with Isis. Admittedly, Isis is not the only Pagan goddess so honored on this early 1800s structure—other portions of the building are adorned with images of other gods. However, Isis is the most prominently depicted goddess.

The Hungarian city of Szombathely, on the ancient Roman city of Savaria on what was once the Amber Route, delights in its recreated temple of Isis. Inside, icons show Isis riding on the back of the wolflike dog representing the star Sirius. In the nearby region, morever, she is represented on small votive objects made of lead, a plentiful metal in the area. A great Isian treasure of bronze temple vessels inscribed with gold and silver has been excavated at Egyed. One of her titles in this region was Isis Conservatrix, "the one who keeps and protects."

The new nation of Macedonia, formed from the breakup of Russian-dominated Yugoslavia, is the first modern nation in many years to show Isis on its money. A representation of a headless statue of Isis, found at a temple site Ohrid, adorns the widely circulated ten-denar note. As a result, most residents of this area will find Isis still functioning as a very practical symbol of abundance and plenty.

For Further Study

Fellowship of Isis. http://www.fellowshipofisis.com. A webpage about an international Isian organization.

The Mysteries of Isis: Her worship and magick. deTraci Regula. Llewellyn Publications, 1995. My book on the worship of Isis, ancient and modern.

Wilderness Magic

By Kenneth Johnson

There is a wonderful passage in one of the old epics of King Arthur. It says that whenever the knights began their quest for the grail, they plunged straight into the wilderness where the woods are thickest.

Clever knights. They knew where to find the magic.

But then perhaps they were not so clever. After all, don't most of our European fairy tales begin in much the same way? The tree spirit, the elvish helper, the old Witch, or the magic fountain—all are discovered when the heroine or hero of the story wanders away from the well-ordered village, the peaceful town, the easy and well-marked path, and enters the wildness. Perhaps it was simply common knowledge back then that the primal chaos of trees, rocks, and water was the most potent magical energy source available.

In many, if not most, magical and folk traditions, the world is the body of the Earth Mother herself. It is no wonder, then, that the trees who constitute her beautiful hair and the rocks which constitute her strong bones are the source of so much magic. Whoever we may be, of whatever cultural origin, all our ancestors were tribal at one time or another, and hence they all lived close to the magic. Wherever we now live, wilderness is generally not that far away—perhaps in the closest state park or forest area. And there are many ways you can touch the magic of the wilderness for yourself.

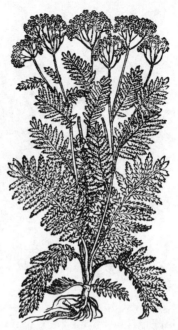

First, like most traditional peoples the world over, pre-Christian Europeans seem to have believed that the center of shamanic power lay in our midsection—between the lower diaphragm and the middle belly. Once you are in the woods, focus your attention on this spot on your body. Don't worry too much about its exact location, it's a little different for everyone. Your body will find it for you if you simply focus on seeking a primal source of internal energy. Keep your awareness there, as if it is the actual center of your being.

Once you have done this, you will find that the paths of energy in the Earth itself just seem to pull you along. When you're really focused, you will be aware of zones of power in the Earth. When you've found such a place of power, there are a number of things you can do.

First, you can work with the rocks. Most rocks, whether tiny stones or great boulders, have a "soft spot" somewhere which allows you to enter into them in the spirit. Use your intuition, eyes, and sense of touch to find that spot. Then, meditatively, go inside. Many people report seeing visions of long ago—the very past of the Earth itself. The whole record of Mother Earth's experience is stored inside her bones, the rocks.

If there is a stream or a lake, you have a wonderful place to get rid of some of your emotional baggage. In European folk songs, sad lovers are always sitting by the banks of a lake or river. Why? Because it is believed that water purifies our sexual selves and washes away negativity. Give your sorrows to the water, and meditatively feel them slip away from you forever.

If there are plenty of trees, you may be able to locate one that "likes" you. I'm not joking. Place your back against a tree so it can feel your aura. If it likes you, you will know. Then you can become one with the tree. Feel its essence go into your center of power. Then open your eyes. If you are lucky, you will be able to see the world through the tree's eyes. Believe me, when this works it's better than any psychedelic.

Finally, you can simply dance. That's right. There's no particular reason to sit still in a place of power. You might as well just dance, moving to your own inner music and the music of the Sun and the wind. The rocks and trees will enjoy it.

Enchanting East Malaysian Tribes

By S Y Zenith

The island of Borneo was thought to be joined to Peninsular Malaysia about 15,000 years ago by Sumatra and Java. In the midnineteenth century when Borneo was not ruled by the Sultan of Brunei, it was rich in British adventurers and traders.

Over the centuries, northern Borneo's natives, namely the Ibans, Muruts, and other tribes have fought against pirates and European traders. Parangs and poison darts were the main weapons. The mode of transport for navigating along the many rivers were dug-out wooden boats. These peoples ambushed other tribes and lopped off their heads for use in fertility and death rites. The skulls also represented male valor according to the native belief systems.

Borneo is strong in ethnic traditions to this day. In particular, East Malaysia is akin to one of its innumerable forest spirits which lure visitors deep into the interiors where the magic and mysteries of the world's oldest and richest rain forests unfold. The regions are diverse and rich with plant and wildlife, and one can trek for several days by river and through dense jungles without seeing another soul.

In remote parts of Borneo, there is no access to modern medicine. Villagers are simply too distant for the "flying doctor," or helicopter services, to reach. As a result, these peoples have long relied on traditional Bornean plant remedies.

The most famous native healers are the nomadic Penans who live in the remotest and most inaccessible parts of the interior. These people are acknowledged by other indigenous tribe of the region to be experts in the administration of all manner of medicinal plants and herbal remedies.

In medicinal system of the Penans, jungle roots, stems, stalks, flower buds, and petals are ground into pastes for applying to the navel parts of the body to relieve stomach pains, soreness, and a host of other ailments.

There are numerous medicinal plants that are made into infusions and potions not only for curing physical conditions but also for people inflicted by spirits or affected by malevolent forces. For instance, digestive teas are made by boiling the barks of certain medicinal trees. To make a massage oil or insect repellant, lemongrass oil is used. For smoothing and beautifying the skin, the *bayam pasir,* or *amaranthus spinosus,* is commonly applied. The *jerangau,* or *acorus calamus,* helps control fevers and dysentery. The buds of the world's largest flower, the *rafflesia* which makes its home in Borneo, are sought after by women after giving birth. These buds, when boiled, produce a tonic which, when drunk, is said to return the uterus to the original healthy state. However, lest you get any rash ideas, modern studies of the *rafflesia* flower by botanists acertained that the buds contain great amounts of tannin which may endanger women who consume the tonic.

The Melanau constitute about 6 percent of Sarawak's population. They once lived in huge defensive houses erected fourteen or more meters above the ground, and they were known for making "sickness images" to treat any and all illnesses. These images were in fact intricate carvings utilized by shamans in elaborate healing ceremonies.

In Sabah, the three main tribes are the Kadazans (also called Dusuns), Muruts, and Bajaus. The Kadazans have in modern times spread from the hills of Gunung Kinabalu to urban parts. Many have abandoned their pagan rites, totems, rice crops, and symbolic stones. The Muruts were the last Bornean tribe to abandon headhunting. Today, they occupy the hilly regions between Sarawak and Sabah where they continue to hunt with blowpipes. Like the Kadazans, the Muruts believe in the powers of certain animals and wear bizarre charms made for protection and other reasons.

Despite massive logging of Borneo's rainforests, the many indigenous peoples of the land have not relinquished traditional medicinal practices of their ancestors. They continue to carry on these traditions for future generations.

THE ART OF MEMORY

BY JOHN MICHAEL GREER

The modern renaissance of the magical arts has brought many branches of traditional magic and occultism back into common use. Many more, however, still remain to be rediscovered. One of the most fascinating of these is the ancient Art of Memory. Once an important part of magical training in many traditions, the Art of Memory is a system of training that allows the human memory to hold enormous amounts of information at will.

The Greek poet Simonides of Ceos, according to legend, invented this discipline. Simonides was hired to recite verses at a banquet, and in the usual fashion started off with a few lines in honor of the gods, in this case, Castor and Pollux, before settling down to the serious business of praising his host. The host, piqued at the introductory diversion, gave Simonides half the amount agreed upon, and told him he could get the rest from the gods he had praised.

A few minutes later, a servant came to Simonides and told him that two young men on horseback were at the door, asking for him. The poet went outside, and saw no one. As he looked around, the roof of the banquet hall collapsed behind him, crushing the arrogant host and his guests. Castor and Pollux, traditionally pictured as two young horsemen, had indeed paid their half of the fee.

Such stories were commonplace in ancient Greek literature, but this one has an unexpected moral. When the rubble was cleared away, the story continues, the bodies of the dead were so mangled that no one could figure out who was who. Simonides found, though, that he could picture the banquet hall in his mind's eye and remember the order in which the guests had been sitting. This allowed him to identify the dead. As he pondered this, it also gave him the key to the Art of Memory.

That key is the use of visual images in an ordered arrangement. The human memory recalls images far more easily than abstract ideas, and it remembers an ordered chain of associations more accurately than a random assortment. Just as Simonides could remember the guests at the ill-fated banquet by picturing them in the setting of the banquet hall, masters of the Art of Memory in later centuries turned information into striking visual images and arranged these images against fixed backgrounds in order to memorize them quickly and effectively. '

These methods reached dizzying levels of efficiency. It is recorded of one famous practitioner, the Roman orator Hortensius, that he sat through a day-long auction and then recounted from memory the item, purchaser, and price for every sale of the day. In the Middle Ages, the practice of the Art of Memory was seen as an act of prudence, one of the seven cardinal virtues, and monks and friars—especially members of the Dominican Order—put it to work in countless ways. Later still, with the coming of the Renaissance, the Art of Memory became a common pursuit of educated people throughout Europe. From here, the Art passed into use among ceremonial magicians. The arrival of printing, and of cheap plentiful paper, barely cut into the popularity of the Art of Memory. It was only with the coming of seventeenth-century rationalism and the Scientific Revolution that it finally fell into obscurity.

The Methods Of the Art

In using the Art, every piece of information that was to be remembered was turned into a striking symbolic image. The image might be beautiful, repulsive, hilarious, or shocking, but it had to be memorable, and it had to contain a clear reference to the information being memorized. Puns, double meanings, and every kind of wordplay could be put to use in this system. Another common habit was to devise an alphabet of images, using either the shapes or the names of objects to refer to each letter of the alphabet. Thus a figure representing a word beginning with the letter *V* might stand in front of a forked tree or carry a vixen under its arm.

Each of these images was then placed in order against a known setting, usually the inside of some familiar building. Students of the Art of Memory would commit as many buildings to memory as they could, and use each one to store different kinds of information. Each building would be divided up into loci, or "places," specific spots where a memory image could be stored. Every fifth place might be marked with a Roman numeral V, every tenth one with an X. Once the images were placed in their settings, the practitioner of the Art simply had to walk through the building in his or her imagination, taking note of the figures there and recalling their meanings. The effect of the Art of Memory can still be discerned today. It's from this practice that we learned to say "in the first place" and other such expressions when going over the points of an argument.

As the Art spread through medieval and Renaissance culture, other systems came into use as well. Some masters of the Art took the heavens as their memory building, placing figures on the different planetary spheres and the constellations. Others worked out ways of creating imaginary buildings for memory use, or developed dizzyingly complex systems of rotating circles in which every position created a different set of "loci."

All these techniques may seem strange or pointless. Still, they make systematic use of the strong points of human memory. The mind recalls images better than ideas, and it recalls emotionally charged images best of all. One's most intense memories, for instance, are rarely abstract ideas, but rather highly visual, highly intense events or places. The mind tends to use chains of association rather than logical order to connect one memory with another; simple mnemonic tricks like the loop of string tied around a finger rely on this propensity. The mind prefers rhythms and repetitive formulae over randomness. It's for this reason that poetry and music are much easier to remember than prose. By combining all these factors with training and practice, the Art of Memory produces a mind that works in harmony with its own built-in strengths to make the most of its own potential to remember.

THE USES OF THE ART

In today's world of gigabyte hard disks and million-volume research libraries, learning the Art of Memory may seem about as relevant as studying the best way to make clay tablets for writing. Still, the Art of Memory has a real place in the tool kit of the modern magician. The magical traditions of the West have always focused on expanding the inner powers of the individual. Memory is one of those powers, and a trained memory capable of storing information quickly and accurately is a powerful tool for meditation and many other magical disciplines.

The Art also helps make sense of some of the mysteries of magical tradition. The images of the tarot cards, for example, are closely related to memory images, and in fact may actually have started out as images in someone's private memory system. So are many of the bizarre magical images in medieval and Renaissance grimoires. Knowing something about the Art of Memory can open unexpected doors of understanding in a wide range of magical traditions.

This practice also has its practical side. The methods of the Art of Memory work so much better than ordinary rote memorization that even a little experience with it can make a startling difference in those situations when one has to rely on memory. And such situations are anything but rare, even today. Once your learn the Art of Memory, you will be able to recall anything from shopping lists to class notes quickly and efficiently. And you will never forget your memory at home when you go to the store or to your final exam.

FOR FURTHER STUDY

The Art of Memory. Frances A. Yates. Routledge, 1999.

The Book of Memory: A study of memory in medieval culture. Mary J. Carruthers. Cambridge University Press, 1990.

MOTHER GOOSE AND OTHER OLD WIVES' TALES

BY LILY GARDNER

Open a book of Mother Goose rhymes and you will hear the echoes of ancient ballads, half-remembered plays, and spells for making butter and bringing on dreams. Mother Goose is our oldest written link with European folk-life.

In older days, Pagan culture was spoken, not written, leaving little record for us to read. Fortunately, the body of Mother Goose rhymes, consisting of over one thousand separate texts collected by folklorists from 1744, with the publication of *Tom Thumb's Pretty Song Book,* through 1849, when James Halliwell published his *Popular Rhymes and Nursery Tales,* represent an important literary treasure for the Middle Ages. In 1650, a French newspaper referred to a story as "like a Mother Goose story." To say something resembled the tales of Mother Goose was in France to call it an old wives' tales. Old wives were the "silly" old women who spouted folk wisdom. In 1697, Charles Perrault published his first group of tales for children, titling the work, *Tales of My Mother Goose.* From that time forward, folklorists collected and published the rhymes under the umbrella of Mother Goose.

Because Mother Goose rhymes were transmitted orally, it is difficult to age them with any accuracy, but Iona and Peter Opie, the leading authorities on Mother Goose, estimate that one quarter of the rhymes were familiar to Shakespeare. What makes Mother Goose unique from other folklore is how the rhymes remained intact for generations. The beauty of a rhyme is that since it is passed on from memory, and children insist on repeating it "just like you said yesterday," such texts are easily passed on from generation to generation.

The other surprise found in Mother Goose is the range of adult subject matter used to amuse the young. This includes, for instance, a wealth of Pagan spells. Mother Goose rhymes percolated up from the memory of the peasant class who farmed the countryside, raised animals, scrubbed floors, and tended babies. In other words, Mother Goose rhymes are truly the magic of the people.

NATURE LORE

The caprice of weather often spelled well-being or doom. Observing patterns in the wind, rain, growth of plants, and behavior of animals determined whether people harvested enough food to see them through the winter. This Mother Goose rhyme is an example of ancient weather-lore:

> *When the wind is in the east*
> *'Tis neither good for man or beast.*
> *When the wind is from the north,*
> *The skillful fisher goes not forth;*
> *When the wind is from the south,*
> *It blows the bait in the fishes mouth;*
> *When the wind is from the west,*
> *Then 'tis at the very best.*

Pagans recited charms to drive away the rain and wind or to urge the snow to fall as in one Mother Goose spell. The old woman is likely Holda, the Teutonic sky goddess who was said to shake her eiderdown quilts to make the snow fall.

> *Snow, snow faster*
> *Ally-ally-blaster;*
> *The old woman's plucking her geese*
> *Selling the feathers a penny a piece.*

Many examples of animal-lore exist in the Mother Goose nursery rhymes such as this observation:

> *If the cock molt before the hen,*
> *We shall have weather thick and thin;*
> *But if the hen molt before the cock,*
> *We shall have weather hard as a block.*

And:

A swarm of bees in May
Is worth a load of hay;
A swarm of bees in June
Is worth a silver spoon
A swarm of bees in July
Is not worth a fly.

Pagans also sang about plants:

When the blackthorn blossom's white,
Sow your barley day and night.

If the oak is out before the ash,
Then we'll have a splash;
If the ash is out before the oak,
Then we'll surely have a soak.

WHEEL OF THE YEAR

Country people may have adopted a Christian veneer, but they still believed that certain rituals needed to be performed to turn the wheel of the year. We know that the Pagans from the Middle Ages to the nineteenth century lived by the wheel of the year and recited charms. For example, Pagans beat pans and drums and wassailed apple orchards on Twelfth Night as in this rhyme.

Here's to thee
Old apple tree!
Whence thou mays't blow
And whence thou mays't bear
Apples enow:
Hats full!
Caps full!
Bushels, bushels, sacks full,
And my pockets full too!
Huzza! Huzza!

They hung garlands of flowers on their neighbor's doors on May Day to ensure fertility for the summer.

A branch of May I have brought you,
And at your door I stand;
It is but a sprout, but it is well budded out,
The work of our Lord's hand.

Each year on July 15, St. Swithin's Day, the country folk burned a fire in their orchards as a blessing on their apple crop. It was said that if it rained on St. Swithin's Day the apples would keep through the winter. This Mother Goose rhyme commemorates the old belief:

St. Swithin's Day, if thou dost rain,
For forty days it will remain.
St. Swithin's Day, if thou be fair,
For forty days 'twill rain na mair.

Samhain marked the end of summer, and Pagans practiced divination to see what the new year had in store for them. This rhyme was said after throwing hazel nuts into the fire:

If you love me
Pop and fly
If you hate me
Lay and die.

SPELLS

We know that our ancestors made wishes on stars, had a charm to churn butter, and a charm for dreams. Pagans knew that a red sky in the morning foretold a storm. They cured warts and planted their gardens by the Moon. They probably practiced sympathetic magic every day. We know this because the charms survive in part in nursery rhymes. One example of a love spell from Mother Goose involved plucking a sprig of rosemary and a sprig of thyme and sprinkling them with holy water three times. The women placed the herbs in a pair of shoes and positioned one shoe on either side of her bed, saying:

St. Valentine, that's to lovers kind
Come ease the trouble of my mind
And send the man that loves me true
To take the sprigs out of my shoe.

Another spell required a branch of ash tree with an even number of leaves on it. The lovelorn said:

The even-ash I double in three
The first I meet my true love shall be;
If he be married let him pass by,
But if he be single let him draw nigh.

OPPRESSION OF MOTHER GOOSE

The Mother Goose literature survived through centuries of persecution of Pagans because it was sung by people from the lowest rung of society: peasants, women and children. As long as the servants followed orders they escaped further notice.

During the Middle Ages, St. Augustine denounced all acts of magic as "pagan," and all Pagan goddesses and gods as "demons." Any belief system outside the narrow confines of Christianity was branded heresy. Heretics were tortured and killed. The Pagan faith was driven to the remote corners of the kingdom, but there were many remote corners in medieval Europe. Small villages, where a number of families grouped together around a lord and farmed adjacent fields, lived in relative isolation. The villagers likely continued practicing their sympathetic magic and Moon worship. One Mother Goose rhyme recorded an ancient prayer to the Moon.

Luna, every woman's friend,
To me thy goodness condescend,
Let this night in visions see
Emblems of my destiny.

The village priest would have tried his utmost to reform his heathen parish. If disaster destroyed the village crops, it was easy to believe the priest's moralizing that the cause of the village misfortunes as the devil's work. Christian priests could explain famine and illness as the work of demons and Witches or God's retribution for the villager's sinful ways. Every calamity could be explained by the priest as it related to the Pagan beliefs he hated. In an era of invasions, war, famine, and plague it was easy to blame one's misfortunes on a misunderstood system of faith.

Incidentally, women had the worst lot in those days. The Bible blamed women for man's fall from grace, and until recently the Catholic Church declared that women had no souls. Women could not own property once they were married, nor could they obtain an education. They were banned from the priesthood and the healing profession: the two areas they dominated before the Catholic Church usurped their rights. A Mother Goose rhyme illustrating women's place in society was recorded in 1620:

Who marrieth a Wife upon a Monday
If she will not be good upon a Tuesday
Let him go to the wood upon a Wednesday
And cut him a cudgel upon a Thursday
And pay her soundly upon a Friday
And she mind not, the devil take her Saturday
Then he may eat his meat in peace on Sunday.

PERSEVERENCE

Many Pagan gods and goddesses were changed into demons or saints, but some Pagan customs—the use of evergreens at Yule, colored eggs and May baskets in the spring sabbats—survived in the nursery because women continued to pass on their traditions to their children. Although alphabet rhymes and lullabies were created for children, the bulk of Mother Goose rhymes were adult material for teaching Pagan beliefs. Fragments of old ballads, lines from plays, military songs, political satires, and riddles all became part of the Mother Goose literature as mothers and wet nurses recited rhymes from memory to entertain themselves and their children. An example of an adult riddle that found itself preserved in a nursery rhyme is:

Hoddy doddy,
With a round black body,
Three feet and a wooden hat.
Pray tell me, what's that?
(The answer is a cauldron.)

Little judgment was exercised as to what was appropriate for children to hear. Until the Victorian era, children shared the same stories, songs, and games as their parents. No one thought to shield them from coarse language, bawdy songs, or Pagan spells. Most children at the time were raised by peasants. From the fourteenth to the nineteenth cen-

tury, city people employed wet nurses for their babies because it was believed that a woman could conceive sooner after the birth of her child if she didn't nurse. Having many children was essential in that time of high child mortality. The majority of the wet nurses lived on farms in the outlying villages. The result of this practice was that most children spent their first two years in the country where the old ways prevailed. A young noble was likely to hear the same nursery rhymes as the peasant children:

> *Come, butter, come,*
> *Come, butter, come,*
> *Peter stands at the gate*
> *Waiting for his butter cake.*
> *Come, butter, come!*

At age seven, children were considered old enough to work as farm help, servants, apprentices, or vassals; thus, they continued to learn the nursery songs of the peasantry. The Mother Goose songs can be compared to the folksongs in the United States that slaves sang to communicate with one another.

The farmyard connotation of Mother Goose seems an apt symbol for the rich literature that has passed down to us. The goose as bird goddess is one of the oldest symbols for the Mother Goddess. The figure of Mother Goose may be based on

Berchta, the Teutonic crone goddess. She was the patron of spinning and said to be very fond of children. Often Mother Goose is pictured as a crone behind a spinning wheel and surrounded by children. Berchta and her followers were often seen in the autumnal skies as a flock of geese.

Despite the centuries of oppression, torture, and burning, the rich heritage of Mother Goose rhymes, which were not written down but passed on through word of mouth by Pagans, and in particular by women, represents the wisdom hundreds of voices. Mother Goose folk wisdom continues to survive, thanks to women over the centuries who have given us a body of work where we can glimpse the lives and ways of our Pagan ancestors.

FOR FURTHER STUDY

The oldest charms in print originate from the Mother Goose collections. To prepare your own grimoire from Mother Goose rhymes, I recommend the following books.

The Annotated Mother Goose. William and Ceil Baring-Gould. Meridian Books, 1962.

The Oxford Dictionary of Nursery Rhymes. Peter and Iona Opie. Oxford University Press, 1951.

To learn more about folk-life, I recommend two books that are treasure troves of information about rural living.

Life in a Medieval Village. Francis and Joseph Gies. Harper & Row, 1990.

Everyday Life in Renaissance England. Kathy Emerson. Writer's Digest Books, 1996.

For a powerful perspective on the role of the Christian Church in the oppression of women through history, read:

The Crone. Barbara Walker. Harper & Row, 1985.

Tara

By Natalie Harter

O nce, in an age without beginning, there lived a Tibetan princess named Yeshe Dawa, Moon of Wisdom. The young woman was very accomplished in her meditation practice, and word spread throughout the land of her skill. Several holy men came to meet her, and they advised her to request rebirth in a male form, for then she would surely achieve enlightenment. She thought on this for some time, and replied, "Here there is no man, no woman, no self, no person, and no consciousness. The labels of 'male' and 'female' have no essence, but worldly beings are often deluded by such."

Then monks stood, taken aback, as she continued. "There are many who desire enlightenment in a male form, but few who work for the welfare of beings in a female form. Therefore, I vow to be reborn only in a female body until the suffering of sentient beings has ceased, and the cycle of birth, death, and rebirth is empty." From then on, Yeshe Dawa saved a million million beings upon awakening and before resting, and defeated a million million demons at midday. For these acts of fierce compassion she became known as Tara-Savioress, Star, and She Who Leads Across.

Tara in Tibetan Buddhism

Tara is the most popular devotional deity in Tibetan Buddhism, and she is worshipped daily. She is arguably the most revered woman in the Buddhist pantheon. Tara holds high honors not only as goddess, but also as *buddha*, one who attains the bliss of complete enlightenment, and *bodhisattva*, an enlightened being who, rather than leave the worldly realm, vows to remain and aid all other sentient beings in their quests. Regular devotion to Tara ensures a long life of health and good fortune. For devotees, she is ever-present, forever waiting in the wings in case of need. All the individual in distress need do is speak Tara's praises, call her name, or think on her and she is there to lead you across the ocean of your fears.

Tara functions quite similarly to the Virgin Mary of Roman Catholicism. Both are believed to be more accessible, more understanding, and more nurturing than their austere male counterparts. Tara's vow is important to women who long to see themselves reflected in the face and body of the divine.

TARA'S MANY FORMS AND FUNCTIONS

Tara exists in many forms and can fulfill most any function. The Green Tara and the White Tara are the most popular, but she has at least twenty-one distinct forms and 108 different names. Tara is most often depicted sitting on a lotus in front of the Full Moon, her hair and body adorned by jewels, her left hand by her heart in the gesture of protection, and her open right hand on her knee in blessing. She holds an *utpala,* a blue lotus flower, as a symbol of the purity and beauty.

The Green Tara is the form from which all others originate. She provides protection and luck and helps one to overcome fear and other obstacles. She is known in Tibetan Buddhism for saving beings from the Eight Great Fears: pride, delusion, anger, envy, ignorance, avarice, attachment, and doubt. The White Tara grants longevity, healing, and wisdom. Her white color is compared to that of a thousand autumn Moons. She sits in the full lotus posture of meditation, and she has seven eyes, so that she may better see suffering and swiftly end it.

The twenty-one Taras come in various combinations of color, arms, faces, instruments, and moods. They can be black in color, have three heads or four arms, and can be clad in tiger's skin adorned with skulls. Some are peaceful and meditative figures who grant invisibility or cure disease. Those familiar with the goddesses of India may find some of these descriptions very familiar. In fact, included amongst Tara's 108 titles are the names of Kali, Sarasvati, and Brahmani. Tara also finds a sister spirit in the East Asian Buddhist goddess Kwan Yin; both are seen as the embodiment of perfect compassion.

TARA IN MAGIC

For every imaginable magical need, there is likely an appropriate Tara. If for some reason there is not one that you know of, merely speak your need and she will rise to the occasion. She cam be particularly helpful in overcoming fears of all kinds, and aiding in the formation of a braver self. Before enlisting her help as a ritual aid, it is best to develop a personal relationship with her. There are many stories from which to learn of her many traits. From a basic understanding of Tara's history and mythology, the easiest way to begin a working relationship with her is through simple devotion, or *puja*.

Most Tibetan Buddhist convents and monasteries perform Tara puja daily up to three hours in duration. They are replete with continuous chanting and full body prostrations. Such complexity and endurance is of course welcome, but certainly not necessary. I had my first experience of Tara puja in the Pharping village of Nepal, where an image of the Green Tara miraculously rises out of solid stone.

My personal puja to the self-arising Tara consisted of first showing my respects. This is done by raising your hands in a position of prayer to your forehead, lips, and heart three times, symbolically offering up your body, speech, and mind to her. I then lit a candle and placed some incense and a *khata,* or white silk scarf offered to honored teachers in Tibetan Buddhism, on the altar. Most of us do not have such an idyllic location in which to worship Tara. An image of her on your altar or nightstand, a postcard or a statue, would work nicely. Envisioning her in

...nd also is sufficient. Remember, Tara does not much of her devotees.

Another simple devotion is mediation with the aid of a *mantra,* a powerful Sanskrit phrase that is thought to contain the essence of a deity. The mantra is most often recited by counting it out on beads, or *malla,* in similar fashion to using a rosary. Both Hinduism and Buddhism employ the practice of meditating with malla. You can make your own by stringing together 108 beads or seeds. In the beginning you may wish to simply recite the 108 names of Tara names along with the beads, or any other phrase that brings Tara to mind. Her official mantra is *om tara tuttare ture svaha* (the last word is pronounced "soha"), but recite at your own risk, for it is said that the words are so powerful that when spoken by the uninitiated they may cause the mind to explode.

Tara is an extremely powerful, compassionate, and practical goddess to work with. She can cross all cultural and continental boundaries. Above the self-arising Tara shrine in Pharping hangs a little red sign that reads Drolma, Tara's Tibetan name. Underneath it is the name Sarasvati, the Hindu goddess of music and learning. Though Tara is worshipped by different names and in different languages, her essence remains the same. Call her Tara, Sarasvati, Kwan Yin, or even Mary, and she will come in whatever form you need most.

FOR FURTHER STUDY

Longing for Darkness: Tara and the black madonna, a ten-year journey. China Galland. Viking, 1990.

The Day of a Buddhist Practitioner. Bokar Rinpoche. ClearPoint Press, 1998.

Teen Witch Survival Guide

By Ellen Dugan

Hello teen Witches. I am a Witch and a mother of three teenage Witches, and if I've learned anything over the years it's that you should forget what you've seen on TV or in the movies. Witches are real people with real problems and real expectations.

You know what I mean—getting good grades, helping with household chores, paying for car insurance, not engaging in hand-to-hand combat with siblings. Sounds familiar. right?

So, how does a modern Witch survive in a Midwestern town? Simple. Keep a low profile, stay away from gossip, do not boast about your religion. In fact, there is a pretty big downside to going public with your religious beliefs. Once you let the cat out of the bag, that's it; there's no going back. It will take years for people to forget. It still amazes me that with all the good information available the average person isn't better informed about witchcraft.

Teens who are interested in magic need some straight talk. There is no Pagan utopia out there. The truth is that you are going to have to be around people who don't believe in magic. Some folks can be hostile or horrified by anything that even hints at the occult. This is true both at school, your job, and maybe even at home.

My teens keep a very low profile. They are active in several different sports and in band at their high school. They dress casually and in style. All three make good grades and are well liked by their coaches and most of their teachers. In other words they blend in as normal teens.

To be a Witch means that you try to work in harmony with the world around you. Discretion is the better part of valor, as they say, and sometimes to do this you must strive to blend in.

If blending in is a problem for you, here are some suggestions.

Lay off the all-black, flowing ensembles. Most of us, when we are young Witches, go through this phase. However, contrary to popular belief there is no Witch dress code. Witches come in all races, genders, ages, shapes, and sizes. You normally cannot spot a real Witch in a crowd unless they want you to.

Keep magical jewelry to a minimum. Or be clever with it. You do not have to wear a large obvious pentagram to be a real Witch. My sons will sometimes wear Celtic knot jewelry. My daughter likes small crescent Moons or faeries. You might try an attractive crystal point on a necklace. If you want to wear a pentagram, fasten it on a long chain and keep it tucked out of sight.

Consider covering your magical books. You could make attractive coverings with fabric, wrapping paper, or even brown paper bags and stickers. I often take my covered craft books to the public pool. Not only are they protected from splashes, but the contents are kept private from prying eyes.

Need an incognito altar for your room? Use a natural representation for each of the four elements. Make it small enough to sit on your nightstand and not be noticed. Use a small houseplant for earth, a feather to represent air, a sea shell for water, and a lava rock or a red candle for fire. My sons use a quartz crystal cluster for earth, and a dragon statue for fire. A few feathers they found to represent the element of air and their aquarium to represent the element of, you guessed it, water.

FREQUENTLY ASKED QUESTIONS

How do I do spells when I'm not allowed to burn candles in my room?

You can still perform spells without candles. This is not a problem. Can you do glitter? Go to the store and buy some little tubes of different colored glitter. Match the color of the glitter to the candle color that was called for. When it comes to the candle lighting part of your spell, put a small pinch of glitter in the palm of your hand. Ask the element of air to speed your spell safely on its way. Then gently blow a small amount of glitter into the air. Or, if you prefer, you can wait until the end of your spell and go outside to blow the glitter to the winds.

I can't burn incense. How do I perform a cleansing if I can't use incense?

Don't worry, there are several ways around this dilemma. You can open a window and let the breeze in, or perhaps turn on a fan. Ask friendly sylphs, the air elementals, to cleanse the room of all negativity. Remember to thank them when you are done. Stir a little salt into a glass of water. Then sprinkle it at each cardinal point or direction. This is called asperging. For an alternative, use a drop of lavender oil or some lemon juice in the water.

What do I need to study magic for? I just get everything I need off the Internet.

Allow me a moment to shudder. The Internet is useful for many things, but it is not a good source for scholarly information. And you should know that Witches are folk who never stop studying and learning. You should therefore seek out good books, and read everything you can get your hands on. Where do you start? Do you have a favorite magical book that really helped you at one point? Check that book's bibliography. Then track down more books. Go to the public library and look up titles on goddesses, folk magic, world mythology, the Celts, the Druids, and pre-Christian Europe.

Now I have a question for you. Have you ever heard of the Witches' pyramid? It teaches you the following: "To know, to dare, to will, and to be silent." These are the building blocks of magic. "To know", means to know yourself—who you are and what you're about. You are seeking knowledge. "To dare", means that you are daring to study and practice on your own. You are daring to be wise. "To will", is to will positive changes in your life with your magic. And "to be silent" is pretty self-explanatory. To be silent is the foundation that the other principles are built upon. And often the hardest to achieve.

Wicca is called the craft of the wise for a reason. I am sure you can take these ideas and add them in a crafty way quietly into your life. There is nothing wrong with keeping a low profile. Now and again, it's the smart thing to do. You can still be and feel magical and no one will be the wiser. That is, except for you.

THE MAGICAL JINN

BY JIM WEAVER

Ever since the days of ancient Arabia, people have sought to gain magical knowledge from the *jinn*.

Of all supernatural beings, few stir the imagination as do the jinn. For many thousands of years legends about them have inspired poets, writers, and musicians. The prophet Mohammed was a sincere believer in the jinn, and even devoted a chapter to them in Islam's holiest book, the Koran. In popular literature, the jinn can also be found in the *Arabian Nights*.

Known as genies in the West, jinn are magical spirits found in Middle Eastern folklore. According to Islamic lore, thousands of years before humans appeared on our planet, Earth was inhabited by a great race of jinn. Unlike angels, which were created from brilliant light, or humans who were created from clay, jinn were created from pure smokeless fire.

In the realm of magic, jinn are unique for two reasons. First, they are treated in Islamic tradition as intelligent beings who, along with humans, have the ability to choose a religious or spiritual path. Second, they are the alpha and the omega of the spirit world; that is, not only were they believed to have inhabited the world before humankind, but some believe after the human race passes from the earth the jinn will once again rise and control the world.

A *jinni*, or a single jinn, could be good or evil. In all, there were five classes of jinn. The *marid* were the most powerful of all jinn, but also the most evil. The *ifrit* ranked second in power and enjoyed leading humans astray. These were followed by the *shaitan*, the *jinn*, which is now used as the term to describe all of the race, and the *jann*, the least powerful.

Originally jinn were thought to be invisible nature spirits which inhabited trees, plants, and rocks. Many inhabited desert regions and forests, while others existed in the oceans and in the air. Jinn also could be found dwelling in marketplaces, abandoned houses, wells, and at crossroads. Many jinn were also attracted to food and were believed to live in gardens and pantries or in specific foods such as rice and chickpeas.

The magical abilities of jinn are legendary. They were able to take on many forms such as snakes, wolves, dogs, human beings, or other animals. Some jinn were said to have the ability to fly, and if angry, they would charge across the deserts in great whirlwinds, raising the hot sand into the air. Jinn that appeared as men and women lived much like humans—they ate, loved, and had children. Some jinn, it is said, intermarried with humans, their children taking on characteristics of each parent. Romantic tales of the love between a jinni and a human have charmed audiences for centuries.

Friendly jinn were also known to grant wishes to people and to teach magical techniques such as scrying.

The jinn were well-known for their ability to construct great monuments. Stories persist which say the jinn were called upon to help build Egypt's pyramids and to assist Solomon in constructing the Temple of Jerusalem. To do this, Solomon was believed to control the jinn with his magic ring. Some accounts say the ring was set with a diamond, while others describe it as being made of bronze and iron and inscribed with the secret name of God. It is also thought that before recorded history, when the jinn dominated Earth, they built great cities, now lost to us.

For all their power, jinn were not without certain weaknesses. They had a great fear of iron, and they tried to avoid it. Jinn who took human form had no blood in their veins. Instead, fire, the element from which they were created, was believed to run through their bodies. So if a human-looking jinni was wounded, they were supposed to burst into flames and be destroyed. Although the jinn are thought to be supernatural, they are not immortal. After living extremely long lives they will die and according to legend, return to *Qaf,* a mythical mountainous region which surrounds our Earth.

The history and lore of the jinn is complex and fascinating. As Islam spread, different nations and ethnic groups added their own stories about the jinn—some serious, some delightful. Many believe jinn still coexist with humans and can act as friendly guardians even today.

The jinn will always be with us as long as there is magic in the world. They were here in the beginning, and they will be here in the end.

FOR FURTHER STUDY

The Encyclopedia of Witches and Witchcraft. Rosemary Ellen Guiley. Facts on File, Inc., 1989.

TEEN PAGANS

BY TYGER'S EYE

Teens and "young adults" worldwide have embraced the Old Religion for a spectrum of reasons. Whether it was because the religion they were raised with did not satisfy, or simply because magic of the Old was too alluring, the reasons to take to the craft are many. After all, the craft is more accepting of alternative lifestyles, and in general more accepting. No matter what the reason for your choice, the Old Religion gives name and structure to the beliefs that we carried with us despite the religion we were born into.

In the craft, age isn't as large a factor as you might expect; people of all ages can celebrate its mysteries and magic. Still, a teenager's overeagerness, enthusiasm, and still-maturing vocabulary tend to take away some of the credibility they may need to legitimate such a choice.

Often, when a teen embraces the Old Religion, she will find herself faced with elders who question her sincerity. The struggle between our parents' instinct to protect us from the evils of the unknown, and our desire to walk our own path, only complicates this highly personal decision. As teenagers are walking a bridge between childhood and recognized adulthood, they regularly have to deal with privacy, credibility, and personal issues. That the choice to practice Witchcraft or Paganism involves religion only causes that much more scrutiny on the part of parents and elders.

In today's world, teens often find themselves pushed away from by elders who don't understand them. This occurs at the moment with an elders wisdom is often most sorely needed. Fortunately for most teens, there are learned Pagans and open-minded parents who can supply such assistance. A teenager does need to take some care whom she confides in, of course. But overall I find most elders involved in the craft to be caring and interested people.

Still, many adult pagans do not always take the desire of teenagers to learn very seriously. Yes, there are youths who will walk around with a book on Wicca or Witchcraft, imagining themselves as the Halliwell sisters on *Charmed* with their "book of magic." But chances are, when the media-Witch-wannabes are faced with the spirituality behind the craft at some time in their lives, they will likely have already moved onto the next fad. In the face of the work that such spirituality demands, these folk will decide that the Old Religion is too much work for them. Those who are serious about the spirituality behind all the magic and rebellion will still be around, however. And these are the young people that older Pagans and Witches need to seek out to help and provide guidance to.

There are, as some of you may know already, those of us who walk with the God and Goddess by our sides. We have understanding in our minds and peace in our hearts, knowing that magic comes from within. There is an assortment of us who have found the Old Religion in our search for something more.

At times, we need encouragement and guidance, not distrust and stern lecturing. Just because we're younger in age doesn't mean we are all younger in mind or spirit. Teen Witches don't need things dumbed-down for us all the time. A little patience and gentle tone is what we need. Give us some faith, and we will soar with it.

SACRED MONUMENTS

BY SEDWIN

T he ancient people of Europe left their legacy in stone scattered across the continent, around the Mediterranean islands, and in the British Isles in the form of circles, alignments, single standing stones, and *dolmens*, rooms formed of standing stone. Several thousand mysterious structures were built from 5000 to 500 BC. There are many theories as to how and why they were built, but the evidence is clear that many sites accurately mark the rising and setting of both Sun and Moon at the Winter and Summer Solstices, indicating there was something more to them than met the eye.

In recent years, researchers have found that these structures also tracked lunar cycles—and not only the 18.61-year cycle, but also the triple cycles of 55.83 years. While the ability to notice and monitor these cycles requires great skill, the fact that early people managed it without the help of calculators or written language is a testimony to their intelligence and ingenuity. It is thought that the stone alignments were tools used to maintain count of these cycles, as well as other astronomical events such as eclipses. Furthermore, the placement of the stones in relationship to hills and mountains suggest that the landscape itself functioned as part of these observations.

The use of sacred geometry, or the mathematical determination of the relationship of an object with its surroundings to maintain a harmonious balance, has been noted when studying the placement of ancient stones circles. As a general rule in these sites, the landscape seems to envelope the structures, though at least one side is left open for a long-range view of the horizon. This type of harmony with the Earth seems to have been used in later times for the placement of the Palace of Knossos in Crete, and the temples at Delphi in Greece. On an even wider scale, many of the Neolithic monuments are in alignment with each other along ley lines, or Earth energy lines. And in fact, if you were to draw lines on a map of England to connect the major sites, you would create a triangle.

Stonehenge and Ireland's Newgrange are the most well-known sites of this sort, but the Brittany coast of France has the greatest concentration of Neolithic monuments in the world. The Gauls called Brittany the "land on the sea," and a map of the Neolithic sites there reveals that they are scattered around inlets, rivers, and on a peninsula across the bay from the Grand Menhir. Note: The word *menhir* comes from Welsh—*maen* (stone) and *hir* (long). Now broken and lying on the ground, the Grand Menhir would have been sixty feet tall. Within a five-mile area there are 3,000 stones. Approximately one-third of them stand in rows running east to west several kilometers toward large semicircles of stones. The height of the alignment of the stones gradually increases from two to twelve feet as they near the semicircles. Major sight lines for the Midwinter and Midsummer moonrises and moonsets intersect at the Grand Menhir.

Material from burials in the chambered mounds at Carnac have been dated to 4700 BC. While the area is densely populated with monuments, archaeological work around the sites reveal that not many people actually lived in the immediate vicinity. This suggests that it functioned as an observatory and place of ritual. Here as well as other sites in Europe, level areas of paving stones would suggest an ideal route for processions and dancing. To the people who built them, science and religion were probably not separate compartments of exploration and belief. To observe and honor the natural world and feel truly connected with it must have made for powerful rituals and celebrations at Carnac. Even well into historical times, the people of Brittany marked the quarter days of the year with festivals and dancing among the standing stones.

We can only imagine what it was like to move among the menhirs and ritual bonfires under a sky full of stars or a luminous Moon. The sacred stone circles, the meeting point of earthly and heavenly energies, likely cast long solid shadows as human shapes flickered between them. Today, we can merely try to reach into the past to capture this experience as we dance in our own rituals, renewing our connection to Mother Earth and all who dwell here with us.

FOR FURTHER STUDY

Great Stone Circles: Fables, fictions, facts. Aubrey Burl. Yale University Press, 1999.

A Guide to Stone Circles of Britain, Ireland and Brittany. Aubrey Burl. Yale University Press, 1995.

Megaliths: Stones of memory. Jean-Pierre Mohen. Harry N. Abrams, 1999.

Sanctuaries of the Goddess: The sacred landscapes and objects. Peg Streep. Little, Brown and Company, 1994.

The Standing Stones of Europe: A guide to the great megalithic monuments. Alastair Service and Jean Bradbery. George Weidenfeld & Nicolson Limited, 1996.

Korean House-selling Spell

By S Y Zenith

To this day and age, Koreans in their native country remain staunch in their belief in shamans and fortunetellers. This ritual was related to me by a fortuneteller in Seoul for those who have difficulty selling their property:

Get four pairs of your clean underpants, and in each place a silver or gold coin. Fold up the underpants with the coins within, and place them in the four corners of your home. In a short time, a buyer will come along and make a reasonable offer to buy your home. This is a tried and tested spell.

THE SACRED SITES OF HAWAII

BY BERNYCE BARLOW

Hawaii is the only one of the United States that does not lie on the mainland of North America. It is made up of 132 volcanic islands that emerged from the floor of the Pacific Ocean. Of all the islands, eight are considered the main part of the state—Hawaii, Maui, Molokai, Lanai, Kauai, Niihau, Oahu, and Kahoolawe. It is amidst these islands that some of the most powerful sacred sites in the world are located.

MAGICAL KAUAI

The island of Kauai is the oldest among the Hawaiian Islands, and it is the northernmost island in the chain. Kauai is where we are going to begin our armchair sojourn to the sacred places, or *heiaus*, where the Hawaiians went to seek out power and to recognize their gods and goddesses through offerings, rituals, dance, and chants.

Kauai is nicknamed the "Garden Island" for good reason. The power and ancient imprint on this island can sometimes feel overwhelming because many of its many sacred sites. Kauai is a lush paradise—in fact, the northern slope of Kawaikini Mountain claims the most rainfall on Earth. Kauai's sacred sites are considered the earliest among the ancestral power centers. It is on Kauai where the fiery goddess Pele is said to have originally lived before moving on to the other islands. Kauai is also considered the first home of the Menehune, Hawaii's lost tribe of little folks who possessed mystical abilities.

Lydgate State Park on Kauai is located and is host to many heiaus such as the Havola "Place of Refuge" and the Hikina Akala Heiau. Hikina Akala Heiau, built around AD 800, was the first temple site erected near Wialua and the first place the rays of the morning sun touch the island of Kauai. Havola "Place of Refuge" is just north of Hikina Akala at the sacred coconut grove. A Place of Refuge was a site that sheltered the very old, the very young, and the injured during the exacting island wars. A Place of Refuge was also a place of pardon where a lawbreaker could seek absolution from a *kahuna pule,* or prayer priest. Most of the main islands had at least one Place of Refuge, and the Hawaiian culture still considers the refuges hallowed ground.

One cannot talk about Kauai without mentioning the Salt Ponds of the Menehune. The Menehune, who were said to be a race of little people who lived among the islands, were very industrious and could perform great feats of strength overnight using their magical ways. Legend tells us if a task was not completed before the Sun rose, the task would never be completed at all, unless it was completed by someone other than a Menehune. Many of the fish ponds on the islands are said to have been built by this lost tribe. Near Lihue there is a fish pond that is said was not completed by morning. Although the gap in the pond was closed many generations later, the work is noticeably inferior to the original works. Appropriately named, the Menehune Fish Pond can be found near the Huleia National Wildlife Preserve.

This region is also home to the Bell Stone that when hit in a particular manner resonates throughout the Wialua Valley. It was used to announce the royal births. The Poliahu Heiau is also nearby, and is considered the largest heiau found on Kauai. Poliahu is the name of the snow goddess who is said to reside on Mauna Kea. This site displays stone carvings, terraces, and idol sites that were an integral part of the Hawaiian ceremonial rites.

Over on the north shore of Kauai along the Na Pali coast there is another heiau that remains sacred to Hawaii. Located at Kiloe near Kee, it is called the *Ka Ulu A Paoa Heiau.* This was the site of an ancient hula school. At one time on the terrace above the boulders advanced students would test their chanting skills by walking on the smooth boulders at the edge of the sea and chanting *meles.* If they could be heard above the roar of the sea and wind, they passed their test.

The hula was not always a form of entertainment, at one time it was only used as a tribute to the gods and goddesses, as a form of preserving history or to highlight a royal birth or war. But it was also used in the magical rituals of the Hawaiians. The hula schools were very strict, and to change a dance was considered a serious offense. The goddess Laka is the primary goddess of the dance although Pele's sister, Hiíaka, is also associated with the dance. Hula dancers have the ability to tell beautiful stories and cast powerful magic, through their dance.

On the north side of Kauai, there is a beautiful trail that will give you a lovely view of the Na Pali Coast. The trail, which begins at Kee Beach where the highway ends, is called the Kalalua Trail and will take you two miles inland to Hanakapiai Falls, where a three-hundred-foot drop ends in a beautiful pool of fresh water. It is said the Honopu Valley was the haven of the Menehune. Kalalau Trail takes you right into the heart of the Menehune's homeland so be sure to leave a gentle offering for the spirit of the place during your hike.

No exploration of Kauai's sacred sites would be complete without mentioning Wiamea Canyon, sometimes called the Grand Canyon of the Pacific. Wiamea Canyon is said to contain a powerful energy vortex that can knock your socks off. The canyon is only 2,000 to 3,000 feet deep but it has the same feel of the canyon lands of Utah and Arizona. Waimea Canyon was formed by the run-off waters of the dormant volcano, Mt. Waialeale. With an average of 460 inches of rain each year, there is a lot of water here.

There are many other sacred sites on the island of Kauai. This is but a showcase of some of them. Indeed, the entire island is a sacred site with its breath-taking waterfalls, unsullied beaches, rugged coastlines, deep canyons, and high-spirited rivers. These sites are the places where the ancestors walked among the gods and goddesses and left a veiled reflection here and there. To visit this ancient island is to feel the aloha spirit as it was meant to be experienced—with awe, reverence, and an appreciation for a kind magnificence that is rarely found except in paradise.

Using Trees as Medicine

By Ellen Evert Hopman

Many common North American trees can be used as medicine. Their advantage over medicinal herbs is that tree medicines can be used year round. In fact, trees make among the most versatile medicine you will find.

In early spring and summer the leaves of trees are useful healing agents. In fall and winter, the bark of the twigs or of the roots may be used to treat common ailments. Some simple rules must be learned, however, and followed for tree medicines to work.

Preparing Tree Medicines for Use

Here are several rules to ensure you are mindful in gathering tree medicines. First, never cut the bark off of the trunk of a living tree. Especially avoid girdling the tree by removing the bark as this will kill the tree. To gather bark use that found on a twig or a root of a felled tree. In these cases, it is a simple matter of stripping the bark off of the twig or root with a sharp knife. Medicinal

agents are found in the cambium—the living green or greenish yellow layer just under the outer bark.

Once you have gathered the bark of a tree you can use it immediately or dry it for later use. To dry the bark, carefully lay it to dry in the shade, making sure that the strips do not overlap. Leaves can be tied together and hung in bunches from a string or rope in a dry, shady area.

To use the bark, simmer two teaspoons of bark per cup of water for twenty minutes in a nonaluminum pot with a tight lid. Strain and drink. The dose is one-quarter cup, taken four times a day not with meals. This assumes a 150-pound adult. A child weighing 75 pounds should take half as much, and a child weighing 40 pounds should take half as much again. The tea may be stored in a glass jar with a tight lid, in the refrigerator, for up to a week.

When using the leaves they should be picked in the early spring no later than Summer Solstice. Steep two teaspoons of fresh or dried leaves per cup of freshly boiled water for about twenty minutes, in a nonaluminum pot with a tight lid. The dose is the same—a quarter cup, taken four times a day not with meals. Add lemon or honey to the medicines as desired.

If you are making a tea to use as a wound wash or to add to the bath it may be much stronger. Use more of the tree parts and less water, and simmer or steep for longer periods.

To make a tree leaf poultice, use fresh leaves, or dry ones that have been soaked in enough boiling water to make them soft. Place the leaves in a blender with just enough water to make a mush. Pour into a glass or ceramic bowl and then add powdered slippery elm bark, a little at a time, until a pie dough consistency is achieved. Spread the poultice onto a cotton cloth and apply to the affected area. Leave on for one hour, and then discard the poultice material. Repeat daily.

A fomentation may be made of the bark or leaf tea by soaking a clean cotton cloth in the tea and then applying it to an affected area. Tree leaves, bark, and nuts may also be used in healing salves. To make a salve simply place the plant material in a large nonaluminum pot, and just barely cover with cold-pressed virgin olive oil. Simmer with a lid for about twenty minutes.

In a separate pot melt beeswax, and bring it to a simmer. After the oil mixture has simmered for twenty minutes add three tablespoons of melted beeswax for every cup of olive oil used. Stir and then strain into very clean glass jars. Allow to cool and harden before putting on a lid.

Some tree parts are used to make massage oils or oils for other purposes. Take the fresh tree parts, and put them in a shallow nonaluminum baking dish. Cover with a light oil such as almond, cover, and bake in a slow oven at 110 degrees for several hours until the plant material wilts.

To tincture buds, barks, or roots, place the chopped plant material in a clean glass jar. Cover with vodka or other alcohol (80 proof or higher), cover tightly, and allow the tincture to sit for eight days. Shake occasionally. Add 10 percent spring water and a teaspoon of vegetable glycerine. Strain and bottle for later use. Store in a cool, dark place. For leaves and flowers; pack the plant material into a clean glass jar, barely cover with alcohol, and allow the tincture to extract until the plant material begins to wilt. Add the spring water and vegetable glycerine, and strain and bottle as above. The dose is about 10 drops, three times a day, taken with water.

GREEN ETIQUETTE

It is only polite to thank a tree when you have used its parts for medicine. Make a habit of giving back to the trees. A meal of fertilizer, a drink during a hot spell, or offerings of herbs such as sage or tobacco are always correct. In ancient European tradition, vervain, honey, or apple cider were often given. Or a simple prayer was spoken, that the tree and its relations always have abundant sunshine, pure water to drink, healthy winds, and the companionship of birds and other friendly spirits. In this time of global warming it is wise to plant trees wherever possible and to nurture living ones. Trees are cooling. They prevent evaporation of rainwater, hold back water to prevent floods and erosion, purify stagnant and polluted water, and maintain the balance of oxygen and carbon in a world increasingly polluted by greenhouse gasses. Ancient trees especially should be honored and protected.

Some Tree Medicines

Alder

Alder is a small tree that thrives in damp areas such as wetlands and river banks. It usually has several grayish trunks, and its female catkins develop into what look like tiny brown pine cones. Alder bark is simmered in water to make a healing wash for deep wounds. It is astringent and will help to pull the edges of a wound together. The leaves and bark can be made into a tea that will benefit tonsillitis and fever. The leaves are also used in poultices to dry up breast milk. Alder bark tea can be used as a douche or for hemorrhoids. Fresh alder sap can be applied to any area to relieve itching.

Apple

The bark of the root of apple trees is used for fevers. Apples are rich in magnesium, iron, potassium, and vitamins C, B, and B_2. When peeled, they relieve diarrhea. Stewed unpeeled apples are a laxative. Eating apples regularly promotes restful sleep. Baked apples can be applied warm as a poultice for sore throats and fevers. Apple cider is important in this time of antibiotics, which destroy the intestinal flora. Raw, unpasteurized apple cider will restore the correct bacteria to the bowels after a course of antibiotics. Apples reduce acidity in the stomach and help to clean the liver. Add garlic and horseradish to apple cider to clear the skin. Use the mixture as a wash externally and take it internally as a drink.

Ash

Ash is a tall tree whose compound leaves are composed of five to nine, or seven to eleven leaflets. Its bark is very tightly and regularly furrowed, and its winged, canoe-paddle-shaped seeds, called keys, hang in clusters until they turn brown and drop off in the fall. The tender new spring growth of the twig tips and leaves can be simmered to make a laxative tea that will benefit gout, jaundice, and rheumatism.

Beech

Beech trees have a distinctive, smooth gray bark that resembles the skin of an elephant. The bark is used as a tea for lung problems, including tuberculosis. It is also cleansing to the blood, though pregnant women should avoid it. Beech bark tea makes a good wash for poison ivy. Beech leaves are used in poultices for burns and for frostbite.

BIRCH

Birch trees have thin papery bark that peels easily—so easily that birds actually use it to build their nests. It can range in color from chalky white and reddish brown to golden gray and yellow. The sweet birch (black birch) and the yellow birch both have a nice wintergreen flavor in their twigs and bark. Birch leaf or twig tea is a laxative, and healing to mouth sores, kidney and bladder sediments, and gout. The tea also helps rheumatic pains. Make a strong decoction of the twigs, bark, and leaves and add it to the bath for relief of eczema, psoriasis, and other moist skin eruptions. Modern medicine has recently confirmed that betulinic acid, found in birch sap, has anti-tumor properties that help fight cancer.

CEDAR

The northern white cedar is an evergreen with a branched trunk, conical shape, and flat scalelike leaves. It has reddish-brown bark that hangs in hairy shreds. Another name for the tree is *Arborvitae,* or "tree of life," a name given to it by the French explorer Jacques Cartier after it saved his crew from scurvy. A tea is made from the leaves and twigs, and is very high in vitamin C. Among the Algonquin it is considered a sacred tree, and they will not perform a ceremony without it. Its branches are used on the floor of the sweat lodge, and it is dried and burned as incense because it harmonizes the emotions and puts one in the proper state of mind for prayer. The tea of the twigs and branches is simmered until the water in the pot begins to turn brown. It is then used for fevers, rheumatic complaints, chest colds, and flu.

ELDER

Elder trees are quite small. They have clusters of white flowers in spring and black or deep purple berries in the fall. They thrive in damp, moist areas. Elderberries are used to make preserves, pies, and wine. Taken as a tea, either fresh or dried, the berries benefit the lungs and nourish the blood. The young leaves of elder are used in salves and poultices for skin healing. A root bark tea clears congestion, eases headaches, and is used in poultices for mastitis. A tincture of the flowers lowers fevers by promoting perspiration. Elderflower water is a traditional remedy for skin blemishes and sunburn. Cold elderflower tea is placed on the eyes as a soothing compress for inflammations. Elderflower oil makes a soothing balm for the sore nipples of nursing mothers.

ELM

Slippery elm is a medium-sized tree with grayish bark, usually found near streams. Unlike the American elm its crown does not droop. Its leaves are also larger than the American elm's, with coarsely toothed margins. The inner bark of the slippery elm, which is sticky and fragrant when fresh, is used medicinally. Slippery Elm bark is available in dried and powdered forms from herbalists. It is made into a paste with water and then applied as a poultice to injuries of flesh and bone, on gunshot wounds, ulcers, tumors, swellings, chilblains, and on the abdomen to draw out a fever. Slippery elm is very high in calcium, and a pudding or tea of the bark can be ingested to help speed bone healing. The powdered bark in water makes a jelly that soothes bowel and urinary problems, sore throats, and diarrhea. It makes a perfect substitute milk for babies who are allergic to cow's milk. Try adding a little lemon and honey for flavor.

HAWTHORN

Hawthorne is a small, broad, round, and dense tree with thorns and edible red fruits. The fall berries and spring new leaves and flowers make a cardiac tonic that benefits virtually all heart conditions. Be aware however: Prolonged use does cause the blood pressure to drop. Use it for a few weeks and then take a week off to prevent a precipitous decrease in blood pressure. Use caution when combining this herb with other heart medications to prevent a sudden drop in blood pressure. For maximum benefit eat fresh raw garlic as you undergo a hawthorn regime. (Garlic provides extra cleaning of plaque in the blood vessels.)

Hazel

Hazel is a small tree with small rounded nuts that grow two to four in a cluster. Hazel twigs are traditionally used by dowsers to find hidden sources of water. Hazel nuts are said to benefit the kidneys. Huron herbalists used the bark in poultices for tumors and ulcers. The Iroquois mixed the nut oil with bear's grease to make a mosquito repellent. The Chippewa used a decoction of hazel root, white oak root, chokecherry bark, and the heartwood of ironwood for bleeding from the lungs.

Holly

Mountain holly is a small tree with ovate, fine saw-toothed leaves and large orange-red berries. The buds and twigs were used by Native American herbalists in decoctions and as an external wash for ulcers, herpetic eruptions, jaundice, fever, and diarrhea. The leaves alone were used as a beverage tea. English holly or European holly is a familiar evergreen usually seen as decoration at Yuletide. It has spiny, elliptical leaves and shiny red berries. The leaves can be used as a tea substitute and in infusions for coughs, colds, and flu. Be aware: The berries of all holly varieties are strongly purgative.

Linden and Basswood

Linden is a large tree found in moist, rich soils near other hardwoods. It has heart-shaped leaves with toothed margins. The bark is dark gray, and its fruit is nutlike, downy, and pea-sized. It has clusters of yellowish-white fragrant flowers in the spring. Basswood, or American linden, is a close relative. Linden flower tea is a popular beverage in Europe for nervous headaches and upset digestion, hysteria, nervous vomiting, and heart palpitations. Linden flower tea can be added to baths to calm the nerves. Linden flower honey is prized for medicinal use. Native American herbalists used the roots and bark of basswood for burns and the flower tea for epilepsy, headache, spasm, spasmodic cough, and general pain. The buds were eaten as famine food, and the bark was pounded and added to soups.

Maple

Maples are large trees with deeply lobed, toothed leaves. The bark of the younger trees is gray and smooth, on older trees it breaks up into ridges and fissures. Maples have winged seeds that hang in clusters of two. The Ojibwa and the Cherokee made a decoction of the inner bark of red maple to use as a wash for sore eyes. The leaves of striped maple, or moosewood, were used to poultice sore breasts. A decoction of the inner bark of sugar maple was used for diarrhea. The Penobscot used striped maple bark in poultices for swollen limbs, and as a tea for kidney infections, coughs, colds, and bronchitis. Young maple leaves can be made into a massage oil that will be soothing to sore muscles.

Oak

Oaks are large trees with lobed leaves and acorns topped by bowl-shaped caps. The best oak for internal use is white oak, though all oaks are valuable as external washes. The tannins in oak bark and leaves are helpful in pulling the edges of a wound together and is antiseptic and antiviral. White oak bark tea is used for chronic diarrhea, chronic mucus discharges, and piles. It makes a nice gargle for sore throats and a wash for skin problems such as poison ivy, burns, and wounds. The tea of the leaf or the bark may be used by women as a douche for vaginitis. Use caution: Prolonged ingestion of oak is potentially harmful.

Pine

All pines are evergreen, with needles that grow in soft, flexible clusters. Pine trees are revered worldwide as healing agents. Any pine, or other evergreen such as spruce, larch, and cedar, will have antiseptic properties useful as a wound wash. The most palatable pine for internal use is the white pine. Its needles and twigs are simmered into a tea that is rich in vitamin C. The tea is used for sore throats, coughs, and colds. Chinese herbalists boil the knot of the wood because of the concentrated resins found there. Pine baths aid kidney ailments, improve circulation, and are relaxing to sore muscles. The aroma of pine is soothing to the nerves and the lungs. Pine tea makes a wonderful foot bath.

Poplar

Poplars are distinguished by their drooping catkins and rounded leaves with pointed tips. Balsam poplar was used by Native American herbalists who scored the bark and applied the resinous gum to toothaches and swellings. The sticky spring buds were gathered in May and used in salves for skin problems, sprains, sore muscles, wounds, headaches, tumors, eczema, bruises, gout, and on the chest for lung ailments and coughs. The buds were decocted and used internally for phlegm, kidney and bladder ailments, coughs, scurvy, and rheumatic pains. The root was combined with the root of white poplar in a decoction to stop premature bleeding in pregnancy. The warmed juice of white poplar was dropped into sore ears. Poplar barks are high in salicin, making them useful in treating deep wounds, gangrene, eczema, cancer, burns, and strong body odor. The inner bark of young poplar trees is edible in the spring and can be simmered into a tea for liver and kidney ailments.

Rowan, or Mountain Ash

The American mountain ash and the European mountain ash have identical uses. The former has bunches of orange berries that look like tiny apples, and the latter has red ones. Both are small, sturdy trees with compound leaves of nine to seventeen leaflets. Their clusters of white flowers, composed of five petals each, appear in spring. Rowan berries are bitter, astringent, and very high in vitamin C. They should be picked just after the first frost when their color has deepened. The fresh juice of the berries is added to sore throat gargles, and a jelly made from the berries will treat diarrhea in adults and children. Rowan berries are added to ales and cordials. In ancient Scotland, a syrup for coughs and colds was made from rowan berries, apples, and honey.

Walnut

Walnuts trees are tall and have compound, alternate leaflets. Their spring flowers are drooping green catkins that mature into large, round nuts covered by green, spongy husks that stain the hands brown when cut open with a knife. Walnut husks are medicinally active. They are antifungal and rich in manganese, a skin-healing agent. Gather them when fresh, and rub directly onto ringworm. The tea of the hull may be used as a douche for vaginitis. For stubborn old ulcers apply the dried, powdered leaf, and then poultice with fresh green leaves. Do this for about twenty days, daily. The leaf tea increases circulation, digestion, and energy. The fresh bark may be applied to the temples for headache or to teeth to relieve pain. The dried and powdered bark, or pounded fresh bark, can be applied to wounds to stop swelling and to hasten healing.

WILLOW

There are more than forty varieties of willow growing in the United States. They are water-loving trees, a good indicator species if you are looking for a regular water source, either above or below ground. Willows have slender flexible twigs and long, narrow, simple leaves. In early spring, willows bloom with golden catkins that mature into small seed capsules in late summer. All willow barks have salicylic acid, which is a natural form of aspirin. Willow bark tea treats muscle pain and inflammation, diarrhea, fever, arthritic pain, and headache. Used externally it makes a wash for cuts, ulcers, and poison ivy. Willow bark in teas and capsules is sedative and eases insomnia. It reduces the risk of heart disease and may delay cataract formation.

FOR FURTHER STUDY

The Audubon Society Field Guide To North American Trees (Eastern Region). Elbert L. Little. Knopf, 1988.

Eastern/Central Medicinal Plants: Peterson Field Guide series. Steven Foster and James A. Duke. Houghton Mifflin Company, 1990.

Medicinal Plants of Native America. Daniel E. Moerman, with a foreword by Richard I. Ford. Museum of Anthropology, University of Michigan, 1986.

Tree Medicine, Tree Magic. by Ellen Evert Hopman. Phoenix Publishing, 1991.

WORKING WITH GOD ENERGY

By Cerridwen Iris Shea

Many people turn to Wicca because they are tired of regimented and patriarchal religions. Working within the female pantheon in a sacred space is wonderful, empowering, and life changing. But we shouldn't forget the God, the Goddess's consort and sometimes her son. Working with the energies of both the God and the Goddess in tandem keeps life in balance, and can create a polarity of energy that can be used to enhance spellwork and life work.

The first challenge for Wiccans is to toss out preconceived ideas about what is male and what is female. Jung promoted the theory that each of us contains a seed of the other gender within, which is supported by a modern understanding of the yin/yang symbol. We all know men who are aggressive, protective, and embody the qualities we are taught to think of as "male." But, on considering the issue, we probably could also say we know men who are gentle and quiet—qualities often considered "female." These men, of course, are no less "male" for possessing these qualities, and if anything are perhaps more male because of their gentleness and sensitivity. At the same time, we all know plenty of strong, independent women whose strength does not make them any less female. So when dealing with people, one needs to consider each as an individual, rather than a generic gender.

But how does this translate to action considering the energy of the deities? Well, we must first and foremost remember that we are all One. In point of fact, we give names to different aspects of this Oneness in order to make the concept more understandable to our human minds. Giving something a name makes it more real and more accessible to us. It is up to each of us as individuals to refine our own definitions of these general concepts.

There are many ways to start connecting with God energy. You may choose to read myths and legends, for instance, and find divine male figures that inspire you. Gather up pictures or statues of the Green Man, the Horned One, Lugh, or Baldur. Take out your tarot deck and study the male figures—the Emperor, the Joker, and so on. Pay attention to the men in your life that you admire, and specify the qualities that make them attractive to you.

Once you have considered these things fully, light a green or white candle that you have anointed with a forest oil such as juniper or pine. Burn an incense that feels leafy or oaky or piny to you. Then, follow your breath, and gaze into the candle flame. Open yourself up to experiencing the God energy. Let the God speak to you, or even appear to you. Tell him that you are not used to working with God energy, which is of course different than the energy experienced inside a church of an organized religion, but would like to learn. This experience will feel different for everyone; just let it happen. As you get more comfortable

with God energy, you may want to invoke the God in ritual from time to time.

You may wish to stand in the God position as you perform this ritual. That is, stand straight with feet together and arms crossed at your chest, right over left. On the other hand, the Goddess position is useful for invoking the Goddess in ritual. For this, stand with your arms and legs outstretched, forming a pentacle shape with your body.

Since deific experience is so individual, you will experience your own feelings in invoking the God or Goddess. It may feel like a tingling current is entering your body, reaching into depths beyond the physical. In my own experience, when I invoke the Goddess it feels as though my energy is being enhanced with a "sameness," located at a very high frequency. It's my own energy, but more so than I could imagine. When I work with God energy, meanwhile, there's a difference. It's difficult to describe, but instead the energy feels quite different, while still very intense and complementary. It is unfortunate that our language is too inadequate for us to describe these feelings with clarity.

The experience of working with God energy is one of fusion. Not being male, I won't venture to speak for their experiences. But men with whom I've discussed this agree that when they work with God energy they feel enhanced, and when they work with Goddess energy they feel fused.

When raising energy for a specific magical working, it makes sense to decide which of the two sensations you feel will enhance your goal the most. Sometimes you might not

know, and you will have to try more than once. Other times, you might want to use both energies for a cohesive and complete ritual experience. In the end, it's trial and error. As you get more familiar with how the different energies feel in your body, you will know whom to call on and how to align your energy for a specific goal.

As much as I like working with Goddess energy, adding the God energy to the mix has been such a boon to my workings and to my life in general. There is a sense of completeness rather than otherness, and it truly makes my life more magical.

FOR FURTHER STUDY

Celtic Myth and Magic: Harness the power of the gods and goddesses. Edain McCoy. Llewellyn Publications, 1995.

The God of the Witches. Margaret Murray. Oxford University Press.

Lord of Light and Shadow: The many faces of the god. D.J. Conway. Llewellyn Publications, 1997.

Norse Magic. D.J. Conway. Llewellyn Publications, 1990.

To Stir a Magick Cauldron: A witch's guide to casting and conjuring. Silver RavenWolf. Llewellyn Publications, 1995.

The Witches' God: lord of the dance. Janet and Stewart Farrar. Phoenix Publications, 1989.

Best Friends Magic

The Power in a Circle of Two

By Edain McCoy

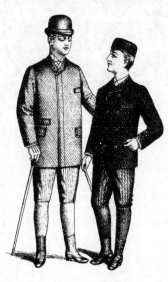

Allll too often, two witchy friends will waste time in search of a coven who will take them in, never realizing the incredible magical potential in their coven of two. If you and your best friend always seem to known what the other is thinking and feeling, and find you're always in agreement on how a situation should be handled, then you have the raw material for making very powerful coven magic.

Best Friends Magic

The concept of Best Friends Magic is simple, but effective. A magical coven works best when all members are in accord over goals, and are able to communicate these concepts to one another so that there is a unity of purpose. To enact magic, the group mind must be as one. When you are perfectly attuned to someone, you can easily overcome the sort of stumbling blocks that interfere with the efficacy of group magic. With your best friend, you will tend to have similar vizualizations and goals for life in general that reflect each others values.

Best Friends Magic is the ultimate in trust and intimacy. It is much like a love relationship—it is exclusive and can start strong and seem so perfect it will last a lifetime. Still, in time such a relationship may break down. Take care, then, when you choose to create such a relationship. Should you ever sense that your friend and partner is grudging of your personal goals, or seems jealous when you start to achieve them, this may be a sign that the magical relationship is eventually doomed.

If you are certain that you and your best friend really want the best for each other, and there is no threat of magical sabotage, then begin experimenting to find the best ways to merge and send forth your combined magical wills. That is, forget about the so-called coven "rules" that Hollywood has planted in your mind, and focus on each other. You may be surprised how well it works.

BASIC BEST FRIENDS MAGICAL TECHNIQUE

With your best friend, begin experimenting with raising and sending energy by sitting on the floor or ground facing each other. Position yourselves so the soles of your feet are touching, then lean forward and place your palms together. Visualize drawing energy deep from within the Earth and seeing it flow into you through the root chakra at the base of your spine. Try to sense when the energy is filling you each to capacity without speaking or signaling one another. Let the gift of spiritual communication you already have with each other do the work for you.

When you are each ready, silently will the energy to begin moving within the circle of your bodies—going out into your friend's palm through your right hand, circling around his or her back, coming down the right arm to the hand, and being received by you through your left palm. Don't worry that the motion is moving counterclockwise. This does not mean negative magic is afoot. These are traditional sending and receiving correspondences, and they are best for beginners because they are easy to sense.

Take turns switching the direction of the energy at random. You may verbally or visually communicate at this point. How you communicate will be just as important as how accurate you become in sensing your friend's energy shifts. See if you can sense when your friend is pushing the energy in another direction. You should in time gain a sense of the resistance to the flow of energy you are sending. Also try moving energy through the soles of your feet. This is harder to do and much harder to sense, but it is possible. A nice variation is to send energy in a predetermined direction from one friend's hands into the other. Send it in two separate circles down to the receiver's feet where he or she will become the sender who projects the energy into the feet of the partner. An advanced version of this variation is to make each arc of energy travel in a different direction.

MAKING MAGIC WITH YOUR BEST FRIEND

When you've both had a chance to sense and change the direction of your energy in various ways, you are ready to use this technique to cast spells. To do this you will need to agree in advance on a single magical goal. This can be a spell for one of you or both of you, but the goal must be exactly the same for each. For example, you can attract a date for one or both of you, enhance your brain power on an upcoming exam, find your friend the perfect job, and so on. Remember that your strength in making this work for you is that you're already very close to one another emotionally and spiritually. You should be able to help each other achieve magical goals with ease because your connection gives you a magical advantage.

Once you have a goal you will need to create a two or four line rhyming chant. Don't worry about crafting fine literature, just make it easy to remember. Chant together in rhythm, and begin moving your hand to hand energy in the direction that seems best for enhancing the goal of the spell. Magic to stop or decrease something is best done with counterclockwise energy, and magic to start or increase something is best done with energy flowing clockwise. Let the energy build in intensity. Enjoy it. Laugh, shout affirmations of your goal, and enjoy the merging of your energy as you work toward the same end. As you feel the peak of energy approaching, begin chanting the couplet or quatrain you created while vizualizing your desired outcome. When you are ready to end the spell, release your hands and let your arms fly upward and outward, directing your magical energy toward your goal.

Owl Medicine

By Marguerite Elsbeth

We have all heard conflicting stories about Owl and its "medicine," or its supernatural power to protect, cure, heal, and to prevent or cause harm. Some traditions teach that Owl is beneficial, while others indicate that Owl brings misfortune. The truth is up to you to decide.

Owl Fact & Myth

Owl is territorial, a vicious fighter and a courageous defender of the nest. This is why Owl inspired and protected the Greek armies, and why Roman soldiers believed Owl signified triumph in battle. The Japanese drink a toast to Owl before a hunting expedition, and Russians believe Owl is sacred because it once saved the life of Genghis Khan.

Owl is monogamous in love. Therefore, Australian aborigines believe Owl represents the soul of women. French spinsters call on Owl to help them find a husband. Also in France, when a pregnant woman hears the cry of Owl, her child will be a girl.

Owl's approach to rearing offspring is sometimes brutal. Many Owl chicks starve or are killed by their siblings, depending on food availability. Perhaps because of these cruel survival tactics, African Swahili tribesmen believe Owl brings illness to children. Moroccans believe that Owl's cry can kill an infant. Still, some Owl offspring always survive to produce more Owls; consequently, Owl amulets protect Babylonian women during childbirth.

Dawn, dusk, and the dead of night is Owl's domain. Owl is the Hopi god of the dead, guardian of fires, and tender of all underground things. Owl attends Lilith, the Sumerian goddess of

313

death, and in Mexico is called "messenger of the lord of the land of the dead." Popular belief holds that seeing Owl or hearing its cry means impending death, sickness, or misfortune. Therefore, Owl is too evil to name in Cameroon, and is known only as "the bird that makes you afraid."

You may have Owl Medicine if you frequently see, hear, or dream of Owl, or if you have the gifts of invulnerability, insight, invisibility, keen observation, wisdom, and curative healing powers.

TRUE OWL ENCOUNTERS

Based on my personal encounters with Owl, I firmly believe that it is an extraordinary messenger, even if it often brings distressing news. Consider, for example, a friend of mine, who always spoke of his affinity for Great Horned Owl. Shortly following one such conversation, he suffered a massive heart attack and died. I traveled to an Anasazi ruin in southern Utah, to honor his passing. The first thing I saw upon entering the ruin was Great Horned, dead on the side of the road. I took this as an omen—my friend and his Owl were finally together.

Another time, I was driving home at dusk when I narrowly missed Owl, who swooped past my windshield in a flurry. Two days later, driving the same highway at twilight, I found myself caught in a sudden snowstorm. I almost became road kill too when my truck skidded on black ice and rolled over onto the median. While my truck was totaled, I was unharmed. It was likely because of Owl's warning that I was alert to possible danger that night.

Still another time, my neighbor saw Owl sitting on a lamppost while walking her dogs. She stopped, thinking that she and Owl might have a friendly chat. But she was wrong—Owl flew down, grazed the top of her head, and made off with a talon-full of her hair. Owl then chased her all the way to her front door. The following week she was diagnosed with a severe digestive disorder.

OWL MEDICINE

According to mythology, if a person does something wrong, they may become Owl. Gwydion the Magician turned the unfaithful Blodeuwedd of Celtic myth into Owl for betraying a magical secret. The Supreme Being of Borneo turned his wife into Owl

314

after she told secrets to mortals. In Poland, girls who are married turn into Owl when they die.

Witches and sorcerers transform into Owl. The majority of indigenous tribal people around the world believe they do too, as shape-shifting is a common practice among shamans and magicians of various cultures.

If Owl Comes Calling

If you are visited by Owl, do not panic. Instead, try to interpret what the visit might mean. For instance, you can interpret Owl's cry by number:

One hoot is an omen of impending death.

Two hoots means success in whatever project you start next.

Three represent a woman who will marry into the family.

Four hoots indicate disturbance.

Five hoots denote coming travel.

Six hoots mean guests are on the way.

Seven hoots are a sign of mental distress.

Eight hoots foretell sudden death.

Nine hoots hoots symbolize good fortune.

If you hear an Owl hoot late at night, return the call to avoid bad luck. You can also take off an item of clothing and put it on again inside out, or get up from bed and turn your left shoe upside down. If you see Owl, do the following:

Throw salt in a fire to avert any possible danger.

Propitiate Owl by setting food, a shiny crystal, or some silver coins near the place where Owl appeared.

Dedicate an altar to Owl. Cover it with a blue cloth. Place Owl images, a glass of water, a bowl of almonds, silver jewelry, and moonstone, pearl, or crystal upon it. Ask the lunar goddesses Artemis, Hecate, and Diana for help and protection.

Finally, never injure Owl, as it is our teacher and elder, and should always be respected.

A MAGICAL EDUCATION

BY JOHN MICHAEL GREER

The success of J. K. Rowling's *Harry Potter* novels has had some positive effect in the occult community. Rowling's tales of young wizards and Witches at magic school are a good reminder that magic, like any other craft, has to be learned. This is a point that some magicians try to avoid facing; after all, it's a lot easier to decide that your inborn magical talents are all you need. Unfortunately, as any artist or craftsperson can tell you, raw talent isn't worth much unless it's developed through training and practice.

If our society were less frightened of magic, there would be schools of magic in every large city. Those seeking a magical education could sign up for classes and work toward a degree in magic. If the modern magical renaissance continues, perhaps we may yet see such schools; establishing such a school is a project I've been considering for years. Unfortunately, there are very few schools or teaching organizations offering instruction in the magical arts these days. So, for now, most people who want a magical education will have to provide for it themselves, and even those who have the opportunity to study with a teacher or a group will need to take some responsibility for their own magical training.

The question then arises: What goes into a magical education? Different traditions, and different magicians, have their own ideas. Still, the following comments may help you put together your own curriculum of magical studies.

MAGICAL PRACTICE

The one non-negotiable thing that needs to be in your curriculum is a magical practice you do every day. Just as you can't become a musician without practicing your instrument, you also can't become a magician without practicing your basic rituals and exercises. It really is as simple as that.

Many traditions have a specific practice that's meant for daily use. If you're a Golden Dawn magician, you already know about the lesser ritual of the pentagram and the middle pillar exercise. If you're a student of the Aurum Solis, the wards adamant and the calyx serve the same purpose. If you're Wiccan, a good daily practice is to cast a circle, call the quarters, and invoke the Lord and the Lady. If you practice hoodoo, candle-burning rituals for spiritual development can be done as a daily practice. If you follow some other magical path… well, the possibilities are endless.

MAGICAL APPLICATIONS

Your daily practice shouldn't be the only magic you do. Again, music provides a good analogy. If you're learning to play the piano, you'll spend time on scales and etudes, but you'll also learn actual pieces of music. In the same way, along with basic practices that develop your magical skills, other magical activities will teach you to put those skills to work.

Your options here depend on your level of skill, the circumstances of your life, and the magical tradition you follow. You may choose to pursue theurgy, or workings aimed at your own spiritual development, or thaumaturgy, or workings aimed at bringing about changes in the world around you. Indeed, some systems concentrate on one or the other, but it's best to work both into your magical training. Theurgy builds magical abilities, while thaumaturgy builds confidence and knowledge by showing you what magic can accomplish in your life.

It's a good idea to start with simple workings. The only thing you'll get by tackling a ritual beyond your abilities is frustration and disappointment, while even the simplest working can become a vehicle for astonishing power if it's done with skill, understanding, and focused intent.

MAGICAL THEORY

Training in magical practice should be balanced by a background in magical theory. The theory of magic is crucial if you want to go beyond a "cookbook approach" to magic—the sort that involves nothing more than doing workings by rote out of somebody's book. Magical practice teaches you what to do and how to do it; magical theory teaches you why it works, and how it can be taken in new directions. Your choice of a tradition will guide you to a theoretical system that fits the magic you practice.

The core theoretical system of Western magic is the Qabala. (You'll also see this spelled Qabalah, Kabbalah, Cabala, and a dozen other ways; the original word is in Hebrew, which has sounds that are hard to express in the English alphabet.) Originally a fusion of Jewish mysticism and Greek philosophy, the Qabala was borrowed by magicians in the Renaissance and has been used in magical circles ever since. There are several excellent books on the Qabala to get you started.

Some Pagan magical systems, on the other hand, have theoretical structures that differ sharply from the Qabala. In Asatru, the religion of the ancient Norse and Germanic gods and goddesses, impressive work has been done on the magical theory that underlies Norse myths and magic.

GENERAL MAGICAL KNOWLEDGE

Just as college degree programs require students to take classes outside their specialties, your magical education should include general magical knowledge. The history, theory, and practice of different magical traditions is a good place to start. Whether or not you practice Wicca or Hoodoo, you'll understand magic more if you know something about all of them. A good general knowledge of other magical systems is also a cure for the "my-tradition-is-better-then-yours" childishness that still burdens too many parts of the magical community.

Mythology and folklore also belong high on the list. The more you know about myth and folklore, the better prepared you'll be to interact with the magical realms of experience. Your mythic studies, though, should always use original sources. Most modern retellings have been cleaned up, watered down, and stripped of most of their magical value. The wonder, wildness, and paradox that marks real mythological stories bears most of its power, and you'll find much more of these in the old sources.

This can be taken one step further, though it's a step that terrifies most Americans. Learning a foreign language is among the most useful things you can do to master magic. Many traditions have a huge amount of material that has never been translated into English, and texts that have been translated often lose much in the process.

The language you choose will depend on the tradition you're studying. Students of Celtic magic should certainly tackle Irish, Welsh, or Breton; Hermetic magicians might consider French,

German, or Latin, any of which can open the door to a wealth of occult lore unknown in the English-speaking world. If Asatru is your style, German will give you the best research on runes and Germanic mythology, while Old Norse or Old English will teach you to invoke the gods in their own languages. If you feel brave, and want to go back to the roots of Western magic, you should tackle Egyptian hieroglyphics. There are several good books on the subject for the complete beginner.

Other branches of general magical study take a more practical turn. If you work with magical herbalism, studying the use and cultivation of herbs is a good idea. If the tradition you follow has a strong warrior ethos, consider contacting a historical combat or medieval reenactment group and finding out what it feels like to swing a sword—and to get hit by one.

The specifics for each tradition will vary depending, but the basic idea is to be prepared to study and learn. As a student of magic in the modern age, you face the challenge and the joy of making your own way from novice to master of a magical art. Your curriculum of magical study is an important tool in this process—one that will change as your understanding of magic develops.

FOR FURTHER STUDY

A reading list for an individualized magical education would fill up dozens of pages by itself. The list below consists of books that focus, to one degree or another, on the issues involved in magical education and training.

Occult Exercises and Practices. Gareth Knight. Sun Chalice, 1997.

Paths of Wisdom. John Michael Greer. Llewellyn Publications, 1996.

Self-Initiation into the Golden Dawn Tradition. Chic Cicero and Sandra Tabatha Cicero. Llewellyn Publications, 1997.

The Training and Work of the Initiate. Dion Fortune. Aquarian, 1987.

True Magick. Amber K, Llewellyn Publications, 1987.

THE ESSENCE OF ANISE

BY NUALA DRAGO

*P*impinella anisum, or anise, is one of the oldest known medicinal and culinary herbs. The ancient Romans were very fond of it. They used it to flavor medicines, baked goods, food, and wines. Anise-flavored cakes were popular then and often served at banquets because anise was said to alleviate the effects of alcohol and excess. The Romans of yore also used anise to stimulate carnal appetites and they gave anise-flavored cakes to newlyweds to ensure fertility.

The seeds of anise, also called aniseed, are the plant's tiny fruits. Its essential oil is highly toxic and should not be ingested. In medieval times, the oil was used to poison rodents and other crop pests. Fresh leaves of anise may be added to salads, but most often it is the dried seeds of the plant that are used for medicinal and culinary purposes. Anise seed may be brewed for a refreshing tea that relieves a cough and sore throat. Anise has antimicrobial properties which also make it a natural antiseptic for topical use.

Anisette is a liqueur flavored with anise seed. It is made the world over under many different names. In France, the most popular comes from Bordeaux, but it is easy to make your own. Simply add five tablespoons of aniseed and a teaspoon each of fennel and coriander seed to three cups of 80-proof brandy. Steep for three weeks in a glass jar, shaking every few days. Strain through cheesecloth, add a cup of honey, and stir. Decant it and enjoy.

Of course, anise-flavored cookies are popular at Yuletide. To make some, try adding about one tablespoon of crushed anise seed to your favorite sponge cookie recipe. Simply toss the crushed seeds into the flour, and bake as usual. You may want to substitute orange extract for the vanilla in your recipe, as it complements anise well. In the spirit of the ancients, don't forget to share your cookies with someone you love.

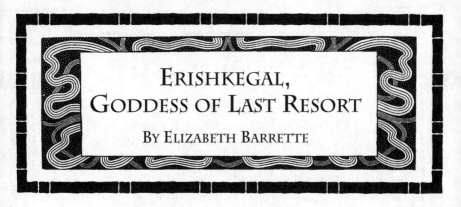

ERISHKEGAL, GODDESS OF LAST RESORT

BY ELIZABETH BARRETTE

When the heavens and the Earth were created,
And all the spheres of influence claimed but one,
The underworld remained, in need of mastery.

"What a nasty job," said Enki. "No one wants it!"
And he discarded the key to the lapis palace.
"I'll do it," said Erishkegal. And so she did.

When the manners of men and women were made,
And Inanna had established the arts of love,
Nergal went and invented rape.

"What a nasty god," said Inanna. "No one wants him!"
So she cast him out of Heaven.
"I'll civilize him," said Erishkegal. And so she did.

When the letters and words were all designed,
And Nebo set them down with stylus and clay,
He discovered that he had invented stagnation.

"What a nasty problem," said Nebo. "No one knows what to do about it!"
Moaning, he buried his face in his hands.
"I'll fix it," said Erishkegal. And so she did.

She broke Nebo's tablet over his hard head, thus creating chaos.
The other goddesses and gods may not like Erishkegal much…
But they'd be lost without her.

THE ART OF CALLING ANIMALS

BY BERNYCE BARLOW

M any folks in the magical community have read stories about people who have the ability to call an animal. I would like to share with you what my teachers taught me about this magical technique.

Of course, animal calling is not a skill one learns overnight. It takes practice and determination, but it can be learned by most people who have good visualization skills. Most often, when a person calls in an animal it is done with thought pictures. Animals respond well to strong mental images—for instance, a dog that does not like baths will hide even before you turn on the tub. That is evidence that animals can pick up on visually oriented thoughts.

With wild animals there is a bit more to it. For instance, if you want to call a bird and hold it in your hand, you will need to project a familiar image to the bird—perhaps a worm. This means you must know everything that the bird knows about the worm. You must know what it tastes like, how it smells, what it feels like to live in the Earth. If you project a picture of a worm from a human point of view this technique will not work; you have to become the worm as the bird knows it.

What I like about modern day shamanism is there are now tools to help us in this process. There are small pieces of plastic or glass now that project how an animal or bird sees things. This helps a lot and has strengthened a weak point in understanding how critters look at their world. You can buy a bird's eye or a rabbit's eye lens and understand how an animal views their world.

Once you know everything that the bird knows about the worm, you project a thought picture to the bird that embodies the whole thought picture—the sight, taste, smell, texture, feel, look, living environment. Only then should you approach the bird and hold it in your hand.

In shamanic practices, this technique is sometimes taken to an extreme, especially with larger wild animals. The process becomes less benign than thinking like a worm. That is, if one wished to call a cougar by envisioning its favorite food, let's say a deer, using the above practice things get a bit more complicated. One should know the taste of raw deer meat, know what it feels like to carry a deer skin around you, know how to make the sounds deer make, and so on. Also, if you lose your train of thought while the cougar is present, it will turn on you out of fear and confusion. This technique is best left for those who have the time to thoroughly study it.

There are also less dangerous ways to call in certain animals. The use of sound and scent is effective in attracting animals—behold the duck hunter with his duck call whistle and duck decoy. There are recordings of animal sounds that are intended bring in other animals. Sundancers use eagle bone whistles that sound like an eagle's call to attract eagles for their medicine ceremonies and dances.

It is important to say at this point anytime you call in an animal it should be for teaching, learning about a totem animal's behavior, or for some other kind of good reason. Using our knowledge for anything other than good amounts to bad medicine for us and for the Earth's creatures. Use your power and knowledge wisely or it may come to bite you in your backside, if you catch my drift. The Lakota teach that we are all related. All things organic and inorganic on Mother Earth and in Father Sky should act as if each thing on this planet or in our sky is brother and sister. If we keep this in mind while working our magical techniques and calling in our relations, we will honorably be able to use their magical, spiritual, and practical medicine and strength to empower ourselves and those around us.

MAGICAL ETHICS

BY JIM WEAVER

L iving a magical life is a powerful and positive way to live. However, it does come with a great deal of responsibility. If you are already following a magical path, you know what I mean. But, if you are just beginning to think about bringing magic into your life, you must understand that there is a moral code of spiritual ethics to follow if you wish your magical journey to be positive.

Whatever area of magic you are interested in, you will find that your magical work will not only affect you, but also those around you. Some of you may be interested in the Wiccan tradition or perhaps in various forms of divination. No matter where your magical interests and abilities may lead you, learning the ancient Wiccan Code will serve you well as you travel the path of positive magic. It consists of only eight words: "If it harms none, do what you will." This creed should be at the core of any magical work you do, even if you don't become a Wiccan.

Over the years I've developed a more extended set of magical ethical principles. I hope they aid you in your practice:

Never speak a charm or spell in a language you don't understand.

Never perform any form of revenge magic; karma will even things out.

Never let anyone coerce you into joining a magical group you don't feel comfortable about.

Never let anyone force you to do any type of divination when you're tired or just don't feel like it.

Never perform a spell to help someone when they haven't asked you. This is a form of manipulation.

Don't brag about your magic—besides being rude, blabbing about your magic weakens it.

Never use magic to harm a person, animal, or plant.

During a love spell never mention a specific person; again, this is manipulation.

Do give thanks when a spell has brought your desire into your life.

When people ask you to perform any type of divination, don't let them become too dependent on you.

In general, negative magic has no place in the life of a true magical practitioner. To further understand this, may I suggest you read Raymond Buckland's *Complete Book of Witchcraft* (Llewellyn Publications, 1986). Also, any book by the late Scott Cunningham will give you solid advice on practicing positive magic.

What you do in magic will come back to you. Positive magic will bring you unexpected blessings, while negative magic will eventually harm the practitioner. Of course, there are times when negative magic can be used in a positive manner, such as trying to destroy a bad habit. Not all negative magic is evil; what's important in most cases is intent. People sometimes ask if they can use revenge magic when someone is trying to hurt them. The answer is still "no." It is better in this case to use a spell for protection, or even a blessing. Concentrate on positive magic to heal any hurts, and get on with your life.

The one of area of magic which gets people into lots of trouble is love magic. If you're trying to attract love, you may perform a ritual to bring the type of person you desire to you. However, never name a specific person, as this violates a person's free will and will have only negative results.

As you journey along the magical road, you will come into contact with people who don't agree with your spiritual path. That is their right. Let them go in peace and never try to force your ideas on them. It is also your right to follow your own way.

Following a code of positive magical ethics will keep you spiritually healthy and will serve you well in all areas of your life. Your positive magic will come back to you threefold.

HOUSEHOLD SPIRITS

BY ANNA FRANKLIN

There was once a general belief that spirits or fairies dwell in human homes, guarding them and occasionally undertaking domestic tasks in return for small rewards, such as a bowl of cream or a warm place by the hearth.

Such spirits are found throughout the world, from the Hawaii to Scotland, from Spain to Russia. A belief in house spirits is very ancient. The ancient Romans honored protective brownie-like spirits called *lares* and *penates*. They gave monthly offerings of garlands on the hearth and daily offerings of food. In return, these spirits protected the house and its wealth. Ovid portrayed the lares as similar to dogs—he said that both guard the house and are faithful to their masters. The penates, meanwhile, were depiced in idols made of wax or ivory and placed on special shrines in the house. They were worshipped along with the domestic goddess Vesta and were responsible for the house's food supply and the success of the harvest.

The lares and penates also played a wider role in Roman society. The *penates publici* were the protectors of the Roman state and

were worshipped in a state cult. There was also a public cult of the *lares vicinales,* or "neighborhood lares."

The annual feast of the lares was the *Compitalia.* It was celebrated soon after the Winter Solstice, when merrymaking accompanied the performance of theatrical farces. Some elements of the festivals gave rise to later Christmas customs. The Compitalia called for the use of artificial light, and the lares traditional sacrificial victim was the pig—sometimes a traditional Christmas fare.

Though some Victorian writers claimed that the concept of household spirits may have spread with the Roman Empire, there is enough evidence to prove that a belief in such spirits evolved independently in places as far apart as China, western Europe, and South America. Folklore tells us that house fairies were once a common feature of English domestic life. In the twelfth century, a spirit called Malekin caused a commotion in the Suffolk home of Sir Osborn de Bradwell by discoursing learnedly in Latin on scriptural subjects. In Persia and China, it was the custom to make offerings to the house spirit before entering a dwelling. In northern Europe, it is customary to take bread and salt when visiting a home. In many parts of the world, blood sacrifices were made to the spirit of the place whenever foundations were laid for a building. Animals or even human victims were buried alive under the cornerstones to provide protective spirits.

Today, house fairies often have a mischievous side and like to play tricks on the human inhabitants of a dwelling. Such pranks might include rattling the fire irons, smashing crockery, hiding objects, or making a mess. House fairies are easily offended. Some house fairies object to the presence of a cat or a dog, and most of them will disappear for good if given a suit of clothes.

Fairies are much associated with the domestic hearth. The hearth was once the central focus of the home, providing warmth and food. House fairies, such as brownies, may be derived from an ancient belief in household gods or spirits that protected the home. The hearth was their means of entrance and egress, their shrine and altar flame. They often try to gain access to a house in order to warm themselves by it and are angered if they are kept out. Some fairy homes lie beneath human hearths, and the hearthstones are their doors.

CREATING A TABLETOP SANCTUARY

BY BREID FOXSONG

Every person needs a private place, a sanctuary where they can find peace and commune with their deities and their innermost thoughts. But a sanctuary doesn't have to be a secret garden, or a separate room in the house. It can be as simple as a picture of your ideal quiet spot, a bowl of multicolored stones, or a gurgling fountain. It doesn't have to be obvious—in fact, the more unobtrusive it is, the better.

Creating your own private escape space is not as hard as it sounds. Soothing tabletop fountains are commercially available for fifty to several hundred dollars. And you can create your own tabletop sanctuary for much less money. It would be much more meaningful, of course, for you to create your own.

In fact, tabletop sanctuaries are not difficult, and you can create a one-of-a-kind sanctuary to suit your personal needs. The only price in this case is time, labor, and the personal investment of energy that will make this sanctuary a fine and private place.

To start, you will need a submersible pump. It's the same kind of pump that a small fish tank would use, so look for it at your local pet supply shop. You don't need a large pump, actually the smaller the better, since you will only be pushing less than a gallon of water. You will also need about a foot and a half of plastic tubing for the pump. Again, use the same kind as for fish tanks. It happens to be a lot cheaper at the pet store than at the garden center.

Remember that it's much easier to shorten the tubing than it is to lengthen it, so, although you might not need more than a

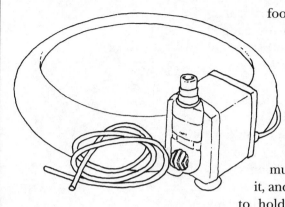

foot, you are better off buying eighteen inches to start with.

The next thing you will need is a bowl for your fountain base. There must be no holes in it, and it must be able to hold water without rusting or leaking. You can find beautiful ceramic bowls at gift stores if you look. Some of them even have painting on the sides that may assist in your visualizations. The electric cord on the pump will go over the side of the bowl, so keep that in mind when you choose it.

Also needed: two small- to medium-sized planter pots. They must be big enough to cover the pump, but smaller than the large bowl that is the base They must also have drainage holes large enough to fit the tubing through. You can use terra cotta or colored pottery for this. Remember that the colors should harmonize so that you get the maximum magical effects. Since the purpose is to be a sanctuary, I prefer shades of blue, brown, or green—all colors indicating harmony, growth, protection, and balance.

Gather a selection of seashells, rocks, gravel, and plant clippings. The eventual goal is to make this resemble a natural scene, and the water will allow the plants to take root, so you want to have a variety of materials. Its a good idea to incorporate a few stones for grounding, such as Apache tears or hematite. Other stones that I personally find useful to combine are agate to bring calm, bloodstone for healing and courage, carnelian to banish depression, fluorite for clarity of thought, and sodolite to aid meditation and banish guilt. For the rest, I like small rounded river rocks, particularly if they come from somewhere that I have good memories of. I have stones from all over the

United States in my sanctu- ary, and I have exchanged stones with friends from all over the world. As a result, my sanctuary has links to their love and friendship.

As a rule, I do not use crystals in my fountain, because I am usually trying to reduce psychic connections when I meditate, rather than increasing them. Still, many people find the addition of a quartz or amethyst to be of value. Experiment and find the right combination for yourself. The plant clippings you choose can include ivy for strength in adversity, mint for cleansing, baby's tears to banish guilt, small ferns for peace and serenity, rosemary to aid memory and concentration, African violet for protection, and a tiny hemlock or fir seedling to provide strength.

DIRECTIONS

If you choose to paint runes or symbols on the bottoms of the bowls in order to enhance the magic a bit, do so first and let them dry thoroughly. I recommend that you use symbols that enhance the feelings of protection, serenity, and meditation. This is, after all, a sanctuary—a place to relax and unwind rather than rev up your engines.

To build the base of your fountain, place the pump in the middle of the large bowl. Arrange the cord over the edge, but do not plug in the pump. Be aware that if you run your pump without water, you will ruin it.

Attach the foot or so of tubing to the pump, and have it going straight up and out of the bowl. Turn one of your medium planter pots upside down, and thread the tubing through its hole. It should cover the pump, and the tubing should come out of the hole. Place the other medium planter pot on top of the first, facing right side up. Again, thread the tubing through its hole, and cut the tubing so it is slightly below the top of your upper pot.

Now it's time to decorate. Choose what side the pump's electrical cord will come out of, and place the garden so that the cord will be concealed. The more you make it look like a manicured rock garden, the better it will look. Fill the top pot and sides of the base pot with large rocks and shells. Make sure that any gemstones are visible so that the vibrations will reach you more clearly.

Tuck your plant clippings in, using the rocks and shells to keep them upright. Make sure that the taller ones will be in the back, and, if possible, arrange them to conceal the electrical pump cord. I find that dwarf ivy works very well in the front of the top pot, as it will cascade down over both pots and trail over the sides. Any plant that will root in water will do well. The plants will begin to root as if you placed them in a jar with water.

When you have finished decorating, fill the bottom basin nearly to the top with cool water, leaving a quarter-inch space. Do not fill the top planter.

Turn on your pump, and let it suck the water from the bottom to the top, making a fountain and eventually overflowing into a waterfall. If your fountain is shooting up too high, cut the tubing shorter. You don't have to use plants for your fountain, but if you do make sure you only clean the fountain twice a year. The plants will lose their nutrients otherwise.

To take yourself away to your place of sanctuary, simply sit and watch the waterfall. Feel yourself standing underneath its cool and refreshing waters. Smell the plants and feel their shade and protection surrounding you. Add a stick of incense and your sanctuary becomes an instant altar. If guests come to your home, they will have no idea that this is your sanctuary, your refuge from the world, but they will appreciate the beauty of the fountain and your sacred space.

WORKING WITH MAGIC MIRRORS

By Raven Grimassi

The magic mirror is one of the oldest tools employed in both divination and spell casting. The classic magic mirror is a dark concave surface of reflective material. You can construct one for yourself by using the curved glass face of a clock and painting the convex side with glossy black paint. Antique stores are a good source for old clocks with rounded glass faces.

Traditionally, the preparation of a magic mirror begins on the night of a Full Moon. It is particularly effective to do this when the Moon is in the sign of Pisces, Cancer, or Scorpio. Consult an astrological calendar for Moon signs and phases.

Once you have painted the glass and it has thoroughly dried, then bathe the mirror in a herbal brew of equal parts rosemary, fennel, rue, vervain, ivy, and walnut leaves or walnut bark. If you want to hold to the oldest of traditions, then pour some sea foam into the mixture. If you are unable to obtain these items, consult a book on magical herbs and substitute other herbs associated with psychic vision, oracles, or divination. While the glass is still bathing in the potion, hold both your hands out over it, palms down, and say:

I awaken the sleeping spirits of old,
Whose eyes reveal all that in darkness is told,
Give to me visions within this dark well,
And make this a portal of magical spell.

Visualize a silver mist forming around the mirror. Take a deep breath, then slowly exhale outward upon the potion. Mentally envision that your breath moves the silver mist into the mirror. Repeat this three times. Next, remove the mirror from the potion and dry it off thoroughly. Prop the mirror up vertically with a sturdy object and make sure the support does not obscure the mirror. Hold your right hand out in front of you so that your palm is facing the convex side of the mirror. Then place the left palm facing the concave side, about three inches away from the glass surface. You are now ready to magnetize the mirror to your aura. With the left hand begin making a circular clockwise motion staying within the dimensions of the mirror. Do this for a few minutes and then perform the same motion on the convex side of the mirror with the right hand. The opposite hand is always held still while the moving hand circulates.

Once completed, take the mirror out beneath the Full Moon so that its light falls upon the concave side. Slowly fill the glass to the brim with the herbal potion. Hold it up toward the Moon, almost level with your eyes. Don't worry about any spillage that may take place. While looking at the Moon, allow your eyes to unfocus slightly. If you are doing this correctly, you will see three lines of light seemingly emanating from the Moon. Continue to squint until the vertical line coming from the bottom of the Moon seems to touch upon the mirror. Once the moonbeam is touching the mirror, speak these words:

> *Three are the lights*
> *Here now that are seen*
> *But not to all*
> *The one in-between,*
> *For now the Enchantress*
> *Has long come at last*
> *To charge and empower*
> *This dark magic glass.*

Quickly close your eyes so that you break eye contact. Open them again looking down towards the glass. Kneel and pour out the potion upon the ground in the manner of libation. Then rinse the mirror off with fresh clear water, and dry it thoroughly. The final step in preparing the mirror is to glue a strip of snakeskin to the back side. The snake is a symbol of the underworld, which has long been associated with divination, the oracle, and fate. Once the glue has dried under the snakeskin, wrap the mirror in a silk cloth to protect its lunar magnetism. Never allow sunlight to fall directly upon the mirror. The mirror is now ready to be used for divination or spell casting.

MIRROR DIVINATION

The technique for this is a very ancient one common among shamanistic traditions. Divination is the ability to see what patterns are forming and becoming manifest. What you see is actually what is likely to occur if nothing changes the pattern being woven in the astral material.

The following technique will provide you with the basic foundation for performing the art of divination known as scrying. Place two candles as your source of light, so that the light does not reflect directly upon the mirror. They should be off to the side about a foot or two, flanking the sides of the mirror.

Next you will perform a series of hand passes over the mirror, slowly and deliberately. Magically speaking, the right hand is of an electrical nature and active charge, and the left hand is of a magnetic nature and receptive charge. A left-handed pass will attract an image and cause its formation, and the right-handed passes will strengthen or focus the image. Begin by making left-handed passes over the mirror, in a clockwise circle, just a few inches above it with palms open and facing down. Stop and gaze into the dark reflection—not at it but into it.

You will need to repeat these passes as you await the vision. Alternate between the left hand and the right hand. This requires patience and time. Use your intuition as you sit before the mirror. Make sure the setting is quiet and free of distractions.

The magic mirror can also be used for spell casting. This is a simple technique involving reflections or sigils. Light two candles and set them off to each side of the mirror about three inches away. Place a photograph, image, or sigil representing the focus of your spell so that it reflects in the mirror. Gaze into the mirror and imagine the desired effect. Make up a short rhyme if you like so you can state your desire without breaking your concentration. If you desire to be rid of an influence or situation, you can sigilize it and then burn the sigil, gazing into the reflected flames in the mirror.

Another effective method is to gently blow incense smoke onto the mirror as you gaze at the reflection. Allow yourself to stir your emotions, then deeply inhale, and slowly exhale across a stick of incense. Imagine the smoke to be a magical vapor carrying your will. As it touches the mirror, imagine the target responding as you wish it to. Do this a total of three times. Creating a short rhyme for your spell can be helpful in this technique as well. Once you are finished, combine the melted wax,

ashes from the incense, and the photo or image you used. Dispose of this in a manner in keeping with the elemental nature of your spell. Matters of love and feelings generally belong to water. Creative or artistic ventures belong to the air. Situations of loss, separation, or destruction are associated with fire. Endurance, strength, fertility, and stability are typically linked to earth.

When disposing of your ritual remnants, bear in mind that tossing something into moving water will merge it with the water element, and so connect it on a macrocosmic level with the higher nature of the spell. This act will help to empower your ritual of magic. For any earth-related spells that you try, you should bury your object afterward in an area somehow connected to your target. Spells related to the element of fire, on the other hand, should involve burning the links. Finally, for an air-related spell, make sure to use steam or smoke.

Spirit Familiars

By Donald Tyson

The history of familiars extends as far back as that of magic itself. Familiars are thought to be pet animals that possess magic power and preternatural intelligence. The image that immediately comes to mind when you mention the word is a Witch's black cat. Familiars are supposed to come and go in a twinkling to carry out the secret purposes of the Witch.

As is true for most clichés, this conception is not completely incorrect, but it is limited and misleading. Familiars are not animals, but spirits. Witches may have familiars, but so do many others who practice different kinds of magic—even those with no interest in the esoteric.

What Is a Familiar?

A familiar is any spirit that maintains a personal relationship with a human being. In fact, it is the close contact and communication between human and spirit that makes a familiar relationship, not the type of spirit or the magical practices of the person. And communication is the key factor.

336

A spirit who intervenes in the life of a human being cannot be classed as a familiar if the person lacks conscious awareness of the spirit. Everyone is said to have his or her own guardian angel, but a guardian angel usually does not qualify as a familiar simply because, in most cases, it does not communicate with the person under its care. Were a guardian angel to begin appearing and interacting on a regular basis with an individual, it would then be a familiar. This phenomenon sometimes occurs in ceremonial magic, and is known as the Conversation of the Holy Guardian Angel.

Several common misconceptions about familiars must be dismissed before we examine their nature. They are too often understood to be the slaves or servants of the Witch or magician to whom they are attached. They are also thought to be bound against their will to their master by the force of magic, and constrained to obey by threats of punishment. Sometimes, familiars are even considered to be evil spirits summoned to the service of a Witch or magician by black magic, or appointed by the Devil to serve those who make a black pact.

While it is true that some Witches and magicians do summon and bind lesser spirits to act as their servants, in general familiars are not always lesser spirits, nor are they always constrained against their will. More often, the bond between a human and a familiar is one of friendship and mutual respect. In these cases, there is no need to bind or threaten the spirit, who acts in cooperation with the magician as a partner to aid his or her purposes. The feelings between human and familiar are usually affectionate, even loving. Spirits constrained to serve by threats of punishment make very poor familiars who cannot be trusted, but those who help willingly from a motive of friendship or love need no constraint.

In truth, familiars are often spirits of a high order, capable of full communication with human beings. They may even possess an intelligence superior to that of their human partner, and act as a guide and teacher—especially in spiritual and esoteric matters. Traditionally, establishing a relationship with a familiar was the first step in learning magic. The familiar conveyed the practical ritual procedures needed by the magician, and enabled

the magician to make first contact with other spirits and to learn their names and sigils. Indeed, the view expressed in some grimoires are that the method for forming a link with a familiar is all that is required to create a magic relationship, since at that point the familiar will give any additional information the Witch or magician needs.

Familiars are seldom evil spirits held against their will. This would make little sense, since such spirits would forever try to escape or betray their masters and require constant vigilance. Such spirits would be far more trouble than they were worth. The notion that familiars are evil arose from the antimagic propaganda of the Church during the Witch craze of the sixteenth and seventeenth centuries. Since all evil was supposed to arise from the actions of the Devil, priests viewed all relationships between humans and spirits are inherently evil. Women accused of witchcraft were coerced into confessing many untruths, among them that they kept as their servants familiar spirits who helped them commit acts of evil, that they suckled and fed these creatures on their own blood, that the familiars took the forms of pet animals with monstrous or fantastic features and could appear or disappear at will, and that these familiars or imps were assigned to the Witches as servants by

Satan himself, after the Witch signed a pact pledging her life to works of evil in return for magic power.

These malicious lies were told and published so often that many otherwise sensible people believed them. They are still believed by members of the Christian fundamentalist movement, who view a devil with horns and a pitchfork as a real and ever-present threat.

The truth is less black-and-white. As there are good and evil human beings, so are there good and evil familiars. Care must be exercised when choosing a familiar spirit, just as we must exercise caution before entering into a sustained partnership with another person. Spirits are capable of deception, but also of honesty. Some are malicious, others loving and kind. They have their own complex personalities and may be cheerful one day but moody the next. They exhibit great nobility, but also spite and pettiness.

What is true of spirits in general is also true of familiars, because familiars form a broad cross-section of the spirit population. Almost any type of spirit may become a familiar.

ESOTERIC TRADITIONS OF THE FAMILIAR

There are four areas of the Western esoteric tradition where familiars play a prominent role: shamanism, witchcraft, ceremonial magic, and spiritualism. It is worth considering each briefly when seeking to understand familiars.

SHAMANISM

In traditional shamanism, familiar spirits were vital to the ability of the shaman or shamaness to enact magic. A young shaman was chosen as a partner by a spirit, who remained with him throughout his life. This spirit became the shaman's celestial or heavenly wife or husband.

Often the shaman had no say in the matter. He was chosen by the spirit. In time, this spirit bride of the shaman would often become the most important single component in the success or failure of his career. The more powerful the spirit bride, the more powerful the shaman. Be aware too: The relationship was sexual. A shaman was not prevented from having a mortal wife, but the spirit wife was always first in his affections. In addition to this primary familiar, shamans used a number of lesser spirits as servants to fulfill specific functions. These would also be classed as familiars, although they were subordinate in importance and power to the spirit wife of the shaman, who was the equal, if not the superior, of the shaman.

The animal spirit interacting with the shaman was a kind of ruling spirit of the species, and expressed the species' collective intelligence and life force. Shamans interacted with other spirits on a regular basis, chief among them the totemic spirits of animal species such as the bear or the wolf with whom the shaman was believed to share a common ancestry. The bond between the shaman and these animal spirits was not as close as the bond between the shaman and his spirit wife, but it might rise to the level of a familiar relationship. The shaman shared mutual obligations with these lesser familiars. He was required to help and respect the species related to him, and in return expected some consideration from these beasts who were his distant relatives.

WITCHCRAFT

Ancient witchcraft arose out of shamanism, so it is not surprising that they would share characteristics. The familiar spirits of witchcraft are the descendants of the heavenly wife and spirit servants of shamanism. The familiar pet of the medieval Witch is a kind of shamanic animal spirit guide, though much reduced in stature.

In witchcraft, there are practical reasons why a familiar spirit would choose to inhabit the body of a pet animal. Possession of the animal allows the spirit to use the animal's senses to perceive the physical world. After all, spirits can only perceive the material world through the senses of living creatures. Also, by inhabiting the body of a pet, the familiar is able to remain in close contact with the Witch, receiving her affection and attention without attracting unwanted notice.

During the Witch craze, there was confusion as to the exact nature of animal familiars. The general consensus of the priests was that a familiar was a demonic creature that had assumed a material form resembling a pet animal in order to remain near the Witch while concealing its identity from others. It was thought that familiars were corporeal, yet possessed the power to change their shapes at will. The truth is somewhat more complicated. Familiar spirits did at times possess the bodies of pet animals in order to draw upon their vitality and to use their senses to perceive the physical world. They could enter or leave these animals at will, and did not always remain within them. They also sometimes appeared in the images of beasts, but without solid bodies of flesh and blood. To an onlooker they might appear as a dog or cat, yet still be able to change shape or vanish in an instant. Familiars might also appear to a Witch in human form, or remain invisible, while communicating with the Witch.

The fable that Witches fed their familiars on the blood of their bodies also has a grain of truth. Familiar spirits derive a form of vitality from the emotions of their human associates— particularly from strong emotions such as love. This is one reason why spirits are drawn to human beings and form close unions with them. Human emotion and human attention have the effect of fixing or solidifying the forms and identities of familiar spirits, so that over time the personality of a familiar becomes more stable, its self-awareness more consistent.

CEREMONIAL MAGIC

Familiars play a less important, yet still significant, role in traditional Western ceremonial magic—sometimes also known as high magic. Ceremonial magic is all about control. The magician seeks to command the forces of nature, the actions of spirits, or even of gods.

Familiar spirits are more apt to fulfill a subservient role in high magic, though this did not prevent them from becoming the close friends of magicians. The Elizabethan magus John Dee, who established communication with the Enochian angels and received from them the Enochian system of magic (see page 38 for more information) had a familiar Enochian spirit named Madimi that came most often in the form of a little girl. Dee lavished on this spirit the same affection he gave to his own children, and even named one of his children after the spirit.

SPIRITUALISM

Over the past hundred and fifty years or so, familiars have been most often observed within the records of spiritualism. The spirit guide of the traditional trance medium is a familiar. The role of such a spirit guide is to act as an intermediary between the medium and the spirit world, and also to serve the medium as teacher and protector. Its function is similar to that of the heavenly bride of the ancient shaman, though the union between a trance medium and a spirit guide is not always sexual in nature. (Just how often the relationship was sexual is difficult to determine—the subject would not have been openly discussed during the Victorian period, when spiritualism was at its peak of popularity.)

The modern equivalent of the séance medium is the channeler. Channelers rely on less theatrical apparatus than the mediums of the Victorian era, but they function in the same way. They have their own spirit contacts who serve them as familiars. Some of these familiars, such as Seth, the spirit who communicated for many years with Jane Roberts, have written their own books by using their human associates as their physical instruments. It can be difficult to determine whether the channeler or the familiar is in control in such relationships. At their best, these are partnerships between equals.

In the end, familiars have always played a central role in Western esotericism. Whether acting as teachers, guides, protectors, or servants, familiars help bridge the gulf between the human world and the spirit world. It would not be an exaggeration to say that without a familiar relationship with a spirit, the highest attainment in the art of magic is impossible. What is truly esoteric is always conveyed directly to the magician through the familiar and can be learned in no other way.

MEXICAN MAGIC FOR THE DAY OF THE DEAD

By Edain McCoy

T he Mexican festival known as *El Dia de los Muertos,* or the Day of the Dead, falls on November 2. As the name suggests, this is a daylong—and nightlong—festival for honoring the wandering spirits of ancestors who have come through the open veil between the worlds to reunite with family and loved ones. The holiday's unmistakable likeness to the late autumn festivals for the dead in Britain, Ireland, and Germany suggest its European origins. However, its successful blending with Native Mexican folk tradition is what has created a unique and beloved local celebration.

At dawn on the Day of the Dead, villages awaken early for a busy day. Food is prepared to feed both the living and the dead. Homes and public places are decorated with symbols of the festival, and altars are created to honor the ancestors who will be visiting. The local cemetery is also festively decked out with candles, crepe paper, and skeletal images. Nearly all families eat their noon meal picnic-style among the graves of their beloved dead. After nightfall, music, singing, drinking, dancing, and other merrymaking ensues in which Death himself celebrates with the community and its spectral guests. The revelry continues until church bells ring the midnight hour, and the merrymakers procede to the church for prayers and a mass for the dead.

Extend your autumn celebration with the spirit world through the Day of the Dead this year by trying these traditional spells from northern Mexico and the American Southwest.

Day of the Dead Home Purification Spell

Copal is a popular incense in Mexico and the Southwest. Its scent is strong and can be cloying, but is often used on the Day of the Dead to purify the home in preparation for a visit from the ancestors. It is also useful for shielding the home from entry by unwelcome spirits. Take the smoking incense from room to room to purge it clean, and burn it when visiting the graveyard to make it a place only good spirits wish to come.

Calaveras Spirit Contact Talisman

The word *calavera* means "skull" or "skeleton." Calaveras ornaments of all shapes and sizes are seen everywhere as the Day of the Dead approaches. They can also be made into talismans that pave the way for successful spirit contact. After sundown go to your altar and place a calavera at each directional point of your circle. On the altar make an incense of lavender, cinnamon, and wormwood. This is a blend that creates a portal to and from the spirit world. On either side of the incense, place two white candles and two small mirrors that reflect the light of the candle back to the portal. This is a protective device to keep harmful spirits from passing through. Speak this charm:

344

Open wide the portal this night
For spirits whose countenance shines bright;
Entities of love who wish me well
Are welcome here when I ring the bell.

Ring a bell three times to call the spirits, then sit back and await your visitors.

CHICORY PATH-CLEARING SPELL

Chicory can remove obstacles and open locks. Place a bit of dried and crushed chicory in a small bowl, or make it into an incense. Place a symbol of an obstacle you wish to overcome next to the bowl, or pass a lock through the smoke to represent a door you wish to open to you. Speak this charm:

My path is clear, troubles held at bay,
Chicory banishes all obstacles in my way;
No more stumbling blocks,
No more tight closed locks;
Open is my road both night and day.

RED CHILI PEPPERS BANE BURN

Red chili peppers are often strung together and hung up as holiday decorations in Mexico from the Day of the Dead through New Year's Day. Their fiery nature burns away harm that dares enter the home. If your skin has a high tolerance for irritation, you can wipe the peppers gently over your body to draw out the energy of curses placed on you.

ALOE AND GARLIC WREATH

Weave aloe and garlic cloves together in a wreath, and place it in your kitchen to draw luck and protection, especially from burns and kitchen fires. Add some cinnamon sticks and some symbols or pictures of saints or deities to add a true Mexican flavor to your finished product.

HEALING AND CLEANSING RITUAL

To enhance healing or to do a spiritual cleansing, tap a red germanium flower all over your body while chanting a little rhyme that specifically asks the saints or deities to assist you in attaining your wish.

PEPPER TREE BRANCH SCOURGE

Another tool for cleansing and healing is the scourge, an item used to lightly "beat" the body to drive out unwanted elements. This technique is popular in many mainstream religions today, most notably those who teach that we must suffer to find God. Lightly flog your body with a pepper tree branch to scourge yourself Mexican-style.

OBSIDIAN SCRYING MIRROR

The volcanic rock known as obsidian is shiny and black. The Aztecs called it the "shining mirror" and used it in divination rites and for crafting ritual blades. Gaze into a shiny piece of obsidian on the night of the Day of the Dead to peer into the spirit world.

FEEDING THE DEAD SPELL

Feeding visiting spirits is a requirement in spiritual and magical traditions the world over. It is also a central feature in Day of Dead festivities. For the enjoyment of your spectral visitors and any house guests, consider making this simple version of the ever-popular burrito on the Day of the Dead.

SUPER EASY TEX-MEX BURRITOS

1½	lbs. lean ground beef
1	16 oz. can refried beans
1	12 oz. jar salsa, your choice of mild to hot
2	cups shredded Monterey Jack cheese
2	cups shredded cheddar cheese
12	flour tortillas
	Toothpicks

Preheat oven to 325°F. Cover the bottom and sides of two 9 x 13-inch cake pans with shortening, and set aside. Mix the shredded cheeses together and also set aside.

In a large pan, brown the ground beef until it is about half-cooked. As it cooks, keep turning and chopping the meat with a plastic spatula so it browns evenly. Drain any grease, then add the can of refried beans and continue turn and chop until the meat seems done. Remove the meat mixture from the heat and stir in the salsa.

Visually divide the mixture into twelve parts, and spoon one of three parts into a tortilla. Add about three heaping table-spoons of the cheese mixture, then fold the tortilla over. Place this in the cake pan and secure in place with a toothpick. Continue putting all dozen burritos together this way, packing them close in the pans. Top lavishly with the rest of the cheese mixture. Bake for 10 to 15 minutes until the cheese is melted and bubbling on the burritos. Serve immediately.

FOR FURTHER STUDY

The Latino Holiday Book. Valerie Menard. Marlowe and Company, 2000.

Magic from Mexico. Mary Devine, Ph.D. Llewellyn Publications, 1992.

Sacred Mask, Sacred Dance. Evan John Jones. Llewellyn Publications, 1997.

Mexican-American Folklore. John O. West. August House, 1988.

TASSELS

BY LYNNE STURTEVANT

Most people think of tassels as fussy decorative carryovers from the Victorian era. However, in many religious and magical systems, tassels serve as bridges to the mystical realm. They adorn the garments of the powerful, and they flutter from humble shrines and altars. Their swaying skirts carry prayers skyward, and they are used to mark significant life transitions all over the world.

TASSEL HISTORY

The first tassels were functional. Buttons, snaps, and zippers are relatively recent inventions. For thousands of years, clothing was draped around the body and secured by cords that served as belts. Gathering and tying loose threads kept fabric and cords from unraveling.

Although tassels appear on clothing in Egyptian tomb paintings, the Chinese were probably the first to use tassels strictly for decoration. In ancient China, a tassel's length, color, and fullness symbolized the wealth and status of its owner. Tassels are still an important element in Chinese opera. Audiences identify heroes and villains by the color of tassels they wear, and tasseled sticks represent horses because the dancing threads resemble flying manes.

During the Middle Ages, the luxury goods of the Orient—among which came silk tassels—began to appear in Europe. Soon, tassels of all shapes and sizes decorated the clothing, furniture, and weapons of the rich. The royal sleeping chamber in the French palace of Versailles was filled with huge tassels embellished with jewels, ostrich feathers, and golden flowers.

In the thirteenth century, the Catholic Church adopted a red hat with matching tassels for those who had achieved the rank of cardinal. The Church's use of tassels expanded somewhat over the centuries. Today the number and color of tassels adorning ecclesiastical garments indicate an individual's place within the Church hierarchy.

According to the Bible, Moses instructed the Israelites to wear tassels as a reminder to follow God's commandments. Married Jewish men honor the tradition by wearing prayer shawls with tassels called *tzitzit* attached to the corners. The tassels represent the four corners of the Earth, and although a man may be buried with his prayer shawl, one of the tzitzit must be removed first.

TASSELS AS SPIRITUAL SYMBOLS

Tassels are spiritual symbols in traditional cultures too. Folk tassels are made from a variety of materials including plant fibers, animal hair, feathers, shells, beads, and bones. They decorate livestock, dangle from key chains and rearview mirrors, protect infants from disease, swing from the branches of venerated trees, and transform simple sticks into magic wands with the power to attract benevolent spirits and frighten evil ones. On the Indonesian island of Bali, tassels made from fresh flowers flutter from the eaves of temples and brighten the countless small shrines that dot the landscape. If the Balinese spirits enjoy the fragrant offerings even half as much as people do, they are happy spirits indeed.

The next time you see a graduating class switch the tassels on their mortarboards from one side to the other, pause a moment and consider the history and symbolism associated with these seemingly insignificant bundles of threads. Tassels are more than whimsical decorations. They have the power to connect us to the world's hidden magic. The ways we choose to use and display them are limited only by our imaginations.

MAKING YOUR OWN TASSELS

The following instructions will allow you to make a tassel approx-imately six inches in length. Given enough time, you can make enough tassels to add magical energy to your entire wardrobe.

Materials Needed

1   1.4 oz. skein of yarn

1   piece of heavy cardboard to use as a form for wrapping the yarn. A book can also be used. The finished tassel will be slightly shorter than the form.

Scissors

1   tapestry needle

Tape (optional)

First, cut two 2-foot lengths of yarn and set aside. Wrap the remaining yarn around the cardboard or book approximately one hundred times.

There will be yarn left over. Wrap so that the strands of yarn lay neatly side by side. You can keep the yarn from unwinding while you complete the next steps by securing the ends to the form with tape. (See figure at right.)

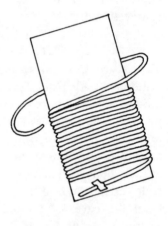

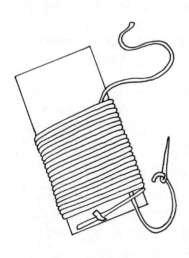

Next, take one of the 2-foot lengths you set aside in step one, fold it in half, and knot the ends together. Hold the knotted end in one hand and twist the other end to make a hanging cord. Thread the twisted cord through the tapestry needle, and pass it through the top of the yarn still wrapped on the cardboard. (See figure at left.) Note: Depending on how you want to use the finished tassel, you may want a much shorter hanging cord. It just depends on your personal needs.

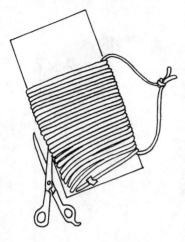

Now, if you want to attach the tassel to a key or other object, thread the cord through the key now and tie the ends of the cord together. (See figure at left.)

If you plan to hang the tassel from a doorknob, or to display it so that it can be moved later, simply tie the ends of the cord to make a loop. Once the hanging cord is secured, with scissors cut the other end of the wrapped yarn, and remove the cardboard or book, leaving a fairly loose collection of hanging thread. Care should be taken at this point not to disturb the form.

Finally, take the remaining two-foot length of yarn and create the tassel's neck and head by wrapping yarn tightly around the tassel about an inch or so below the top. (See figure at right.)

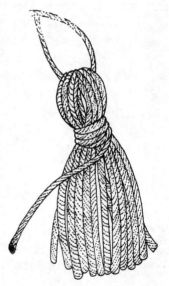

When you finish wrapping the neck, thread the loose end of the yarn through the tapestry needle, draw it into the center of the tassel and the thread. The loose end will disappear within the tassel's skirt.

Shake the tassel and let it hang for a few hours then trim the skirt so that the bottom is even.

FOR FURTHER STUDY

Tassel Making for Beginners. Enid Taylor. Guild of Master Craftsman Publications Ltd., 1997.

Tassels: The Fanciful Embellishment. Nancy Welch. Lark Books, 1992.

FULL MOON ENERGY

BY MICHELLE SANTOS

A coworker of mine said this to me the other day as I sat down at my desk: "Watch out! It's a Full Moon today. Everyone's going a little bit crazy."

I shuddered once, and pasted a smile on my face. I knew I would need strength, for as anyone who has worked with the public knows, things do not always run smoothly when the Moon is full. People tend to be more irritable. They jump from one topic to another. They cut drivers off at tollbooths.

It's been that way since the beginning of time. After all, humans are made up of about 70 percent water, and the Moon visibly affects the tides and other water bodies when it is full. Consider: The very term "lunatic" derives its meaning from the Moon, because eccentric people who lived outside society's rules and regulations were said to be "touched" by the Roman goddess of the Moon, Luna.

On the other hand, Wiccans and Pagans the world over recognize the power of the Full Moon and rejoice in its monthly appearance. They are able to draw the energy of the Full Moon into themselves, and to use that energy to empower their magical workings and spells.

Of course, that's the hard part—making the jump from "Moon crazed" to "Moon strengthened." If you're like me, it's not quite so easy as reading a few books and lighting a few candles. To harness the power of the Moon is to become one with the Great Goddess, and to intimately feel the ebb and flow of nature's monthly changes. You simply must work hard always to align yourself with the Moon.

To do this, you should follow a few helpful steps. First, buy a calendar with the Moon phases noted on the correct dates. Personally, I like wall calendars that give you a month-long view at a glance. (Llewellyn's *Witches' Calendar* is excellent for this purpose.) At the beginning of each month, take a few minutes to familiarize yourself with the important Moon dates, especially the days of the Full Moons. Keep these dates in mind as the month progresses and the Full Moon nears. As people around you start to fret and complain, you can remain comfortably balanced since you have the knowledge of the cycle of the Moon beforehand and are aware that the ebb and flow of the orb is constant.

Another good step to take is to take time during the month to look at the Moon. I can not emphasize this enough. All too often we rush from one appointment to another, from work to home and back again, never realizing nature's beauty. Before long, a month has passed and we are exclaiming, "Where has the time gone?"

You don't have to spend long amounts of time outside to gaze at the Moon. As you wait in rush-hour traffic, get the mail, or walk the dog, take a few minutes to notice her. Before long, you will recognize her many crevices and irregularities, and you will smile as you look up at your old friend in the night sky.

Once you have familiarized yourself with the Moon's monthly journey, and with her likeness in the sky, you can perform an alignment ritual. This is not as scary or as difficult as it sounds. Ideally, the alignment ritual should take place outside, in the light of the Full Moon. If this is impossible due to your living arrangement, do not despair. You can perform the ritual inside as well. However, try to find a spot inside your house or apartment that allows you a view of the Moon.

To start, cleanse the area in which you will be sitting. I usually light a sage wand and smudge the area with its smoke. Sometimes I will cleanse the area with representatives of the four elements as well—dirt or salt for earth, incense for air, a candle flame for fire, and a splash of water for water. Do what feels most natural to you.

Set up your corner with directional candles. I usually use colors that correspond to the different directions—green for north, yellow for east, red for south, and blue for west. However, all-white candles work wonderfully for this ritual as they will mirror and represent the Full Moon.

Cast your circle as you normally do. I start at the north and walk clockwise around the circle three times, pointing my index finger at the ground. (You can use an athame or wand for directing the energy as well.) As you walk, feel yourself depositing energy around the perimeter of the circle, as well as above and below you. You are creating a sacred space reminiscent of a bubble. You can chant something as you walk around, or you can remain silent. It's up to you. Sometimes I make up a rhyme, such as: "I cast the circle thrice around. Let evil begone and good abound." Other times I say: "The circle is cast," over and over again, very quickly.

Once you have created your sacred space, sit facing the Moon. It does not matter which direction you are facing, as long as the Moon is in front of you. Gaze up at her, noticing her many hues, her brilliance, her jagged edges and smooth curves. The Moon has many faces that she presents to the world—waxing, waning, full, and new. You also have many faces you present to the world—mother, wife, lover, worker. The Moon is not a cardboard cutout that can fit

into a specific role; neither are you. The Moon is multidimensional, as are you.

With these thoughts in your mind, visualize your energy reaching up toward the Moon. (I find it easier to visualize if I close my eyes.) See your energy flowing up to the sky in two thin, glowing streams. I see my energy as golden in color, as I am a Leo and gold is one of the colors of that astrological sign. Orange, green, blue, yellow—any color will work, as long as you recognize it as your own. See your energy streams crossing back and forth, over each other, forming patterns in the sky.

Hold the image of the energy streams in your mind, and visualize the Moon's energy flowing down to you in two glowing streams, silver in color. Again, the color is optional but should represent the Moon to you. See the Moon's energy streams crossing back and forth, making patterns in the sky, as they race toward the Earth.

Visualize your energy and the Moon's energy converging. The streams wrap around each other, intermingling in a graceful dance, becoming one. The energy creates a new spiraling pattern of all four streams of energy. It continues in two directions, to the Moon and toward you. The energy enters the Moon and enters you at exactly the same time. You watch the Moon brighten, welcoming your added energy. You feel the energy enter your body, adding the Moon's power to your own. You sit taller, your back straight. From the inside out, you glow.

Eventually—the length of time is different for everybody—the Moon's energy retreats from your body, returning to its place in the sky. Your energy, too, disengages from the Moon and treks back to you. Wait for all the energy to return to its original destination. Once your energy is inside you again, sit for a while, pondering your experience and noticing any differences you feel. Then thank the Moon, and close your circle.

Closing your circle is almost the same as casting your circle. Use the same energy-directing implement as before, and walk counterclockwise three times around the circle. Imagine the circle's energy being released. You can think of it sinking into the ground or dispersing on the wind. Again, you can chant a rhyme, or say: "The circle is closed," or remain silent. It's up to you.

Many Witches and Wiccans end their rituals with the phrase: "Merry meet, merry part, and merry meet again." If this feels appropriate, you can say it too—even though this ritual is designed for solitary practice.

This alignment ritual can be done as many times as you deem necessary. If you currently have a difficult time with the Full Moon's energy, you might want to perform the ritual several months in a row. As you become more aligned with the Full Moon, you will notice that you are happy and excited as the Full Moon nears, and not irritated and upset as before. You will then be able to greet all those "Moon crazed" people with a genuine smile.

Parsley, Sage, Rosemary, and Thyme

Magical Properties
of Common Cooking Herbs and Spices

By Magenta Griffith

Many herbal primers give the properties of various herbs, but often many of the herbs listed are items you have to make a special trip to a particular store to buy. Still, there are some useful herbs and spices you can find in any large supermarket or may very well already have in your cupboard.

Many of these herbs have healing properties. However, you should consult with your doctor or other medical practitioner before you take any herbs for a medical condition.

Anise is said to help you sleep; put a few seeds in a glass of warm milk before bedtime.

Bay leaves are good for purification. A wreath of bay leaves in your house is both decorative and protective. You can also burn the leaves as an incense to induce visions. Scattered on the floor, they repeal evil.

Caraway has a beneficial effect on the digestion, easing or curing flatulence. It also stimulates the appetite, and some herbals say it can relieve cramps. Crush a teaspoon of seeds and add to hot water to make a tea.

Cinnamon is used in many prosperity spells and charms. It is also supposed to "excite the passions," so it would be a good addition to food served to a someone you wish to fall in love with you.

Cloves are antiseptic and anaesthetic. Clove oil is an old remedy for toothache, and still can be found in some pharmacies. Chewing gently on a clove will sweeten the breath. Cloves are also considered a strong protection herb. Soak cloves in water for a few hours to soften them, and put a needle and thread through them to make a string for protection.

Garlic, when eaten, can drive away colds; it has antibiotic properties. It will also keep away vampires and other malicious beings. My grandmother taught me to put a clove of garlic at every door and window to keep out evil. Or buy a strings of garlic bulbs and hang it in your kitchen—both for protection and decoration.

Ginger is an excellent remedy for nausea. Brew one teaspoon of ground ginger, or chop about a tablespoon of fresh ginger in boiling water, for tea. It will strengthen the digestion and act as a mild stimulant.

Lemon, while not strictly a herb, is very useful for treating colds. Squeeze the juice of one lemon into a cup of hot water, and add a tablespoon or two of honey. Drink this, then go to bed. Also, to brighten blonde hair mix the juice of one lemon with an equal amount of water. Put in hair after washing, and rinse out five minutes later. (For brown hair, see rosemary.)

Marjoram is useful in love charms and for drawing happiness. It is an ingredient in some protective mixtures.

Mint is useful both internally and externally. Internally, peppermint tea is wonderful for the stomach and will often ease indigestion. Externally, many types of mint keep away insects. Mint is also an ingredient in many prosperity spells and charms.

Nutmeg is a stimulant and aids the digestion. In the Middle Ages, it was considered an aphrodisiac. My grandmother said carrying a whole nutmeg is a rheumatism charm.

Orange peel, like lemon is not strictly a herb, but it is useful for various sachets and love charms, and can be used in potpourri. Many herb teas contain orange peel.

Parsley is a cleansing agent, and eating it will clear the system of toxins. Chewing parsley will help get rid of bad breath. Parsley contains vitamin C, as well as iron and other minerals. Sprinkle it in salads and soups.

Rosemary makes a useful hair rinse for brunettes. Infuse a cup of water with a teaspoon of dried rosemary for five minutes, cool until just pleasantly warm to the touch. Pour over your hair after you've washed it, and let in sit for a few minutes before rinsing out. It will bring out the luster in dark hair. Rosemary can be used in protection charms, or if you can get the whole plant, make it into a wreath to hang in your house to keep away bad luck and ill will. An old motto is: "Rosemary for remembrance." Indeed, rosemary tea improves the memory, and is good to sip while you are studying.

Saffron is the quintessential solar spice. It can be used to produce a lovely yellow dye, but it is extremely expensive. The ancient Greeks wore amulets containing saffron as a protection against diseases of all kinds.

Sage is used in smudge sticks and for purification. For this, be sure to use the whole leaf, crumbled, or it will just smolder and go out. You can also use sage leaves as part of a purification potpourri. Sage tea is useful for chest complaints such as bronchitis. Use it in soups during the winter to ease respiratory problems.

Salt isn't really a herb or spice—it's a mineral. But we all have it in our kitchen. And in fact, salt is very useful magically. It is the essence of purification and is used in many rituals as a symbol for the element of Earth. Most Wiccan rituals start by blessing water, then blessing salt; the two are then combined, and salt water is used to consecrate the circle. If you have a small object you wish to clear of bad vibes, bury it in salt at Full Moon, and remove it after the New Moon.

Thyme will induce and ease menses. It is antiseptic, and used in a bath it is good for various skin conditions. A small pouch filled with thyme and placed under your pillow is said to cure nightmares.

Tumeric, the herb that colors curry powder, is an excellent dye. You can use it to color cloth, eggs, and almost anything else. But be careful, it is quite permanent and will stain enamel pots and kitchen towels. You can add it to bread if you want to leave out the eggs for health reasons.

Vanilla is said to be an aphrodisiac. You can use vanilla extract as a perfume by putting a drop behind your ear and a drop on your wrist.

FOR FURTHER STUDY

The Herb Book. John Lust. Bantam, 1974.

Herbs and Things: Jeanne Rose's herbal. Jeanne Rose. Workman Publishing, 1972.

Magical Herbalism. Scott Cunningham. Llewellyn Publications, 1982.

UMBRELLA MAGIC

BY CERRIDWEN IRIS SHEA

The umbrella is a much misunderstood and neglected accessory. Often left behind on the bus, or in a restaurant, you would think that anything that's been around for about four thousand years, keeping us dry and safe during countless storms, should get a little more respect. It's time we realize what a truly magical tool the umbrella can be.

The word "umbrella" derived from the Latin root of *umbra* meaning "shade" or "shadow." While there is archaeological and artistic evidence that the parasol, or a simple apparatus used for protection from sunlight, was used in Egypt, Assyria, and Greece, it was the Chinese who turned this basic device into the umbrella—lacquering and waxing paper so that it could protect its holder from rain. In the sixteenth century, the umbrella became popular in rainy northern Europe. A Persian traveler and writer named Jonas Hanway began to use the umbrella in public in England. He did so for thirty years, and the umbrella was nicknamed in that country a "Hanway."

In time, the umbrella evolved into a wood and whalebone device covered in oiled canvas. Then, in 1852, Sam Fox founded the English Steels Company and made umbrellas with a steel-ribbed design. He claimed it was a way to use up overstocks of the steel stays used in women's corsets. Over a hundred years later, the collapsible umbrella was the next step.

In order to use the umbrella magically, as with every tool you first need to find the right one. That is, look for an umbrella that has some sort of meaning to you. It could be one passed down in your family. Maybe your grandfather's big old British umbrella has meaning to you. Or maybe an umbrella purchased at an art exhibit with a rendering of an impressionist painting on it has meaning. Maybe you like an umbrella depicting cats and dogs for when it rains "cats and dogs." Because Iris, the rainbow goddess, is one of my patron goddesses, I picked one where each panel is a different color, giving the umbrella a rainbow look.

Bless and consecrate the umbrella according to your usual tradition—the way you would any tool or piece of magical jewelry. You can name the umbrella if you wish, and ask it to help you with your magic. Since the umbrella generally protects you from the rain, you can use this device for protection magic—from the elements, from people, from difficult situations. Imagine your umbrella as a shield, keeping unwanted energies at bay. They hit the umbrella and bounce off, just like raindrops.

Some umbrellas are good for invisibility spells, although mine, being brightly colored, is not. As you open the umbrella and raise it over you, imagine that the cloth reaches all the way to the ground, cloaking you from others, keeping your energy contained. The problem with invisibility spells is that when they work, people tend to walk into you or "through" you because they can't sense your energy. And this can be a bit dangerous.

A closed umbrella can be used as a walking stick. Therefore it can be used for support magic, healing magic, or in circle the way a stick or a stang is used. When you have a specific goal in mind, take a walk with your closed umbrella. Imagine it guiding you purposefully towards your desire. There's nothing like the tap, tap, tap of the umbrella on the ground to make you feel like you're getting somewhere. For symbolism, place the umbrella on the ground and jump over it to signify overcoming obstacles.

You can open your umbrella up and take a walk in the rain to wash away tension. Think of the umbrella as representing your aura.

As the rain washes over the cloth, it cleanses blocks, tension, and stress. And, of course, your umbrella can be used for elemental magic. Simply point it at the clouds, and ask the rain to go away—or to come closer, if rain is needed. Use it too in polarity magic. As the clouds and rain represent the Goddess, your umbrella represents the God.

If the wind turns your umbrella inside out, it may be time to look at things from a different angle. The element of air is telling you new thought is needed. If you like divination, look at the patterns the raindrops make on the cloth to see what they tell you.

In the end, umbrella etiquette is important, especially on crowded city streets. Make sure you don't jab someone in the eye with your prongs. Be sure you know when to raise the umbrella in passing. Don't keep the umbrella up if you are walking in a covered walkway or under scaffolding—there just isn't room. Take it down, then put it back up. Don't walk on crowded city streets with a long umbrella tucked horizontally under your arm, poking everyone around you and causing them to duck when you turn. Don't pause in the middle of the subway steps and fight with the umbrella, causing a few hundred people stuck behind you to get soaked. Remember, what you put out comes back three times. The best umbrella magic can be simply showing consideration to others.

So, retrieve your umbrella from under your desk at work, or go out and buy one specifically for your magical work. Experiment to see what feels right. And, if you get a chance, dance and sing in the rain.

FOR FURTHER STUDY

Earth, Air, Fire, Water. Scott Cunningham, Llewellyn Publications, 1991.

Earth Power. Scott Cunningham. Llewellyn Publications, 1983.

GARBAGE SPELL

BY LADYHAWK WHISPERS

This article is about garbage—but not the stinky stuff you put in your garbage can. Rather, it's about removing the psychic kind of garbage from your past so that you can live a more fulfilling life, filled with reason and direction.

It recently struck me that all the little nastys—demons, if you will, or bad chi, if you prefer—that are lurking deep inside each of us surely go a long way to sabotaging any attempts at spiritual growth. I had the idea that maybe if I just stuffed those yukkys down where I could not see them they would cease to be a distraction. Therefore, I developed a spell with the help of a very wise crone, who told me her secret to dealing with her own garbage left over from a bad marriage.

When this woman's relationship ended upon her husband's death, she decided she didn't want to carry the heavy burden of old garbage into her new life. So she went to his grave mentally carrying a large garbage bag over her shoulder. Into this garbage bag she put all the turmoil and strife of their relationship. She sat for a moment and talked to him. Then she slung the bag from her shoulder and gave it to him—vowing never to think of it of again. After all, it wasn't going to do her any good to keep carrying the garbage around with her.

I have embellished on this theme a little. In my professional tarot reading practice, I have given certain of my clients the following exercise to do as home-work. I have done this spell myself several times, with great results, finding it to be much like peeling the skin of an onion—the layers are nearly endless.

The Garbage Spell

Do this spell on a Saturday during a waning Moon. The time of day isn't all that important, but you may choose to use planetary hours, if you know them, to plan your spell. What is most important is that you have at least a couple of hours when you are certain you will be undisturbed.

You will need the following items:

Your spirit guide or a guardian angel; if you want, you can call on the archangel Michael, who loves to clean up stuff.

A large piece of paper that can be rolled across your bed or floor

A white candle

A black magic marker

Your favorite music played on low

Sage incense

A clear quartz crystal for clarity

A box of tissues (optional)

A lighter

Warning: Do not do this spell if you are experi-encing deep depression. Looking at the things that are wrong in your life will likely not be good for you; seek medical help instead.

Get comfortable. This is not an easy task and maybe too painful for some people—that's the point of the tissues. Start slowly. Surround yourself in white light, light the candle, and start writing. Have the archangels hold your space while you call the quarters. Then write about your earliest memory of someone hurting you. Move forward from this point to your life at present. Then go back and remember all the missed opportunities. Finally, list all the wrong you have done to others. Write as much as you can without stopping to think too much. Don't worry about grammar or punctuation. Just keep it coming.

When you feel you that you've scraped the bottom of the garbage can and can't bring any more up, stop writing. Now wad up all that paper and sit on it. (You heard me: Literally sit on it!) This is the last time you will own this junk as your own. After you have sat for a while, take the crumpled paper to a safe spot out of doors. Call on the Goddess to help you by saying:

Goddess of love and light I bring to you this outpouring of regrets, that you might take them from me, never to burden my soul's progress again.

Set the paper afire. Watch as the wind takes the ashes away. Take three cleansing breaths—in through your nose, out through your mouth. Fill your being with rainbow light to replace what just came out of you. Whenever something painful from the past rears its ugly head again, just remember that you have the ability to rid yourself of it. Tell youself: "I can give my garbage to the Goddess. She will always know what to do with it."

Know, too, that with this spell you are not ignoring past troubles, but simply examining how your life got to be what it is today. There is no reason to carry all the past garbage along with you, because you can't change the past. You can only, with the help of this spell, look forward to walking on a better path.

The final step is to take a hot bath or shower. Make sure you drink plenty of water for the next three days. Remember you have just purged yourself of a lot of negative energy, so you will want to treat yourself as if you were just getting over an illness. Be gentle to yourself. Remember: You can do this spell any time the past holds you back. Good luck and many blessings.

FOR FURTHER STUDY

Working magic is not simple, but with a little reading and some effort you can take some wonderful magical journeys. A must-have for any beginner is Ray Buckland's *Complete Book of Witchcraft* (Llewellyn, 1986). Buckland writes about everything you know need to know about putting a spell together. He gives you information on the history of the craft, how to work magic, rituals, circle casting, and much more.

Silver RavenWolf is another excellent author. Her books give you very good information, as well as hands-on exercises for making your everyday life more magical.

Finally, Dorothy Morrison's book *Everyday Magic,* (Llewellyn, 1998) is a good source for tips on how busy Witches can put things together in a hurry.

ASWANG VAMPIRES
OF THE PHILLIPPINES

BY S Y ZENITH

The following story was related to me in 1999 by a young man from the Philippines. It is about one of the most feared creatures of the night—the *aswang* vampire.

By day, the aswang vampire is a beautiful woman who lives an ordinary life—in a house, with a job, rearing her children. Seemingly normal, her neighbors have no suspicion of how terrible she can be.

The aswang takes on the form of a flying terror at night. It usually appears extraordinarily large and completely black in color. It is led by night birds to victims' homes where it inserts its long, thin, hollow tongue through cracks of the roof so it can suck the blood of victims. When an aswang leaves its home, its head and intestines are transformed into a flying creature while the rest of is body remains on its bed. The aswang can also assume the forms of a dog, pig, horse, or other animal when it roams at night in search of prey.

A good way to spot an aswang is to look into its eyes. Your reflection in an aswang's eye would be upside-down. It is important

not to look away but to stare down the aswang as it usually doesn't take long before it surrenders to your stare and shifts its gaze. If you are the first to look away the aswang will harm you. One other method for detecting an aswang is to use a special arcane oil prepared in a complicated ritual only on Good Fridays. When brought near an aswang, this oil will boil.

Pregnant women, young children, and sick persons are especially appealing to the aswang; it supposedly preys on those who sleep in the middle of the bed, but not those on the edge. Most horrible of all, an aswang's preference is for unborn babies, which it extracts from expectant mothers' wombs with its tongue.

To repel an aswang, mothers rub garlic under children's armpits for protection before they go to bed. If the aswang licks someone's shadow, the person will die soon after. People are warned never to touch a strand of cobweb extending from a tree at night, as it may be the tongue of an aswang waiting to catch an unsuspecting victim.

People are wary of sleeping with their bellies exposed, as the aswang may steal their intestines as they sleep. When an intended victim is not yet asleep, the aswang will stand upside-down and emit a strong odor which paralyzes the prey. The aswang then proceeds to eat the internal organs of its victims.

The word *aswang* itself is often misinterpreted or translated as "sorceror." This is misleading, as sorcerors do what they do of their own free will. An aswang is actually in an altered state wherein it is completely unable to control itself. When an aswang blows air down a person's neck, this person will gradually transform into an aswang. This can be cured with the help of a native healer, known as the *mananambal,* who forces the person to drink certain potions that induce vomiting of all sorts of weird objects such as eggs, birds, and the like.

Whether the aswang is something of the imagination or real, it remains a part of the core beliefs of the Philippino culture. Present-day Philippinos, especially rural folk, continue to believe in, and fear, the aswang.

THE CROSSROADS

BY SUSAN SHEPPARD

Does the dark side of the paranormal make you feel a bit squeamish? Do you dread ghosts, banshees, and the living dead?

Then you would do best to avoid the crossroads—a lonely, haunted intersection in every community where the four directions meet and roads cross.

According to legend, the crossroads is where various forms of spiritual power tend to lurk. It is a place where menacing ghosts and the ancient dead linger and haunt travelers. This is especially the case if there is a cemetery is nearby.

Why the crossroads? In ancient lore, at the crossroads is where psychic powers—ghostly powers if you will—would be the most focused and strong. The meeting and parting of ways is associated with the crossroads, and ancient peoples were suspicious over intersecting paths and their confusing mishmash of energies. There is a lot of power in changing direction and crossing over, and such powers can be used for good or for evil; it all depends upon the individual. Indeed, the more sinister elements of the supernatural—such as vampires and devils—have always been associated with the power of the crossroads.

It was once believed that all kinds of creepy beings hung out at crossroads waiting for a chance to gobble up the immortal soul of the weary traveler. For instance, the Christian devil, or Satan, has been associated with the crossroads. This is true in both African American folktales and in European lore. The most powerful Witch's poppets and voodoo dolls are made from sticks gathered at the crossroads.

Not only is the devil associated with the crossroads, fairies are said to frequent there—but not the benevolent sprites in children's fairy tales. These are wicked fairies of mischief and wrongdoing. Be certain, therefore, that you never fall asleep at the crossroads. All manner of misfortune will fall upon you. You may wake up "bewitched," or "fairy led." You may even wake up in the land of the dead.

Not so long ago, the gallows where condemned men were soon to die were built at the crossroads. Suicides and victims of murder were buried at the crossroads as well. This was done so their restless souls wouldn't wander around seeking revenge upon those who harmed them in life. Some believed it was the power of the Christian cross, as symbolized by the crossroads, which protected the living from vengeful acts of the murderous dead. But legends of the crossroads are much older than the Christian cross, so who's to say...

Contrary to popular opinion, menacing ghosts, who are not always the earthbound souls of the departed but sometimes an evil component of a person's personality that survives his or her death, are believed to lack authority and direction. Thus, these are the types of the ghostly powers that can be summoned on occasion at the crossroads.

Folklore also has it that evil ghosts are easily confused. It is believed that a malevolent spirit will stand at the crossroads all night long trying to make up his mind which way to go. Then at sunup, the golden rays will send the ghost screaming into banishment. The same holds true for vampires, who are said to carry their shrouds to the crossroads in search of fresh victims.

Positive things can happen at the crossroads as well. If you bury three pieces of silver at the crossroads on the night of the Full Moon, this will shield you from evil and increase your ability to attract love and money. If you drive a three-pronged stick painted red and decorated with black crow feathers into the ground at the crossroads, your psychic powers will increase, and you will gain unimagined mystical abilities. Certain stones gathered up at the crossroads can also protect you from evil and various toxic influences—as long as you carry the rock in your pocket or your purse. Stones gathered up at the crossroads on a Full Moon will always protect you and the ones you love.

Various other types of powers can be brought forth at the crossroads, but you must be very careful. Ghosts that haunt the crossroads tend to latch on, and they can become troublesome.

The magic and mayhem of the crossroads goes further into history than our recorded memories. The legend is very old—having appeared in Asia, Africa, and North America well before European influences reached these places. This gives proof to the idea the concept of the crossroads go far back into our subconscious. On the whole, ancient peoples thought that magic was at its most powerful at the crossroads, and thus they associated this place with witchcraft. Hecate, the goddess of witchcraft, lurks at the crossroads, along with howling black dogs and midnight madness. When you hear barking dogs at the crossroads, you can be certain that Hecate, the three-faced goddess, is prowling about.

In ancient times, offerings of food and cakes were set out at the crossroads to appease Hecate and her mysterious forces for good and evil. Such cakes were then called "Hecate cakes." It was traditional to place a lighted candle in the center of these cakes for good luck. This was also done to light the way so Hecate could find her food after dark. This is where the custom of candles on birthday cakes originates.

Voodoo gives great spiritual significance to the crossroads. Voodoo spells are often performed there, so that the crossroads can lend its magical powers to the spellcaster. Crossroad dirt, as well as graveyard dirt, is still used as protection from the evil eye and other negative forces. The concept is similar to Europeans putting gargoyles on their churches to scare away evil. The worse the gargoyle looks, the more successful it is in chasing away evil spirits.

In Voodoo rituals, the priest or priestess who casts the spell waits at the crossroads until an apparition, some say it is the Devil, appears. If this ghost does not make himself known immediately, the spell will be more difficult to work. However, if a devilish ghost arrives right on time, you can be assured the spell will work, but in the most dangerous and diabolical way.

In the end, one should not challenge the mysterious and foreboding forces at the crossroads. Certain things might happen there. Uspeakable ghostly things...

Remember: A crossroads exist everywhere. Even in your town.

MAGICAL ETHICS FOR TEENS AND THEIR PARENTS

BY ESTELLE DANIELS

Magic and Wicca are everywhere these days—on TV, in the movies, and in books of fiction and non-fiction. It's so popular that many people have become very interested in learning more about, and possibly becoming part of, the tradition. Unfortunately, though, having an interest and willingness to learn does not guarantee you will be able to find a good and ethical teacher.

TIPS FOR BEGINNING YOUR STUDIES

The first thing you should know about magic is that what is depicted in popular media is not at all like the real thing. In the years I have been a practitioner, for instance, I have never met anyone who could merely wave their hand and cause things to happen. The truth is magic is much more subtle and slow-acting than would ever serve a Hollywood plot. In the movies, the actors only have a short time to get done what what they want to get done, so of course magic is made to appear more dramatic, visual, and quick than it is in real life.

In truth, magic and Wicca are studies which can be pursued and perfected over a lifetime, or more. As with most worthwhile

things in this life, no one book or secret recipe will be able to make you an instant expert. Becoming a magic-worker takes practice and intensive labor. Of course, there are many aspects of magic that you can master in a short stretch of time—such as learning to read tarot cards, for example, or learning a simple incantation. But these are just small facets of the magical life.

CREATING A MAGICAL LIFE

Many people who choose to become magical find they create a magical life for themself. They begin to view the world differently, paying attention to things others might miss. Their ideas, values, and priorities change and become somewhat different from more mainstream people.

Of course, a magical person still has to go to school or work in order to bring food to the table, but these workaday trappings of modern life can take a back seat to knowledge and experience in the magical realm.

That said, the most effective way to learn about things magical and Wiccan is to find a solid, ethical teacher or become part of a good and nurturing group. Of course, this sounds easier than it is. Few groups advertise for members, and the best groups are relatively small and have little turnover. Classes are available here and there, but not all are accessible in terms of time or sometimes money. Plus, the exchange of money does not necessary bring ethics into the matter—in fact, often the opposite is true.

TEACHING MAGIC TO TEENS

A further complication occurs for teenagers who, inspired by what they see on TV perhaps, want to learn about magic and Wicca. Many teachers won't teach minors; this is not out of prejudice, but rather for solid legal reasons. In the past few years, parents, grandparents, and stepparents have all sued and won cases against people teaching their children about Wicca and magic. The law in our society makes children the sole responsibility of their parents, and if parents don't want a child doing something, any adult who helps work against that can be sued or criminally prosecuted. Alternatively, some teachers may have parents or guardians sign a waiver before they take minors on as students. This is for everyone's protection in the event of future litigation.

If you are under eighteen, then, and want to learn about magical traditions and the religion of Wicca, your options of somewhat limited as far as finding a teacher. Still, there are many things you can do on your own. First, look to attend any public lectures, seminars, classes, or book signings that you can. If there are psychic fairs in your area, go and watch, ask questions, and observe. Some people are willing to talk in informal settings, even if they refuse to take you on as a student. Any event open to the public is a safe zone for the exchange of information—in other words, parents will have a hard time suing a teacher for the information they give in a public lecture.

Of course, at these events you might have to pay an admission price. Do so, and feel free once you are there to talk to people. Be friendly and eager to learn. Don't be a pest. Respect boundaries, but ask questions. Sometimes you can get into conversations and learn things. You may even ask an elder if they might meet you and talk to you over lunch—again, in a public place. Always be sure you can pay your own way.

If people are busy or can't talk, don't take it personally. Just move on, and keep trying. Occasionally you will find someone who is willing to talk and teach you informally. There is certainly no harm in trying.

If you find a metaphysical bookstore in your area, go there and ask the employees if they know of any classes or open groups. Ask them for help and advice. Sometimes they will be more than willing to share. Furthermore, you can just go and browse the books and listen to the conversations of customers. You might be able to pick up some interesting information; at the very least, you will get some useful reading done. If you can, try to get a part-time job at the store. Working in a place with such materials on hand, and with such customers, is a great way to pick up a magical or Wiccan education.

Certainly, as you already must know, you can learn much about magic and Wicca by reading books. But these sources are not intended to be the end of your education. You should also go beyond the books by trying to practice things yourself. Don't be afraid to experiment. If you cannot find a teacher, get a few friends together and work it out among yourselves. Don't be worried about looking or sounding strange. Simply keep your activities private. Don't impose your beliefs or practices upon those who aren't interested or might be uncomfortable. Wicca and magic are part of your private life, and though they may seem wonderful to you not everybody will feel the same. Cultivate discretion, it will serve you well in the future.

Read magical fiction too. This is not to say that if you read all the *Harry Potter* books, you can become Harry Potter. We all would love that, but it isn't possible. You may think fiction is simply at best an interesting and diverting pastime, but you should know too that reading such material does train your mind to think in magical ways. Reading about magic and spells can get your mind used to understanding what it might feel like to do magic and Wicca.

Be careful to choose positive and helpful literature, not the darkly horrific or negative stuff. In your books, look for people who are active, who take care of themselves, and who make a positive mark on their world. If you like Harry Potter, there are many other books in the same vein. Ask your librarian or bookstore clerk. They will probably have a list of other books and authors to read. The genre is called science fantasy, though it covers much more than just magic. Realize that when you read, as when you watch TV or movies, these are fantasy worlds, and things are exaggerated for plot and effect.

Okay, you can also continue to watch your magical movies and TV shows too. Again be careful to choose the positive ones, and be sure not to become dazzled by the special effects and quick plot resolutions. As mentioned before, real-life magic does not reach its fruition so quickly and neatly. Life is a lot less flashy and takes a lot longer to resolve. Sometimes things don't even get resolved or even solved—that's life.

Finally, in your studies you will find there is a lot of information on the Internet. Be careful here. The most effective people generally don't have time to hang around chat rooms, and frequently the people who are the loudest and boast the most know the least. Information on the Internet isn't always reliable. Unfortunately there are few restrictions here. If you find a cool website with loads of "secret" information that nobody else has, be cautious. If their stuff is so secret, why are they putting it on a website? If someone says on their website that they know best, and everyone else is wrong, be wary. Do your research; take your time; do not commit to anything—especially if a Website asks for your money before they will dole out the truth. Usually the only truth you learn is that a fool and their money are soon parted. The Internet is anonymous, and many shady people rely on this anonymity to do their shady deals. If it feels wrong or bad, just say no, and go elsewhere.

YOUR OWN ETHICS

As you begin to learn more, here is a word of advice: Be careful about proclaiming yourself to be an expert simply because you have read a book and practiced a bit. There are people who have devoted many years to study and practice, and nothing turns others off faster than the instant expert.

That is, try to keep an open mind about other people and their opinions and practices as you learn more about what you like and what works for you. Just because you read a book that makes one claim, don't assume all other approaches are wrong. Different people have different ideas. Be open to new and different ways of doing and thinking about things. Listen and think about what someone says before automatically saying they are wrong. At the very least, express your thoughts in the form of an opinion: "I think you might be mistaken," or "I got different information from this book."

Magic and Wicca should make you feel good about what you do and make your life better. Be patient, and learn what you can. Many of us started the same way, and we are still around. Good luck.

PARENTS AND WICCA

If you are the parent of a teen who has expressed an interest in magic or Wicca, there are many things you can and should do to help your teen. Your key role might well be to check things out to be certain your child is getting good reliable and honest information.

My first and best advice to parents is: Do not panic. After all, the majority of teens who are interested in these subjects eventually go on to other pursuits. It's a fad. If you don't make a big deal of it, they will either stay with it out of honest interest, or find something else to freak you out.

Next, you might be well served if you do some research. If your teen is reading books about magic and Wicca, read some yourself. How do they seem to you? You will likely be surprise how harmless they are, and how positive and motivating. If they scare you because they clash with the beliefs you were brought up with, take a look at the underlying mindsets. These practices, like most religions or spiritual pursuits, are designed to make a person more self-aware, motivated, thoughtful, helpful, caring, sensitive to others, and interested in making the world a better place. As a result, the practices of magic and Wicca may suddenly seem not as awful to you. You might realize you are simply objecting to the way things are done, rather than the mindsets.

Still, there are bad people everywhere, and Wicca and magic are no exceptions. Focus your attention on the individuals your child is associating with—as opposed to the mindset of the spiritual practice. Be certain to watch for attitudes or practices that are selfish, dominating, nihilistic, destructive, or encouraging of practices which are dangerous to self and others. Separate the individuals from the general practice, and be sure to talk to your child about these things.

If your teen is on the Internet, be sure to monitor their activities. Ask about the websites they have visited, and look at them yourself. Lurk in a few chat rooms, and monitor what goes on. Most of the time, it's just boasting and bravado. Be sure to let your child know that you will continue to take an interest, and that you will not tolerate any bad practices or behavior.

If your child sends away for materials or goes to classes, look at the materials yourself. If your teen wants to take a class with a private teacher, check the teacher out. Call and ask about what will be taught and what goes on in the class. Ask to sit in. Some teachers won't teach minors at all. Some teachers require parents sign a waiver granting permission for a minor to study. If the teacher won't talk with you or you get bad feelings, err on the side of caution. It will be difficult to give your reasons to a teenager, but if you are uncertain about the particular practices of a teacher or group, you will have to tell your child to wait until they reach adulthood and can make the decision alone. The anger and frustration your child may feel after this is preferable to having him or her get into a bad group and be damaged.

If there is a great deal of money involved, be extremely wary. Most Wiccans for religious reasons cannot charge for teaching the craft—outside of reimbursement for supplies and books. Few people will teach magic for a fee, and if one promises to teach everything quickly, you have special reason to be skeptical. It just doesn't work that way.

If your teen finds a teacher that you agree may be good, you should ask many questions: What they will be teaching; what books they will use; how long the course will take; what the workload and time commitment will be for your teen; what the rules are, and what your child will have to commit to; what you as a parent will have to commit to; how long the teacher has been teaching; how many students are in the class; and where the class will meet (though rules about secrecy may prevent the teacher from saying exactly). You may even want to ask for references.

You might not get full or understandable answers to these questions, but use your instincts. The teacher may speak in jargon, but listen to their tone and attitude. Are they upset that you are checking up on them? Are they resentful, secretive, misleading, or obfuscating? Those are not good signs. Are they patient and willing to answer your questions? Do they seem knowledgeable, have credentials, and are willing to let you sit in? Those are good signs.

Wicca is a religion, and becoming Wiccan means choosing a religious path. This is of course not something to be taken lightly. If you don't want your teen changing religions, discuss it. Give your reasons openly, and be fair to your child. Expect the same from him or her.

If you object to magic, examine your reasons. Is it because you are afraid your teen will blow your house up? Are you afraid they will be possessed by demons? You should know this is silly— these things just don't happen. The worst thing that will happen if a spell is done incorrectly is nothing. Do you object to magic in and of itself? Why? Most magic these days is done for healing or self-help. Prayer itself is a classic form of magic. The practice of Wicca and magic differs very little from the ancient practice of praying—though it is much more involved.

Ask your teen why they want to get into magic. If they want a quick fix or love spells—inform them that this is not how magic works. It takes time and energy, and the practitioner also has to put their energy into making the desired outcome happen. Tell your child that you would be much more impressed if he or she focused on becoming more presentable, cultivating some manners and social graces, and being a person people would like to be around.

Both Wicca and magic require work, study, and commitment to be effective and successful. Many teens when confronted with the work involved are less than enthusiastic. It certainly isn't like it is in the movies and on TV. Harry Potter depicts the amount of work, study, and practice fairly realistically, though the subjects or effects you can achieve are rather heavily exaggerated.

If you let your teen explore and read some books—and there is a whole lot of reading involved in magic and Wicca—chances are they will learn something and will eventually move on. Neither magic nor Wicca has an instant formula for success. Tell your child to be patient and open-minded, and let them know that you intend to do so too. If anything, your tolerance will teach your teen a valuable lesson.

ON NEW YEAR'S DAY

By Denise Dumars

M y mother always told us that whatever you did on New Year's Day you would end up doing the rest of the year. We would usually have black-eyed peas on New Year's Day, which is a Southern and Midwestern tradition for good luck. So today, when I am invited to a party or potluck on New Year's Day I always take my own version of Mom's recipe, which was itself a version of the dish sometimes known as Hoppin' John. My recipe follows as does advice on what to do and what not to do on New Year's day.

GOOD LUCK NEW YEAR'S BLACK-EYED PEAS

Ingredients:

2	2-lb. cans black-eyed peas
2–3	large stalks of celery, chopped fine
1	small onion, chopped fine
4–6	slices of good lean bacon (turkey or beef bacon can be substituted, but do not use Sizzlean)
	Apple cider or white vinegar
	Tabasco or similar pepper sauce
1	small red or green jalapeño pepper, chopped (optional)

Fry the bacon until crisp in a medium skillet. Thank the Celtic sow goddess, Ceriddwen, for her blessings while cooking the bacon if you wish. Remove and drain bacon, then set aside. Pour off all but about 1 tablespoon of bacon fat. Add peas, celery, and onion to skillet. Add a little salt and white pepper if you wish, and the chopped jalapeño. Add just a tablespoon or two of the vinegar so that there is a bit of broth to cook everything. Always stir in a clockwise direction for good luck.

Once everything is heated through and the onion and celery are cooked, add tabasco to taste. Crumble the bacon and add to the skillet and heat through. Now it's ready to serve—over rice or with a sweet potato casserole. The recipe serves four to six people as a side dish, and it can be easily doubled or tripled to serve at a party.

If your altar includes some of the African or Afro-Caribbean pantheon, don't forget to offer a portion of your lucky New Year's black-eyed peas to them as well; the origin of this dish is probably rooted in African cuisine and traditions.

WHAT TO DO ON NEW YEAR'S DAY

Legend has it that whatever you do on New Year's Day you will do the rest of the year as well. In magical terms this means you should plan your activities accordingly. Here are some suggestions.

BE CREATIVE

If you are a writer, musician, artist, actor, or other creative type, you will want to create more opportunities for yourself in the New Year. In order to take advantage of these opportunities, do a bit of writing, painting, or whatever creative art you practice on this day.

BE HEALTHY

Try not to overeat or overindulge in alcohol today. Be good to yourself; take your vitamins and eat your vegetables. Go for a jog or a walk or do some other light exercise.

BE HAPPY

Do something that makes you feel good: Make love, see a movie, read a good book, play a game with your family.

WHAT NOT TO DO ON NEW YEAR'S DAY

There are also some things you probably should not do on New Year's Day. Do not put off the laundry and the heavy housework—ugh, who wants to be stuck with the chores all year? Don't work on your resumé—you don't want to spend the whole year job hunting! Don't work on the car if you want it to remain reliable in the year to come. Try not to argue with family and friends if you wish to have harmonious relationships during the new year.

At the end of the day, sit or lie comfortably before going to sleep. Meditate, pray, or listen to a self-hypnosis or creative-visualization tape. Tell yourself that you will have wonderful dreams about all the exciting possibilities in the year ahead.

Have a happy New Year!